LADIES WHO LUNGE

TARA BRABAZON was born and educated in Perth, Western Australia. She has lived and worked throughout Australia and New Zealand, and is currently a senior lecturer in Cultural Studies at Murdoch University, Perth. Her previous book, *Tracking the Jack: A Retracing of the Antipodes*, was published by UNSW Press in October 2000. She is a wide-ranging commentator on feminism, men's studies, teaching and cultural history.

LADIES WHO LUNGE

CELEBRATING DIFFICULT WOMEN

Tara Brabazon

UNSW
PRESS

This book is dedicated to Dorothy Wren, Doris Brabazon
— and the journey that separates them.

A UNSW Press book
Published by
University of New South Wales Press Ltd
University of New South Wales
UNSW Sydney NSW 2052
AUSTRALIA
www.unswpress.com.au

National Library of Australia
Cataloguing-in-Publication entry:

Brabazon, Tara.
Ladies who lunge: celebrating difficult women.

Includes index.
ISBN 0 86840 421 7.

1. Feminism. 2. Feminist theory. 3. Women — Social conditions. I. Title.

305.42

Printer Griffin Press

CONTENTS

INTRODUCTION

FIND A GOOD WOMAN AND DO AS YOU'RE TOLD

Frequently, I hate myself for being a heterosexual woman. It is like cherishing a scratched vinyl record in the era of compact discs. From macramé to magnolias, I am inept at the feminine wiles. We start with food and those serepax-inducing cookery programmes. I never find the right knife, let alone the courage to commence the cooking. I do not believe that we are meant to *eat* tofu. It looks like a degreaser for my car. And whoever invented hipster trousers has never seen a woman's body. I'm sorry, but I curve there. Heterosexual women do not have the chic of lesbians or the lager-fuelled confidence of straight men. I cannot even ponder romance these days without laughing. Roses die and chocolates adhere to the aforementioned hips. As to dating — do not get me started. It is such a disappointment.

I just received an email from a man who has pulled out of a dinner that I was cooking for him tonight — and asks would tomorrow be convenient? Two hours' notice. The oven is already heating up, I have set the table and the best towels are proudly dangling from the bathroom railing. This social disappointment happens after cancelling the meal last night. Today he offered the pathetic excuse of 'something has come up'. I am sorry, but unless that *something* is the death of a family member or having his genitals caught in the fanbelt of a car, this pretext is predatory.

I hold suspicions. He is a game player — one of an increasingly large group of men trying to ascertain whether or not a woman is desperate for a date, so desperate that she would actually put up with this nonsense. By convincing me to move a dinner from Friday to Saturday (and, he hoped, to Sunday), he was trying to illustrate that I have no life, no prospects and have been left on the shelf. Did he really think that I would fall for this ruse? Of course — to return email — I replied that I was *so sorry* he could not make it to my house this evening. I also informed him that I would feed the fresh salmon to someone else. No, tomorrow night is not convenient. End of email. Seething subtext: you will never see me again, you bastard.

That would be the end of it, except I am left hating myself for my stupidity, naïvety and foolishness. I actually thought he was coming to see me for good conversation and a pleasant evening. Stupid. It gets worse. I wanted to make a good impression: always a mistake, and the trigger of my true stupidity. I bought the best wine, the best salmon, the best feta, the best olives and all those really gross antipasto vegetables — saturated in too much oil and of no use for anything, except as an expensive starter. Maybe they too can be used as a degreaser for my car. It took three hours to find fresh asparagus to pair the salmon. So now I have a fridge full of food that I will never eat. I can hear it quietly going off, laughing at me as it deteriorates. But it does not end there. I have been on my hands and knees scrubbing the floor. I've even deodorised the toilet. A potpourri scent mocks me from the bathroom.

And I bought two new bathroom cleansers, a facial masque (very important not to confuse these items …) and an expensive conditioner to add shine to my locks. I also purchased new floral hair accessories — flowers that do not die — that would co-ordinate with my toenail polish and the dining room carpet. Hey, this amount of detail takes time.

So now, after all of the preparation, thought and energy expended to give this gentleman an enjoyable evening, he sends me an email — an email two hours before the dinner — to inform me that 'something has come up'.

How has this happened? This bloke is fifty-five years old — most men his age would give up their firstborn child to have dinner with a 30-year-old, upwardly mobile, blonde woman. Then again, maybe I am already past it. Men — seemingly — prefer a date they can burp and change. This situation is made even more embarrassing because during our first meeting, a brunch last Wednesday, this man enacted a monologue of monolithic proportions, informing me of his emotionally incestuous childhood, his father's infidelities and genital herpes. This father is blamed for his resultant, recurrent flatulence and numerous other 'anal challenges'.

Just what I need: a man who can't control his mouth or his asshole.

Here I stand, emotionally wading through antipasto vegetables and potpourri toilet cleaner. But I have learnt a lesson. The reason men behave in this way is because women let them behave in this way. We fit in, excuse their rudeness, quietly clean up their mess and forgive them for calling our mothers old scrubbers. These men *should* be scared of our mothers: mums know the vagaries and treacheries of the masculine game. After relating this story to my mother, her response was immediate: 'I would prefer you to flush $200 worth of food, including the bloody salmon, down the toilet rather than ever see that man again'.

Men may say I am being melodramatic. No way, buddy. This is not about the food, it is not about the money, it is not even about the clean toilets. This is about a loss of effort and time. Men simply must not behave in this way. Game players belong on Jerry Springer, not in my dining room. Most of us are accustomed to households with fathers who think they rule the roost and mothers who actually run everything. My parents, who have celebrated their fiftieth wedding anniversary, rarely probe their marital longevity. But when pushed, my father always confirms that the secret to a happy marriage is 'to find a good woman and do as you're told'.

This book is written as a dialogue with our times, an evaluation of contemporary masculinity — and the women who poke, probe and provoke it. I disdain dishcloth-wet writing, essential oil euphemisms and Laura Ashley politics. Beige-frocked psychologists pumping out bland prose belong on lifestyle shows, not in feminism. Instead, I write bristling words for the tough broads who like to laugh and think — at the same time. I do not apologise for the journey of feminism. With confidence and dignity, the time has come to acknowledge that the pain and confusion of both feminism and patriarchy has produced a social system that is flawed and fallible, but also fascinating and provocative. In these pages, truths are excavated and tales told. Feminism is not lost. It is never lost. The movement — and the women in it — are exactly where they need to be.

The way this book is written — *the how* — is just as important as the subject matter — *the what*. Words pour from one person with the purpose of moving another. Gloria Steinem reminded us that 'finding language that will allow people to act together while cherishing each other's individuality is probably the most feminist and truly revolutionary function of writers'.[1] My book is therefore written defiantly, creating a theory that s(t)ings and a politics with punch. I am not happy to relax back in consumerist pleasure — mobile phone in one hand, steering wheel in the other and Gloria Gaynor on the stereo. Feminism is like a toolbox in the back of the car. When the vehicle is cruising along the freeway, we never need to think about tyres, oil or brakes. But when something goes wrong — a tyre blows out or our radiator cooks — suddenly we need the toolbox, and badly. Feminism is similar. When we are young and completely outside of power structures, a mobile phone and Gloria are sufficient. If relationships end, we lose our job or confront sexual impropriety — suddenly we need the toolbox. Steinem replaces Gaynor. This is the role of feminism: to be available, ready and useful, when and how we need it.

There are many attributes and ideas that this book does not address. It does not celebrate individual women's success. It is not a herstory. Nor does it summon over-arching readings of the feminist world — like Susan Faludi's *Backlash* and *Stiffed* or Naomi Wolf's *Beauty Myth* and *Fire With Fire*. Instead, within these pages I focus on moments and movements of meaning — sparks of sharp insight, wit and change. Like the rush of adrenaline on a dance floor, there are instants of access to another — a better — world. I argue throughout this book that disempowered groups, like women, use disempowered sites, like popular culture, to renegotiate their social position.

The book is presented in two parts. The first section — 'Women Moving' — circuits the social, economic and political landscape. The recurrent motifs of revolution, revelation, mobility and movement are exposed through discussions of feminist waves, fashion, cosmetics and sport. Women's history is cut up, restitched and hemmed. The second portion — 'Moving Women' — grants a feminist icon the role of political teacher. These renowned women are summoned from film and television, wrestling, journalism and education, offering seminars about leadership, family, power and writing. These two sections are propelled by the thrill of an operative narrative that unleashes action and alternatives, while sharing words of emphasis and intensity. I also open feminist theories up to histories of (post)colonialism, class and race, all fired within an Antipodean kiln.

Most importantly, I contend that the purpose of feminism and the women's movement is not to make women happy. Happiness is a weak and ill-focussed aim. Instead, my endeavour as a feminist is to make women's lives easier. If a woman is happy, she is content, satisfied, calm — and completely unable to see the inequalities of her life. If an oyster was happy, then it would not make a pearl. It is the grit, the discomfort, the site of irritation that actually forms the precious jewel. It is the same with feminism. When women are irritated, tired, angry or hurt, the vision becomes clear.

We all have a responsibility to value and validate women's choices, cutting away the language of ridicule and hatred. We are also accountable for the testing of ourselves, to risk failure and activate change. In our time — when feminism is everywhere — empowered femininity is ever more difficult to locate. It has been a tough ten years. Political struggle, if it is to produce change, must make all of us uncomfortable. The difficult women featured in these pages do not simply re-play the familiar feminine rhythms of life. Instead they skip a groove and change the beat, which makes women's lives more difficult, but also more defiant. To monitor this jarring syncopation, my words dance in the spaces between women, femininity, feminism and popular culture.

This book is about — and for — the ladies who lunge.

PART I

WOMEN MOVING

MY OTHER CAR IS
A BROOM: MOVING
WOMEN BEYOND
THE HAPPINESS PATROL

Feminism needs a popular cultural equivalent of the movie *Fight Club*.[1]
This film is a testament to angry white men whose lives have been over-
run by pointless jobs and mogadon-triggering consumerism. Stripped
back to an authentic masculinity, the men gather to fight. To regain
control, they must first lose control. Pushing them to their physical
limits is the leader of Fight Club, a gritty, twisted split personality,
Jack/Tyler. Appropriately, attending men's self-help groups pushed
him over the edge. To take other men with him, he pummels out the
painful perceptions:

> You are more than the contents of your wallet
> You are more than your job
> You are more than your Ikea-appointed flat.

In this film, women are part of the problem. Wives, girlfriends, lovers
and mothers have created 'a generation raised by women'. Reclaiming
men's physical strength, aggression and capacity to fight is a way to
shut out the pain of feminised masculinity and channel the anger.

Fight Club is brilliant cinema, one of a highly original stream of
films located in the contradictory space between lived experience and
celebrated societal truths. *Human Traffic*, *Stigmata* and the Kevin
Smith four (*Clerks*, *Mall Rats*, *Chasing Amy* and *Dogma*) offer gritty
commentary on life, death, drugs and faith. The absence from this
remarkable stable of statements is a feminist-inflected film. If women
did have a *Fight Club*, what would they chant? A mantra floods the
mind:

You are more than your womb
You are more than your children
You are more than your husband
You are more than Retinol A
You are more than Target Home
You are more than puckered napkins
You are more than Elizabeth Arden's Red Door
You are more than Lean Cuisine
You are more than your mobile phone's answering tone.

Women's lives are filled with knowledges of anti-wrinkle cream, good fatty acids, calorie control, fluffy towels, more nail polish than it is possible to use in a lifetime and enough perfume to neutralise a metropolitan zoo. It is no wonder that one of the major self-help books of the last few years was titled *Something More: excavating an authentic self*. It is a book geared towards comfortable, white, middle-class, married, reproductive women who find their lives pointless. Their mothers read Betty Friedan's *The Feminine Mystique*. Now they wander (aimlessly) along the *Road Less Traveled*. Letters to women's magazines are filled with this aimless torment:

> It's not that I'm unhappy but I just always tend to feel discontented and restless. My friends tell me I'm having a mid-life crisis (I've just turned 40). No matter what I do or achieve, it doesn't stimulate me — I keep wanting change. What does that say about me? I haven't always been like this — it has just been in the past year. Prior to that, I thought I had everything.[2]

There is desolation in her words. While men excavate the self through a fight, how does *Something More* recommend women rescue the real person marinating in Diet Coke? Go back to childhood photograph albums, cry and ask what happened to the dreams of that little girl. It is pallid reading for a pallid time. I have sympathy for Tyler: 'How much do you know about yourself if you've never been in a fight?'.[3]

Women need a (metaphoric) Fight Club, a place where we can slog out our discord at a devious world. Women are so accustomed to being the scapegoats for the downsizing of white, middle-class men, that we have internalised the blame. How dare we ask for more than 72 per cent of a man's wage for doing the same job? Why should we express anger when expected to complete the second shift at home after a day at work? Why become hostile at the decentring of crucial health care and educational legislation? Why should women demand safe abortions?[4]

A fight is introduced in this chapter — through words and ideas rather than the crunching of cheekbones and powdering of knuckles. The goal is an excavation, not of the self, but of the feminist movement.

There is no need for a bland, overcooked history of women, retracing long-forgotten meetings, personality spats and legislative changes. I remain fascinated with *how* feminism is being used, re-written, forgotten and remembered in the present. All women must be far more attentive to the context of the books, lectures and ideas that have emerged through the twentieth century. It is no surprise that thirty-five years ago women focussed on maternity leave, equal wages and abortion. It is no surprise that younger feminists are focussing on popular music, fashion and the Internet. Bodily rights have transformed into representational rights. A new type of citizenship is being negotiated.

BE MILITANT EACH IN YOUR OWN WAY

If I can't dance, it's not my revolution.[5]

Emma Goldman

Whoever I talk to and whatever I read these days is interspersed with a fear and concern that young women have turned away from feminism. I have always found this 'realisation' somewhat odd. There are more young feminists now than there have ever been.[6] So many women are summoning dreams of difference, dreams of struggle and dreams of power. Those fearful of feminist decline have forgotten that politics is derived from experience, from living a life. While men are most radical in their youth and become conservative with age, women's political realities are frequently an inversion of the male narrative. The most brilliant, radical, controversial and devil-may-care women I know are in their seventies and eighties. They offer level-headed advice to everybody and are not frightened of making others uncomfortable. While men may dismiss 'old biddies' and their 'magging',[7] they are ignored at great peril. These wise women are funny, confrontational and deadly in their putdowns. Their lives — of depression, war, death and/or divorce — have given them knowledge and consciousness. Gloria Steinem has assembled a highly convincing rationale for the changing political truths of ageing women:

> This makes sense in a male-dominant society where young men rebel against their powerful fathers, and then grow more conservative as they replace them, while young women outgrow the limited power allotted to them as a sex objects and child bearers, and finally replace their less powerful mothers. Furthermore, young women haven't yet experienced the injustices of inequality in the paid labour force, the unequal burden of child rearing and work in the home, and the double standard of aging. To put it another way, if young women have a problem, it's only that they think there's no problem.[8]

I have always possessed great respect for Steinem. She is not frightened of asking difficult questions about race or difference and is prepared to think critically while challenging herself to communicate in new ways. It is wise to infer that until young women think there is a problem, *there is no problem*. In the nineteenth century, feminism was led by older women; women who either became chattel — through marriage — or old maids — through spinsterhood.[9]

It is absolutely crucial at this point in women's history that we do not expect young women to genuflectingly continue the movement with only gratitude and deference to prior struggles. It is important that young women are not treated as vessels into which feminism is poured. Life must be lived, struggles fought and consciousness generated. Probably the most radical thing that a young woman can do today is avoid marriage or pregnancy, thereby giving herself some space and choices. Although much rhetoric emerges about girls maturing earlier than boys — as determined by their physicality — young women need time to gestate socially and politically.

Much of the generational controversy in the recent history of Australian feminism was triggered by Anne Summers' article in the *Good Weekend* on 18 March 1995. She argued that contemporary young women had produced little of note for feminism. Indeed, she concluded that 'maybe the third wave will lead the way to a calmer and more reconciled future. I just wish they'd get started'.[10] Although not in Australia, I remember this time well. I was twenty-five years old, working in a full-time, one-year lecturing contract at a New Zealand university. I had just submitted my PhD, completed in eighteen months while teaching. Working 100-plus hours a week, I was about to leave one transitory position for another in Central Queensland. Many were part of this temporary, contract workforce, young people prepared to take any job, in any place. I moved my entire life — traversing two States and two countries — three times in three years. It was a difficult period, trying to earn a living while skidding through a slamming economic door. Pondering Summers' piece years later, I understand her motives and context better, but I still retain the anger that so many of us possessed at the time. We were all doing the best we could under arduous conditions. These circumstances were economic rationalism, a retraction of the university sector, temporary employment and a volatile personal life. Summers' comments provoked some fresh feminist writing, of which *DIY Feminism* is the best known:

> While second-wave feminists have been puzzled by The Next Generation's ambivalence towards their ideology and achievements, the rejection of organised feminism has been constructive.

It is a reaction against constricting dogma and a means of keeping feminism active and alive.[11]

Women have a common bond of affiliation. The most important attribute we share is our subjugation, the structural inequality and demeaning of activities connoted as feminine. It must be the task of all women to listen to others, to understand different contexts and experiences. Most importantly, older feminists who have fought hard — but also gained social and political maturity in a more buoyant economic time — must allow younger women the opportunity to resolve the paradoxes within their experience. No one enjoys having ideas stuffed down a gagging throat. Feminists must not poach an evangelist-like zeal from the pseudo-messiahs of the day. Feminism is not a dogma. It is a series of ideas that holds both a political application and lived integrity.

One of the great mis-representations of the women's movement is the existence of only three waves. Such an analytical structuring device is of little use, except to attack political directives and motivations. Therefore, I avoid the compression of the waves and seek out the movement of ideas. To understand contemporary women, theories of sexuality are inadequate, understanding the media is not enough and histories of education are insufficient. We need to move around, create a diverse checklist, think big and take risks. Of course, it would be handy (for critics) if feminism had an understood and agreed agenda. This will never happen. The movement is wide-ranging, volatile and convoluted. That is a strength. Anti-feminists and the media love a bitch fight. The idea of feminists arguing among themselves makes good copy. If *they* do not know what *they* want, then how can *we* give it to *them*? Women need to develop more advanced models of conflict and change that do not unravel collectivity and community. Men have had much time to institute these structures. The basis of legal institutions, the Westminster system and the rugby field establish the value of an antagonistic system. The organisations that reinforce masculine power — politics and law — actually validate and teach conflict, competition and resolution. Women, frequently isolated in households or in the workplace, rarely have the experience to teach and apply healthy adversarial procedures.

It is obvious that the self-help movement has channelled (some would say stifled) much feminist anger. The audience for these books is overwhelmingly women. Indeed, Australian bookshops have slotted feminist texts into self-help sections. It was a bemusing Saturday morning when I discovered Germaine Greer's *The Female Eunuch* on the shelf next to John Gray's *Men are from Mars, Women are from Venus*. It gave me a great image: a celebrity death match in which Greer punches the diminutive Gray as he tries to calm her with a hug and recognition of her overdeveloped Martian side. While there are rows of books aiming to teach women how to improve their self-esteem and confidence in the public sphere, there are very few texts that pronounce men lacking in their domestic duties. Feminism is both a target and trigger for these texts. Susan Faludi suggested:

> To the vast female readership of self-help manuals, the advice experts delivered a one-two punch. First they knocked down the liberated woman, commanding that she surrender her 'excessive' independence, a mentally unhealthy state that had turned her into a voracious narcissist, a sterile cuckoo. Then, having brought the 'victim' of feminism to her more feminine knees, the advice writers reap the benefits — by nursing the backlash victim.[12]

This self-help matrix moves the reader from a fear of vulnerability to a desire for co-dependency. When the problems of women's lives are internalised, wider structural changes and inequalities are underconsidered. In self-help manuals, of Mars and Venus and not sweating the small stuff, we have the testimony of a silent scream. What is most disturbing about these books and the culture that feeds them is the notion that the solutions are always within the person. To transform life, an individual only has to think differently. No matter how deep the scar or black the bruise, a thought can heal an injured self.

While a feminist consciousness starts with the self, it must not end there. Discussing self-esteem always seems like a luxury. The hyperindividualism of the self-help movement is a concern. Louise Walker is correct in determining that 'an individualist solution to the problems that women face as a group is undoubtedly inadequate'.[13] We all must contemplate, read about and be active in the big issues — racism, colonialism, ageism, health, disability and education. Not surprisingly, the individualism of the feminists who claim the label of third wave is pervasive. Obviously, they have not seen *Monty Python's Life of Brian*:

Brian: You are all individuals.
Crowd: Yes, we are all individuals.
Aside: I'm not.[14]

There are large-scale problems in our economy. The division between the over-worked and the under-employed is pronounced. The childcare revolution did not arrive. Australia and other (formerly) colonised nations have major challenges to confront in the pathway to indigenous self-determination. The force of an individual's will cannot correct these inequalities.

We forget how frequently women pour all their political expectations and hopes into the vessel of a man. Consider Nancy Reagan,

Barbara Bush and the pre-senator Hillary Clinton. Men can temporarily rescue women. They can protect us from failure, while actually conjuring a weight of despair and disappointment not masked by the rhythms of grocery shopping, washing, ironing and vacuuming. I am always fascinated by women who meet a man and, after ten minutes of conversation, are assessing his marriage and breeding potential. Later, while on the phone, they connect his last name with their first, to doodle perspective married titles. They dawdle past jewellery stores with their girlfriends, dreaming of wedding rings. These women are hiding from their own lives. When they marry, they should put that ring through their nose, rather than on a finger. It would be more honest.

When women are attracted to influential, older men, they are drawn to a power that they can never hold. They see a big man, a man so big that a small woman can be enfolded into his life. No self-help book could — or should — make women feel pleased or justified about this sacrifice and fear of failure. Such an attraction lacks courage and a capacity to stand out, to risk mediocrity. Julie Burchill marks the aching shame of this discovery:

> Marriage: it's not all that's wrong with the world. But right here, right now, for healthy women during the closing steps of the twentieth century, it's most of what's wrong. Yoked together, male and female, on the hamster wheel of their own surrender to the system, and each hating the other for being the blood witness of their compromise and shame … You know how lying in bed too long is meant to waste your muscles? Well, lying in marriage too long wastes your brain.[15]

Julie Burchill is the Groucho Marx of feminism. With great humour, she shares life's black humour with her audience. We need her. I am always intrigued by the controversial topics chosen by leading feminist writers. For Burchill, it is a deadly accurate rendering of marriage, love and sex. She effortlessly connects politics inside and outside the home. She in unlike any other woman writer; her style is sharp, combining wit and poignancy.

Burchill's specific talents are revealed through comparison with other feminists. I have enjoyed little of the writing by Betty Friedan or Germaine Greer. My lack of pleasure does not mean that theirs is not important work to read and ponder. Simply, the political inflection and experiences have little connection with my life. I appreciate the lesser-known books. Friedan's *The Fountain of Age*[16] and Greer's *The Change* are superb. While basing their careers on overarching feminist texts, they are better writers when focussing on specific issues, like ageing or menopause. Their research is tighter; their writing sparkles. The collection of Greer's essays, *The Madwoman's Underclothes*, demonstrates her capacity to write blistering, fast prose.[17] Although her theorising of the media is poor, in the essay form she has written well on popular culture.[18] Many cultural critics have underestimated the range of her intellectual work. For example, Paglia mourned the loss of an earlier mode of feminism:

> Germaine Greer ... what a loss! If that woman had stayed on her original track, all of feminism would have been different. She was sophisticated, sexy, literate. What happened to her ... She turned into this drone, this whining, 'Woe is me, all the problems of this world'.[19]

Paglia could talk a glass eye to sleep. What is ironic is that she was not prepared to let Greer age and address new concerns in different ways. If only Paglia had exhibited Greer's range of interests. *The Change* is a fine book. It is not sexy, but it is important. Greer charts 'the difficult transition from reproductive animal to reflective animal'.[20] It is a mix of autobiography, literary analysis and critique of the medical discourse. Her rendering of 50-year-old women is not only an act of historical reclamation, but of political rejuvenation.

My major critique of Friedan, which she has not corrected through time, is the class-based bias in her work. In her memoir published in 2000, Betty Friedan still saw no contradiction between her arguments in *The Feminine Mystique,* stating in *Life so far* that 'I found a woman to clean and watch over the kids when I was writing, except she couldn't speak English'.[21] While she described her target audience as 'we, ordinary American women',[22] how would she label her (unnamed) housekeeper and childminder? Similarly, she has not corrected the historical record concerning her ignorance of the specificity of race. Instead, when African American women resisted joining the National Organisation of Women, Friedan 'wanted to spank them, but they learned soon enough. They eventually came in'.[23] Such statements are paternalistic, condescending and about as appropriate as taking a sleeping pill and a laxative on the same night.

What is odd is that Friedan has re-written her own radical past as a journalist in the United Electrical, Radio and Machine Workers' Union. Her role in anti-fascism and union activism during the 1940s and 1950s has left few traces on the record. Daniel Horowitz has enacted noteworthy historical detective work, considering Friedan would not allow the reproduction of her unpublished papers. He shows that:

> In focussing only on middle-class women, Friedan was following and making even less adversarial the genre of social criticism on which she patterned her own work. In opposition to all that she

knew as a labour journalist, she apparently believed that America had become a middle-class society.[24]

Horowitz has enacted a fascinating picture, charting how Friedan denied her early concern with class-based inequalities. There is something of a feminist mistake, in *The Feminine Mystique*.

Naomi Wolf, along with other self-proclaimed third-wave feminists, occupies a distinct place in media consciousness from Greer and Friedan. Highly visible, in *Fire With Fire* Wolf argues the usual line, that 'we must close the gap between the majority of American women and the women's movement'.[25] Similarly, she was concerned that 'a 1989 ... poll found that 33 percent of women called themselves feminists, and 58 percent did not'.[26] Wolf remains worried that 'some feminists'[27] have created opposition to the movement. Once more she is shooting (her mouth off at) the messenger. Who are 'some feminists'? As the book progresses, it is clear that her anger is fuelled by a desire to label and demean earlier modes of the women's movement.

This is a short-sighted tactic. It is always naïve to proclaim at twenty that we must not trust anyone over thirty/forty/fifty/sixty, because inevitably we become our own enemy. Think about Roger Daltrey singing 'I hope I die before I get old'.[28] His hope was not realised. If the alternatives are ageing or death, then I am heading for the former. I am younger than Wolf and Faludi, but I would never blame earlier feminists for the political flaws of the current age. After all, Greer, Steinem and Friedan are still writing in our present. Their work has changed and they must not be attacked because they do not provide *the answer* to all our problems. Although I do not appreciate *The Female Eunuch*, I know that it changed many women's lives. It is not my place to discredit women's journey. Obviously though, the personal attacks from third wavers are hitting the target. The great Lynne Segal lamented:

> As ... the fractiousness between feminists is matched by the decline in collective political engagements, I wasn't confident I could manage to write at all any more ... no longer sure of whom I would be writing for, or why.[29]

Other feminists are not the enemy. Feminism can change and grow without burning the books of the past. Perhaps the time has come to separate the personal and the political once more. It must be possible to dialogue about ideas without the identity-crushing demolition of women who have produced notable work for our benefit. I own every book Segal has written. They are well-read and well-loved. Those of us who believe in social change must commend our front-line fighters. That they are feeling gassed by following soldiers is a tragedy. Segal is right: 'yesterday's visionaries are today's scapegoats'.[30] The key for young feminists is to contextualise the work of earlier women: understand their purpose and see what of their agenda can be used in the present. Of course, there is precedent for young women's trashing of the past. Greer attacked 'the old suffragettes' for not mobilising their opportunities in parliament, the professions and the academy.[31] We must not forget that these 'old suffragettes' attended, and were ejected from, public rallies, and served prison terms for their beliefs. Greer does not give them this credit. It is far easier — and more exciting — to claim innovation, freshness and disappointment at those boring old women who did not live up to their promises. It is harder — but more honest — to understand the context of past truths and their legacy in the present. As Emmeline Pankhurst affirmed in her first speech after being released from prison, 'Be militant each in your own way'.[32] Every new political leader wants to break with the past. If a single difference separates the second and third wave then perhaps it is the understanding and use of popular culture and cyberculture.[33] I have enormous respect for cyberfeminists.[34] I have enough trouble with Macromedia Ultradev. I fear that when I turn my computer off, it is learning new things without me. Open the pod bay doors, HAL.

From critics of corsetry to cyberculture — feminism is a wide movement. No single sage can convey the agenda of an age. That includes Naomi Wolf. She told of asking 'who in my audiences of several hundred has read Germaine Greer or Betty Friedan,' and lamenting when 'usually fewer than a dozen hands go up'.[35] This is not a surprise. If members of the same group were asked if they had read Marx and Engels, or Dickens and Dickenson, then the answer would be the same. Wolf's audience straw poll does not signify that Greer or Friedan's words have little value. Feminism is not an ideological fire sale, auctioning off ideas to the most popular bidder. It does demonstrate that the literacy of the era has shifted. Feminism is everywhere, but in an altered form. From Madison Avenue to PJ Harvey[36] and Hole,[37] *Bridget Jones's Diary* to 'Sex in the City', the vocabulary and grammar of empowered women is punctuating our popular culture.

I am not suggesting that this is a purely positive force. While respecting Catharine Lumby's *Bad Girls* and *Gotcha*, I am concerned with the consequences of her argument:

> I argued that feminism can't simply be seen as a bunch of academic theories or political interventions, but that it's a set of ideas and practices which percolate right through popular culture. Feminist ideas circulate throughout our media ... it's incredibly easy to send up pop-culture appropriations of feminism and condemn them for turning a serious political agenda into a lipstick-and-Wonderbra fest. Yet it's equally true that popular culture is the

zone where many women encounter and negotiate political notions of sex, gender and the social, and to write this culture off as insufficiently complex means ignoring the politics embedded in these interactions.[38]

Obviously I agree with Lumby, but it must be remembered that such statements are motherhood mantras in cultural studies. If cultural studies has a single directive, then it is to value popular culture and link it with political change. The cultural populist framework, most frequently associated with the work of John Fiske, wove these notions into the cloth of cultural studies. Popular culture triggers heteroglossia. It is no surprise, therefore, that feminism is a part of popular culture. In fact, it would be remarkable if feminism was not ground into the granules of film, television and music. Post-disco popular music has been focussed around stroppy women belting out how men have done 'em wrong. Consider the irony of Britney Spears' 'Stronger', Mya's jealous rage in 'Case of the ex', or the saturating revenge of M People's 'Moving on up'. To see women dancing and singing along with these tracks is to witness a searing flash of empowerment. But the interpretations of these textual moments must not be assumed. Lumby is correct: it is important for all writers to hook readers through a reference that resonates in their lives. But writers must not leave their audience in a zone of contentment. To believe in social change necessitates challenging truths and agitating experiences. Our words must take readers on a journey of difference, distinction and change.

My concern with populist feminists, rather than feminist-inflected popular culture, is more detailed than Lumby's rendering makes possible. While her research into media feminism has been enormously important in Australian cultural studies, it is the political equivalent of a bald man's comb-over. It makes the wearer feel better, but others see through the ruse. No one is ignoring the politics of popular culture. We simply cannot agree on the nature and effectiveness of that politics.

We need Lynne Segal and we need 'Charlie's Angels'. Academically-trained feminists conduct powerful work that must be documented and rewarded. I wish it was read more frequently. I wish everyone would read more. Reading has been the greatest joy of my life. I consider it a privilege to buy a new book, to identify that the author has spent three or four years researching, thinking and writing and that, for the price of admission, I have been invited on a journey. That love of language does not mean that I do not dance, watch wrestling, listen to loud obnoxious music, spend way too much time and energy on my fingernails or scream at horror films. I do not separate reading, thinking and dancing. The aim of feminism is not to trash or celebrate popular culture or academic writing. The real skill lies in linking the two.

If Polly Toynbee believes that 'Feminism is boring',[39] then she has a responsibility to be active and activate change. Actually, writing about feminism is very difficult. The popular and the political, the textual and the economic, must be plaited. There is some powerful popular culture that needs to be mobilised and embedded in academic feminism. I remember the first time I saw Alanis Morissette's video 'You oughta know'. It was played late at night on the Australian national broadcaster's video show, 'Rage'. The woman with the crazy hair and the badly cut white suit shockingly fixated me with her raging eyes. And the lyrics — did I hear them correctly?

And every time I scratch my nails on someone else's back
I hope you feel it.[40]

No wonder Kevin Smith gave her the role of God in *Dogma*.[41] Elizabeth Wurtzel, who has handled popular culture brilliantly throughout her writing career, did not let Morrisette or *American Beauty* speak for feminism. Instead she framed, discussed and questioned their truths, showing their application to the women's movement. Most significantly, she reminded her readers:

Feminism saved these women's lives. It saved your life too, and if you don't know that, you are reading the wrong book.[42]

Wurtzel reminds readers that life was starkly different before the 1960s. Banks would not extend credit to women without a husband or father's 'support', they could not equally access graduate or professional qualifications at universities and were paid less and accorded less status in the work they attained. Their titles were either Miss or Mrs. The former signified either an available (for what?) woman or a spinster. The latter meant that a woman had taken on the name and identity of her husband.

Feminists, much to the angst of the anti-feminists who are gaining increasing visibility, do not hate men. Men are not the primary target of the women's movement. Its aim is to assemble consciousness and collective action. Men are decentred from the political stage. If some men and women confront being (temporarily) ignored with hatred, then — to quote Julie Burchill — they are suffering 'from severe spotlight deprivation'.[43] The women's movement invokes an appreciation and understanding of being a woman, not chattel. Sommers believed that 'certain feminists [are] so eager to put men in a bad light'.[44] She is a '60 Minutes' piece waiting to happen. Her argument is masochistic and simple. To read the biographies of feminists who gained power through the 1970s is to see continual, passionate relationships with men.[45] Sommers, Roiphe and Wolf are too demanding of the feminist ghosts they find in the pages of the past. The aim of the women's movement is not to ensure that women get married or stay single, but to grant them a choice to do either. These self-proclaimed third wavers must be more open to difference and more active in their interpretation of history. Gloria Steinem is not Femmo, a new scary fifth Teletubbie.

We need more than knockers of the past. While I am in favour of earnest, rigorous debate, Greer, Steinem or Friedan should not be judged because they do not have hair like Naomi Wolf or the family connections of Kate Roiphe. Sommers, Roiphe and Wolf need to laugh more and gorge themselves with life. Never trust a woman who does not know how to behave at a (feminist) smorgasbord. It is obvious that these women would head straight for the salad. While the rest of us anchor ourselves to the smoked salmon and prawns, to be followed by a multi-layered chocolate torte *and* a mousse, Wolf would look at us (with pity) while picking at her Roma tomato. There is only one (culinary) rule in life: never eat anything we cannot lift. Part of the joy of life — every now and again — is to be gorged with joy, laughter and chocolate. These women are so self-controlled and so demanding of others.

The goal of radical politics, the point of desiring social change, is to stretch and poke citizens and their lived truths. Only when people are uncomfortable, do they re-think their lives. Popular culture, because it is reliant on both consumerism and capitalism, continually patrols the boundaries of acceptable behaviour. It is not intrinsically conservative or radical. The popular is also hegemonic. The women's movement must not be as guarded. At times, feminists need to be as unpopular as a proctologist with depth-perception problems.

It does not worry me that feminism is not popular. It never was. I never expect it to be. When Sommers whines that feminists 'blame a media "backlash" for the defection of the majority of women',[46] she does not make the obvious realisation that feminism *has never* been popular. She has a naïve, Oprahfied notion of politics. Unless the audience applauds a motherhood statement ('Being a parent is the toughest job in the world.' Tumultuous ovation.), then feminists must be doing something wrong. If feminism was popular, if Wolf reported in one of her surveys that 99.5 per cent of American college students termed themselves feminists, then I would be concerned.[47] When Betty Friedan stepped down as the president of the National Organisation of Women, there were only 3000 members, spread between ten chapters in thirty States.[48] This was no mass movement.

The next section enters one of the most controversial spheres of our era, which accesses popular culture, governmental policies and none-too-popular feminism. It also reveals the profound consequences of excluding feminist directives in the debates of the age. Compliant, hegemonic, popular approaches are not useful when confronting our current educational system and the men working within it. A critical, interrogative, snarling approach is more viable.

BUT CAN SHE REVERSE A TRAILER?

There is trouble in manland. A four-centimetre headline in *The West Australian* on 6 January 2001 screamed 'GIRL POWER'.

The West Australian, Saturday 6 January 2001.
(Photograph: Don Palmer)

The reporter, Geraldine Capp, foreshadowed the end of Western civilisation:

> Girls outsmarted boys in the tertiary entrance exams and blitzed them in Year 12 vocational subjects. Girls took out most of the academic prizes with 21 of the 40 general exhibitions and 20 of the 26 subject exhibitions. They also overwhelmed the boys by winning 17 of 18 subject prizes in non-TEE subjects. These included the traditional male subjects of automotive workshop, furniture design and technology, business information technology, outdoor education and small business management.[49]

Readers could rightly be confused at this emphasis. Those who had watched the preceding night's television coverage of the Tertiary Entrance Examination results on both commercial and public broadcasters would have seen three bright young men, smiling into the camera as they were congratulated for their awards. There were no women in these televised reports. Therefore, the headline was a surprise. What the writer and editor buried in this article of feminine revolution was the fact that a young man topped the State, boys attained the four highest scores and also the Award for Excellence in Vocational Studies. Instead of acknowledging the top student on the front page of the paper, he was not mentioned. Instead, Rachael Ord was photographed, dusting (!) a jarrah table that earned her the award of top student in furniture design and technology.[50] While this achievement deserved much credit and commendation, the parents of the Beazley Medallist would be rightly amazed by a jarrah table overshadowing their son's accomplishment. He had a remarkable story to tell. At sixteen years of age, he had skipped several grades and was also a talented musician. Anthony Phillips was not even named in the page one article. He was given a mid-level article on page eight, with a seven-millimetre-high headline.[51]

There were many other possible emphases in these Tertiary Entrance results. State schools recovered from the disastrous results of the preceding year. Country students were well represented; the second highest result was attained by Samuel Bennett, who attended Northam Senior High School. Also of interest was how students were amalgamating academic and vocational courses into their final year's study. However, *The West Australian* chose to cry wolf over a gender crisis. We need to unpick the nature of this fabricated fracas.

The article reported that 'Girls took out *most* of the academic prizes with 21 of the 40 general exhibitions' (emphasis added). By my calculation, twenty-one is only 52.5 per cent of forty, which is not *most*. It is marginally more than half. Similarly, the article stated that of the top 1000 students, 477 were male and 523 were female. Again, these statistics demonstrate that 52.3 per cent of these high-achieving students were women. This was not 'Girl Power'. It was a minor statistical aberration for one year. Little commentary was made on the pattern of the tertiary entrance results, which men have dominated through history. If men had attained twenty-one of the forty prizes, then no comment would have been made.

With these statistics belying their journalistic interpretation, it is necessary to assess the basis for this analytical framework. Geraldine Capp constructed her investigation on the testimony of four experts — two women and two men. They were highly disparate in terms of professional standing. Guess the gender of the following professionals:

- Professor (and Dean) of Education at Curtin University
- Education Department Director-General
- Principal of a private girls' school
- State School Teachers' Union President

No prizes, or even vocational awards, for guessing that the first two 'experts' were men, the last two were women. No surprise in discovering that the men cried catastrophe, while the women fathomed no surprises or difficulties in these statistics:

> I do not think it is disturbing because in the long term it evens out.[52]

> We have to be really careful not to overreact because the reality is that boys are still getting jobs. When girls leave school they still face many more disadvantages.[53]

These are reasoned responses to a non-story story. Neither the principal nor the union president fixated on a single year's results, but commented about longer-term historical and social trends. Their testimony is decentred because of the power held by the male sources, which actually verifies the argument that 'boys are still getting jobs'. The Education Department Director-General assured his male colleagues that 'the problems come up early in schooling and we have strategies in place which are directed at helping boys'.[54] How great could these problems be, with men attaining the top four places in the State and nineteen of the forty general exhibition prizes? These minor shortfalls in attaining 50 per cent of the prizes require 'strategies' to make the system fairer for boys. Much of this discussion is resonant of the classroom study of boys' and girls' speaking patterns. When girls speak up to 30 per cent of the time, the boys believe the girls are talking more than 50 per cent of the time and are taking over.[55]

The most astonishing testimony, which is the trigger for the remainder of this section, was derived from the Education Dean of Curtin University. He was the first 'expert' quoted in the piece and was cited in the most depth:

> Something needs to be done urgently because there should be no distinction between students on the basis of gender in terms of who can perform better ... We are seeing a gender difference and it is not because girls are better than boys. It is clear that the system is not working as well for boys.[56]

This crisis of the system is not a quirky, wild Western Australian formation.[57] It is part of a widespread 'cry she-wolf' movement in the

United Kingdom and the United States. Female success is not being applauded, acknowledged or appreciated. Instead it is a problem — a problem for boys. By placing attention on the marginal softening of young men's results, there is a serious assumption driving the words of Professor Dellar and others in this international 'crisis': the assumption that men must always be the dominant sex. He does not confront his illogical argument. How could a system not working well for boys allow them to attain the top scores? Of greater concern is the realisation that, as a Dean of Education, most of the students in his care at Curtin University are women. What is he teaching them of 'the system', a system that has installed a male professor and Dean in an occupation dominated by women?

By the middle of 2001, 'The trouble with boys' had become a headline story in *The Weekend Australian*.[58] The illustration featured a glum schoolboy, standing morose and isolated before a large blackboard. The article is littered with unsubstantiated, unnamed sources. Once more, Western Australian principals were trotted out to provide their try-hard arguments, asking 'for anonymity for the purposes of this article'.[59] Most ironic of all is the statement from a Conservative member of Parliament, Brendan Nelson, who believed that 'there is also a problem with people denying there is a problem'.[60] It obviously never occurred to him that there actually *may be no problem*, that the ideology of feminine success has corrupted his judgment of masculine crisis.

We live in an era of experts. Whenever an examination result or an educational policy is released, a greying man in a badly scuffed corduroy jacket is summoned to offer an opinion that, from the mouth of an expert, becomes a truth. Those who hold power rarely wish to lose it. Therefore, it is not surprising that rasping naysayers have attempted to decentre and silence the language of feminism within this debate. The argument that women have now attained equality in education rarely suggests how this notion is being either defined or applied. Indeed, what is the difference between equality and equal opportunity? It is ironic that a meritocratic framework was used throughout the post-war period to demonstrate that women and the working class had a chance for educational success if they took the opportunity. Now that women are able to pull up those bootstraps, the meritocratic system is to be blamed for their accomplishment.

A series of statistics not disclosed by the male Australian educational experts is far more wide-ranging and convincing in terms of both space and time. Question B12 on the 1996 Australian Census data featured the following information about the 'Age left School by Sex'. These statistics surveyed all persons aged fifteen years and over.

B12 AGE LEFT SCHOOL BY SEX
Persons aged 15 years and over

	Male	Female	Persons
14 years and under	927 921	978 632	1 906 553
15 years	1 316 797	1 445 483	2 762 280
16 years	1 289 081	1 351 776	2 640 857
17 years	1 295 937	1 396 968	2 692 905
18 years	876 818	808 031	1 684 849
19 years and over	284 502	239 362	523 864
Still at school	326 732	330 737	657 469
Never attended school	42 424	58 603	101 027
Not stated	456 596	488 496	945 092
TOTAL	6 816 808	7 098 088	13 914 896

Statistics derived from Census 1996, Australian Bureau of Statistics, *Basic Community Profile*, Document number 2020.0.

While the girls' recent success is predicted in the increased number still at school when the census was taken, the rest of the table makes grim reading for any educationalist. Considering the entire population of Australia, men are better educated than women. More women than men have never attended school, more women did not want their educational level listed, and far more women left school at fifteen years or under. If the Australian education system has failed anyone throughout its history, it is women. It will take many years of women 'overachieving' men by 2.3 per cent to overcome the scale of this disadvantage.

The 'problem' for these empowered educators is not underachieving boys, but overachieving girls.[61] Educational testing is a volatile political terrain. My question is: why is gender framed as *the* policy variable, rather than class, race or region? The discourse of boys' 'failure' needs both a rationale and a scapegoat. Young women's success provides an answer to both. Over the last ten years, the language has shifted from equal opportunity for all students to underachievement for young men. The notion that 'we' need to change the pedagogy, subjects and environment — the system — so that boys will learn better is not asking broader questions about the history of both men and women in education. The language through which success is described is highly distinct for young men and women. While boys have 'intellectual gifts ... evident at an early age',[62] girls are 'all rounders' who exclaim that 'I never expected to go this high'.[63] Boys display natural ability, while girls are diligent. In a toss between brilliance and reliable hard work, boys have their excellence validated. Girls play a supportive role in boys' luminosity.

Equality and difference are not static terms.[64] The meritocratic notion that anyone can 'make it' ensures that educational outcomes are riddled with class, race and gender biases. There are at least three distinct curricula circulating in the contemporary school system. The academic curriculum, assessed by standardised tests frequently enabling university entry, values education for its own sake. Extending its origins back to Plato and continued in the Oxbridge tradition, this curriculum organises knowledge into subject areas and ranks their importance. English literature, physics and higher mathematics are granted status over manual arts or typing. To succeed in these subjects is to gain entry into the high-status professions.

The vocational curriculum ties the school system to the workplace. Educational institutions provide young people with work-related skills. The school and university transform into the resource base of employment, offering, for example, graduates with technology-related skills. Throughout the nineteenth and twentieth centuries — and into the twenty-first — schools have taught discipline, regularity, obedience and a reward for effort. At school, like at the factory, workers are called to the job by a bell. Therefore, class-based interests are served. This curriculum has increased in its momentum and range during the last twenty years. As Preston and Symes have apprehended:

> The sad irony must be noted that much of the impetus to vocational education coincides with the push to boost secondary school retention rates, a trend substantially motivated by the huge downturn in the youth labour market. In other words, the effort to get schools to prepare increasing numbers of young people for the workplace coincides with the lack of work opportunities confronting those students.[65]

At the very time of lessening employment opportunities, schools and universities have their purpose geared to work-place preparation. This economic function of education explains the growth of Asian studies, business studies and computer studies through the 1980s and early 1990s.[66]

The other curriculum weaved through the system is a democratic or remedial imperative. Education is granted a social purpose, encouraging participation in citizenship and the nation-state. As schooling became universalised, this curriculum gained in importance, encouraging the use of words like access, opportunity and equality. While feminist and social democratic theories may stress the emancipatory orientation of schooling, it is the academic and vocational strands that are granted the most attention and creditability.

The delicate dance between the three curricula results in difficult decisions for teachers, negotiated on a daily basis. John Knight investigated how the multiple functions of education operate, particularly in disempowered communities, such as those in South Auckland:

Schooling is substantially implicated in the production and reproduction of the social formation, including inequalities ... while schooling may not be able to change the world it should provide some advantage to its users ... while appropriate to their communities, they [South Auckland teachers] sought also to enable their students to succeed in the mainstream of society.[67]

Within these three sentences, we view the passage between citizenship, vocationalism and academic attainment. It is a knotted, perhaps impossible, position to maintain with consistency.

Women believe in education. They approach high school and university with enthusiasm and commitment. However, they are mirroring the faith in education expressed by recent immigrants. It is almost as if women are migrants to the land of power and possess an unshaken belief that a degree will open up a world of success and happiness. Women are finishing high school and gaining degrees during an era when these qualifications have never been worth less. Marginson affirmed that:

... the simultaneous growth in education participation and the number of people holding educational credentials has had a number of effects on the relationship between education and the labour market. First, educational qualifications are now required in order to enter almost any form of long-term career-oriented work. 'Shop floor to manager' is a thing of the past: management training is the fastest growing area of tertiary education.[68]

This degree-inflation means that qualifications are required to attain employment, but are not granted the value of earlier periods. Female university graduates have a lower initial salary than men and, when promoted, clutter up middle management. There is also a highly disparate (un)employment rate for male and female PhD holders. Women believe that the testamur will guarantee equality, but the faith in education is misplaced.[69]

While Australian educators are starting to publicly vocalise their disquiet with a system that does not automatically reward boys for brilliance, their words are unerringly resonant of international commentators. My favourite example of this genre is from Christina Hoff Sommers, whose latest 'research' details *The war against boys: how misguided feminism is harming our young men*. This book is a brilliant historical document of our era. I laughed more while reading this text than when watching the 'Bro' episode of 'Seinfeld'. Offering 'a good word for the capitalist patriarchy and marital virtues',[70] Sommers tells 'a story of how we are turning against boys and forgetting a simple truth: that the energy, competitiveness and corporeal daring of normal, decent males is responsible for much of what is right in the world'.[71] It seems appropriate that Sommers becomes the ventriloquist's dummy for male educational professors.

Alongside motherhood and apple pie resides Christina Hoff Sommers. How do we interpret her analysis? At the end of a century that encouraged boys to finish school and girls to leave, there is a fear that boys are being pathologised, their natural ability remaining inhibited. Throughout much of the twentieth century, there was little panic about the girls who did not enrol in higher science and maths; now it is boys' 'underachievement' that is 'contentious and ideological'.[72] It is an opportunity for much gnashing of gold capping and shrill wailing from neo-liberal pseudo-feminists like Sommers. All these movements, books and ideas aim to return men to the centre of the educational stage, in full spotlight. As Presidents, Professors or Problems — and sometimes all three — we need to focus on the men. That is the important topic for our attention.

It is also remarkable when these American masculine defenders cite the Australian context to verify their 'global' correctness. For example, William Pollack found that:

> In Australia, as elsewhere, regional and national studies that seek to understand the troubles which girls experience in the education system have also uncovered the unexpected news about boys and their struggles to thrive. 'What about the boys?' has become a rallying cry for Australian researchers, psychologists, parents and teachers … It has become obvious that the problem of 'the blokes' runs deeper than mere school performance. The boyhood pain that we are finally beginning to recognize is nothing short of a world-wide epidemic.[73]

The crisis of a system has become a global disease. Men are receiving 'mixed messages' and are feeling 'a sadness and disconnection they cannot even name'.[74] As the Co-Director of the Centre for Men at McLean Hospital and a faculty member of the Harvard Medical School, Pollack does not discuss the power and success he holds. But he has noticed the obvious. If men are oppressed, then it is other men who do the oppressing. What school teaches boys is the range of valued masculine attributes and the subordinate masculinities attached to homosexuality and the feminine. Kenway ponders:

> … there are different ways of being a male, some more valued and prestigious and powerful than others, and that one way of being and feeling powerful as a male is to demonstrate power over other males and over females. Sport plays a major role here.[75]

Girls and women are not creating men's problems. School is not trig-
gering men's problems. Far greater and wider ideologies of power,
authority and responsibility are moulding the notion of crisis. The theorists of this crisis are locked into a vacuum-sealed dialogue. Mclean
showed that 'for men, two things seem to go inextricably together —
the desire for power and the fear of powerlessness'.[76] These protest
masculinities are constructing men as the new victims. But men and
women can intervene in, critique and shape the gender patternings of
institutions. While a lock and load mentality predominates, progressive
modes are rarely offered as worthy or valuable substitutes.

Emerging through the language of equal opportunity and meritoc-
racy is the realisation that young women have triggered a surprise.
Women have started to gain scholastic success. We must recognise
though that, structurally, the system has not changed radically. The sci-
ences and mathematics are still highly valued. Literature is more important than typing. Now that equal opportunity is not working (for boys),
the system must be changed. Social justice in education in the past has
meant equal access by all citizens, but there must be attention placed on
the curriculum — with what is being accessed and distributed.

Children are taught through education about the limits of acceptable
behaviour. What young women and men are being taught in our current
intellectual climate is that when men do dominate a system, the system
must be changed. Popular culture is filled with images and narratives of
men controlling their environment. From Rambo to Dirty Harry, from
the Westerns to the Action Adventure, men temper and mould the world
to their liking. It is a mystery why empowered educationalists are inse-
cure about young men's results in education, when profound and
encompassing sites of masculine power saturate politics, media and the
law. Men's economic influence is profound. As Connell has reported,
'men's average income in Australia is approximately twice women's average income, when all men and women are taken into account (and not
just those in fulltime work)'.[77] Despite these advantages, when women
attain a 2.3 per cent higher ranking than men, a wire of such tautness is
tripped that the educational system must be changed. Men are like Super
Mario: they keep fighting to go up to the next level.

Most distressing in this discussion of young men's 'failures' is the
knowledge that the women gaining success have their achievements
decentred, mocked and problematised. I also believe that these 'education experts' are not accurately considering the consequences of their
actions. Many parents of sons are also parents of daughters. Few would
discredit the achievement of young women who have worked hard and
frequently overcome incredible odds. They are certainly role models. If
a woman can top the State in Automotive Workshop, then I can learn
how to change a tyre. Similarly, Rachael Ord, who won the Furniture

Design and Technology Award, was the only girl in a woodwork class of eighteen students. She stated that 'the boys were conscientious and ambitious but I seemed to set myself bigger tasks'.[78] We can only imagine the difficulties, isolation and questions that were asked of her. She took a risk, stepped outside of a gendered box and was successful. We would like to believe that such ambitious women will attain great success as they move into — and through — the university system. Unfortunately, this imperative has not been sustained.

A GLASS CEILING IN A HOUSE OF CARDS: PONDERING UNIVERSITY WOMEN

People have this fantasy (as I did when I was young) of colleges being liberatory institutions, when in fact they're so much like every other institution in our culture in terms of repression and containment — so now I feel like I'm trying to break out.[79]

bell hooks

In most workplaces, feminism is about as appropriate as finding Kenny G in a mosh pit. Universities are no different. It may be assumed that women have been assisted by affirmative action policies, yet they remained locked in the lower leaves of the academy in traditionally female disciplines. Female teachers are, as a percentage, also well below the participation level of female students.[80] While I have always been suspicious of the phrase 'glass ceiling', it is appropriately applied to the university sector.[81] A-level or Associate Lecturers refer to the staff primarily responsible for tutorials, with some lecturing. B-level staff are accountable for course co-ordination and some administration. When reaching the higher bands, staff are involved in university-based management, while also attaining a level of leadership and visibility in their field. However, a pronounced barrier of feminine achievement separates the Senior Lecturer (level C) from the Associate/Professor (level D/E).

Full-time academic staff in Australia by employment level and gender

		A	B	C	D/E	Total	Number
1988	M%	12	35	30	23	100	19 300
	F%	33	45	13	9	100	7 258
1992	M%	14	35	29	23	100	21 358
	F%	31	49	15	5	100	9 987
1995	M%	15	33	28	24	100	21 906
	F%	32	45	17	7	100	11 030
1999	M%	15	31	28	26	100	20 907
	F%	29	43	20	8	100	11 499

Statistics derived from DETYA (Department of Education, Training and Youth Affairs), 1988–1999, *Selected Higher Education Statistics*.

Much can be read from this table. There is clearly a lack of promotion of women from Senior Lecturer to Associate Professor. While 26 per cent of men hold the title of Associate Professor or Professor, only 8 per cent of women possess the same ranking. This proportion has marginally declined between 1988 and 1999. It cannot be assumed that women will inevitably be promoted to these upper levels, as the entire tertiary sector is declining in numbers. The retiring senior men are not being replaced. In pure economic terms, Marion Sullivan has conveyed the consequences of these figures: 'the average female academic earns 70 per cent of her male colleague's salary'.[82] In 1997 women held only 27 per cent of tenured positions, but comprised 42 per cent of academics on fixed-term contracts.[83] We must probe the unspoken assumptions of the university sector and ask how women can be springboarded into leadership, creating not only a confidence about the workplace, but an ability and space to present gendered concerns. Higher education is suffering a credibility crisis. While there is much talk of efficiency and productivity, fewer staff are completing much more work. The women at the lower end of the seniority spectrum are not only the most vulnerable, but are undertaking the most teaching in overcrowded and under-resourced classrooms.[84]

Competence is determined by the environment. Strong performance is encouraged and framed by an appropriate context. Women are outside leadership positions at universities because their activities are frequently invisible and their modalities of power are distinct from the organisational culture of the workplace. Women's lives in the corporate and public sector make more sense when conceding that managers see the woman first and the worker second. Women's discourse is framed as a problem, invoking descriptions such as nagging, bitching or gossiping. Throughout history, women who speak with authority and knowledge have been labelled either witches or hysterics. The career woman, in a French navy suit, has become a postmodern monster. Through films like *Disclosure* and *The Last Seduction*, she is vicious and ambitious. Such determinations have been particularly marked in Australian history, with a highly segregated workforce.[85]

Feminist educational thinking offers alternatives to iconic representations of the school ma'am and of teaching as an expression of natural maternal motivation. Emerging from bureaucratisation and the social efficiency movements, teaching and learning evolves into a set of quantifiable skills and characteristics. There is a confluence between professionalism and maleness. This means that the subjectivity of female teachers and students is frequently displaced or dismissed.

A very precise mode of feminism must be deployed in the university environment during this volatile time. Jennifer Gore, for example, reported that a female and feminist academic was once asked in a seminar, 'how do you reconcile wearing lipstick with your work on feminist pedagogy?'.[86] There are so few faces of female power: it is not surprising that debates about the appearance of this face become significant. Writing is emerging that profiles the generational tension between women of the academy.[87] This problem is exacerbated because women are under-represented in educational management.[88] Women frequently describe their working lives in universities as 'feel[ing] taut, almost to breaking point'.[89] It is also difficult to diffuse authority between staff and students without intervening in the business as usual mode of teaching, research and management. Students, like other disenfranchised groups, do not have an authentic voice that can be represented by the empowered.

Social justice requires intervention, not an acceptance of conventional structural truths. Men have held power and authority throughout the history of universities. Rarely has this power been overtly misused. A horrifying example of mishandled authority, which is presented as a factual record but I hope is an example of fantastical masculine bragging, was recorded in *Harper's Magazine* in 1993. William Kerrigan, Professor of English at the University of Massachusetts, reported that:

> I have been the subject of advances from male and female students for twenty-five years. I've had them come at me right and left. I've had people take their clothes off in my office. And there is a particular kind of student I have responded to … I'm talking about a female student who, for one reason or another, has unnaturally prolonged her virginity … There have been times when this virginity has been presented to me as something that I, not quite like another man, half an authority figure, can handle … these relationships between adults can be quite beautiful and genuinely transforming. It's very powerful sexually and psychologically, and because of that power, one can touch a student in a positive way.[90]

The notion of a young woman's virginity being 'presented' to an ageing academic turns my stomach. This story conveys the double standards of both age and sexuality. Describing sexual intercourse between an old professor and a young woman as 'quite beautiful' is not the description I would use. It is a flagrant misuse of power. What I find so bemusing is the pride this ageing scholar exhibits in the advances he has attracted from students, assuming that they are interested in him, rather than the aura of his university position. All academics, almost on a weekly basis, must deal with emotional students and situations. Students in our care are testing the limits of their new identity. They cry, they provoke, they fling their problems at us. Part of the job is to handle these situations as delicately as possible, allowing the student's identity to remain intact. To take advantage of, or twist these situations, is the work of an egocentric fool. Kerrigan has obviously forgotten his own vulnerability as an 18-year-old in a new environment. Students do not need to have sexual intercourse with staff members. Students require a bond of trust. While sexual harassment is a highly volatile issue in Australian workplaces, this type of behaviour must be neither justified, nor rendered ennobling or enriching.

The aim for the current generation who are just entering positions of leadership is to naturalise the work of women, not justify it. While I believe that the Faludi-inspired discussions of a feminist backlash were too encompassing and pessimistic, I remain concerned by the gentle, quiet acceptance by women that they will earn less, are not worthy of promotion and are not management material. Similarly, Friedan has started incinerating her own legacy, observing that:

> In the last five years there has been a significant drop in income — nearly 20 percent — of college-educated white American men. Not minority, high school-educated, or blue-collar, but white management men, the masters of the universe ... Of course, women, on the whole are still not making as much money as men. But more women are coming out of professional programs into management jobs.[91]

Friedan's *Beyond Gender* comes close to blaming women's 'success' for men's 'failure'. She sees that women — and family values — will suffer through the economic insecurity of men.[92] Once more the binary of woman versus man has been rendered an adversarial, oppositional, competitive force in society. This division is only highlighted when men are supposedly suffering within the system.

From talkback hosts to journalists and politicians, we live in a time where the prevalent notion of a university scholar is a man or woman encased in an ivory tower, distanced from the gritty world of life and experience. We become the safe targets for ridicule and dismissal, taking from the public purse and living an easy, dreamlike existence of writing, posturing and endless coffee breaks. The campus has been enmeshed in — and at times blamed for — declining standards of literacy, high levels of unemployment and Australia's unreadiness to move into the informatic age. Academics have been granted these responsibilities at a time when universities and scholars are drenched with low credibility.

A university in this position cannot solve the nation's problems. Scholarly work is moulded by experience, but must connect individual narratives with social and political movements. There is a need to arch above the shaming and blaming of women. The most effective way to move beyond this scrutiny of women's behaviour inside and outside the university, and to add complexity to the texture of women's lives, is to enter the realm of representation.

DINNER IS READY WHEN THE SMOKE ALARM GOES OFF
Lots of us, myself included, go to movies to learn stuff.[93]
bell hooks

All women have a little Stevie Nicks inside of them; a woman with an overfondness for crimped hair, big clothes, gothic dancing and shawls with too many fringes. Singers, film stars, comedians, comic book superheros and fashion editors teach us about romance, inequality, injustice, struggle and success. Organising popular culture into narratives of self and society creates the momentum of everyday life. It must be anchored to a recognisable frame. *Notting Hill* was such a phenomenal success because it started in a grimy bookshop and flat, with a hairy flatmate and a series of friends unable to manage successful inter-personal relationships.[94] The women in *Notting Hill* are funny, powerful and honest. The men celebrate their failures and indeed compete 'for a brownie' to determine the biggest loser.

Feminism, alongside anti-racist movements, has crumbled the creamy, white façade of the past. It is no surprise that such a startling, controversial and powerful paradigm has punctuated popular culture. Through disco and the disco(urse) divas Donna Summer and Gloria Gaynor, black women asserted the power of both a voice and body. It was bell hooks who suggested that the point of feminism is to 'make room for self-determining, passionate women who will be able to just be'.[95] There is a need to develop critical, creative thinking towards these artefacts of the age. While young women in particular do not have equal access to the modes of representation, they have made a profound and significant use of available texts. Women use popular culture to renegotiate the social truths of their lives.

Feminists question the representations of the feminine. By finding and naming patriarchal discourses, they offer a critique that opens the public sphere to new ways of constructing ideas and images. In the battle for either equality or autonomy, the aim is to create alternatives to masculine norms.[96] The media's role as an agent of socialisation necessitates a concentration on who is both absent and present within the representational field. The feminist theorists who are open to the media's potential in presenting social alternatives demonstrate great resilience during politically challenging eras. Obviously, theorists have been worried that they must trade too much political specificity to enter the realm of hegemonic negotiation. For example, Patricia Hill Collins presents a case for the important particularities of black feminist thought:

> Oppressed groups are frequently placed in the situation of being listened to only if we frame our ideas in the language that is familiar to and comfortable for a dominant group. This requirement

often changes the meaning of our ideas and works to elevate the ideas of dominant groups.[97]

The conformist nature of the last twenty years has meant that all of us who believe in social change and responsibility have had to accept less and re-cut the fabric of neo-liberalism. Catharine Lumby's *Bad Girls* and *Gotcha* emerged from the conservative John Howard years. Elayne Rapping's *Media-tions* originated from the Reagan/Bush era. Through the times of backlash and attacks on feminist imperatives, there is an analytical need to return to hegemonic contestations.

Hegemony describes how power is renegotiated in culture. It refers to the ways in which the truths of popular culture are agreeable to both dominant and subordinate groups. A disempowered collective wins concessions from the powerful so that it agrees to the conditions of its subjugation. These terms are accepted because the disenchanted communities gain pleasure and reclaim some cultural terrain — this is the payoff for their consent. Hegemony operates in the realm of both consciousness and representations. The aim is not to coerce the disempowered into a position of weakness, but to grant the weak some space to remould commonsense.

An obvious example of this renegotiation of power is found within popular music. Divas singing about Dilberts who done 'em wrong is a significant subgenre of dance culture. While young women are frequently disempowered by the realities of romance, love, sex and relationships, it is in the realm of dance music that this subjugation is not only hinted, but discussed overtly and renegotiated. Consider these lyrical highlights from the genre:

> Don't underestimate me boy
> I'll make you sorry you were born
> You don't know me
> The way you really should
> You sure misunderstood
> Don't call me baby[98]

> Now who the hell are you to treat me
> Like that? I don't care where you've been
> What you've done or where you're at
> Now who the hell are you, to act the way you do?
> You won't be smiling by the time
> I'm through with you[99]

Importantly, popular music is far more than pointed, punchy, empowered lyrics. These sadistic, revengeful words explode from a gleaming backbeat and smooth Philadelphia sound sample. The movement in ideas is delivered via a movement of the body. Both dancing and dance music are culturally demeaned activities, but through these textual and reading tactics, women's consent can be managed and negotiated. From Gloria Gaynor's 'I will survive' to Pat Benatar's 'Love is a Battlefield', women are using popular music to think through the battlefields and disappointments of their lives. The primary structures of these inequalities are not challenged, but the meanings granted to these activities are shifting. This is hegemony in motion.

Popular culture allows us to make sense of the world. There is great pleasure derived from producing meaning at that moment when a song collides with life experience. Popular culture is creative and traverses limitations, borders and boundaries with relish and ruthless precision. There is also pleasure in aligning reading practices with the dominant ideologies of racism, sexism and homophobia. It remains an analytical imperative to sort out, judge and evaluate cultural formations, rather than accepting the pleasure and popularity as either self-evident, or intrinsically — politically — useful.

The problematic compulsion for media-based theorists is a desire to render feminism accessible. Rapping noted that 'a troubling gap has developed between academic and public discourse'.[100] For many feminists, a way to bridge the intellectual/popular gap is to enter the pornography controversy, the most extreme of representational frameworks. I am not remotely interested in pornography. Politically, I am anti-censorship, but am not unilaterally in favour of letting it all hang out, baby. This is the odd nature of the pornography debate. Even as we try to avoid it, the polarised positions crush us within its grasp. What feminists, and others, frequently refuse to acknowledge is that most pornography is boring. Anal probes and bad guitar soundtracks are not the foundation for political change. Without a doubt, pornography is denigrating for women. It is also denigrating for men. It crushes the flesh, blood and bone of sexuality and the tenderness and silences of intimacy into poor editing, rushed scripting and awkward characterisation. If women are the trophy in the pornography narrative, then men are merely the horses in the saddling yard.

Pornographic images and ideas move smoothly through films, magazines, advertisements and novels. When confronted by the genre in its more pure form, it can prove debilitating. When Jane Ussher watched the films:

> I lost sense of myself ... its impact certainly seeped into my personal life and I began to see the boundaries of acceptability in the sphere of sexuality very differently than I had before.[101]

From a libertarian perspective, it is a political reflex to affirm that sexual plurality and a roaming imagination are always beneficial to the forging of a new world order. These myriad visions can empower the already empowered. Pleasure — sexual pleasure — is the reward for consenting to 'the system'. For women, the key node of argument is whether or not sexuality can be separated from violence and domination. Provocatively, Catharine Lumby has asked two questions:

> Why do feminists need porn?
> Why do feminists bother talking about porn?[102]

There are consequences for her questions. Pornography transforms the feminine and the child into a consumable product.[103] It is a provocative genre because it occupies the boundary of what is representable. It is a system that signifies sexuality. The slippage between the object and the subject places women and children in a viscous lattice of representation, the 'indefinite, in-finite, form'.[104] There is no solution to this soluble imaginary. Images of women are dissolved into images of sex. Pornography is not isolated away from other configurations of women or men. The brutish hero, like Heathcliff or Rhett Butler, is perpetuated by Code Men, a bizarre cultural movement to counter The Rules Women. They remind their readers that, 'a Code guy ... never forgets that he is, first and last, the consumer, and that is his strength'.[105] As consumers, men become justified in pollinating women, deserting one bud and moving on to the next. My worry is that too much attention is placed on pornography, deflecting attention away from the popular culture that is productive, potent and pithy. So much of culture is worth fighting for, arguing about — and is a trigger for laughing, dancing and thinking.

The difficulty for the feminist movement is learning how to manage a stance of anti-censorship alongside a concern with some of the excesses of pornography. Steinem's description is an admonition:

> Young girls with tear tracks in their make-up as they experience 'pleasure' in their humiliation, women chained with their legs apart while bottles and rods are forced up their vaginas; girls who smile, apparently on drugs, as their nipples and labia are pierced by needles.[106]

The reason why feminist writing about pornography is so powerful is that it re-tells the narrative and describes the images of the films. For women who have not been exposed to these ideas, it can appear horrifying, shocking and polluting. It reveals the backside, rather than the face, of humanity. However, Dworkin and others are simply describing the images, not analysing why they have such currency.[107] Theorists with interests in feminism must not focus on pornography in isolation. As a genre, it is not unique in demeaning women. Fantasy is not — and

never will be — autonomous. Pornography does teach men to frag-
ment women's bodies and claim the right to control and judge. It is a
Barry White school of sexual etiquette and must be re-located into theories of both hegemony and consumerism.

I often ponder the most effective methods for enacting change in conservative times such as ours. It is so difficult to balance activism and academia, populism and pornography, strutting and writing. Then I hear a
snippet of song, and the heat of consciousness emulsifies my disquiet ...

> But any time you feel the pain
> Hey Jude, refrain
> The movement you need
> is on your shoulder[108]

It is a great privilege to write and enjoy the ooze of words as they align
neatly on a page. We all inscribe our folio for an era. It is one of the
joys of writing that we can observe the stylistic snapshots of a time and
later recognise how far we have moved from our previous selves. To
engrave past events both retemporalises and repoliticises our history.
Elspeth Probyn described herself as 'a sociologist of the skin'.[109] I have
always preferred to be described as a feminist of the pen. Speaking or
lecturing as a feminist, or offering a feminist perspective, still troubles
me. To consider issues of sexuality, gender and self, I need a pen and a
keyboard, so that the complex patchwork of identity can be unfurled,
a word at a time. The result of political change for women is to bring
every moment, every hope, every disappointment, every love, every
loss to the present instant. Writing brings into play all that we have
learnt. For Jude, as for all of us, the movement we need is on our
shoulders. The remaining three chapters in this section grasp the
potential of the head, the mind and critical thinking, through attention
to fashion, cosmetics and sport. Taking the simple rituals of everyday
life, we mark the meanings in the movement.

The feminist exfoliation of ideas reveals more than the aroma of
cheap perfume and cheaper politics. The aim of feminism is not to
cleanse the patriarchal face, but to make effective use of the blemishes,
bruises and freckles that life presents. There is also a need to open our
eyes to reveal the energy and passion of feminist-inflected popular culture. The verve of Shirley Bassey's 'Diamonds are Forever' offers a
shrill boiling of the Oil of Ulan wafting through femininity. Feminism
was never as successful as its critics feared. Considering the scale of
change, no single movement in a short historical period could be.
Feminists did not build a new world or even a new house. They did not
even find the door. But a window was unshuttered and now we can see
what could be. The aim now is to shatter the pa(i)n(e) for a new
scratch 'n' sniff feminism.

WHAT WILL YOU WEAR
TO THE REVOLUTION?

GEN(D)ERATING CHANGE

I have a secret. I am a fashion Nazi. I drive to suburban shopping centres on Saturday morning, sit in a mall, buy a cup of coffee and count
the number of men and women wearing tracksuit pants. Then I wander through Katies and try to ascertain why women *choose* to buy
jumpers and leggings. I have to stop myself approaching a man wearing a blue shirt and brown shoes. He has broken the first rule of fashion: never wear brown and blue simultaneously. Obviously, everybody
worries about these transgressions ... Surely most people notice these
things ... Maybe it is me who has the problem, Oprah.

Fashion allows a quick, precise and devastating devaluing of others.
It remains a cliché that 'you are what you wear'. More precisely, fashion makes bodies speak. It is a language, ordered through a societal
grammar. Like all languages, fashion can only be understood and read
through agreed rules by wearers and readers. There is a literacy, vocabulary and politics of stitched fabric. This chapter follows on from the
discussion of feminist representation, to unpick the cloth of fashion
and ponder how to connect a transition of style with shifts in society.

A 1989 edition of *Marxism Today*, the journal derived from the
Communist Party of Great Britain, headed a page with the slogan
'What will you wear to the revolution?'.[1] This statement showed the
impact of identity politics on Marxism: New Times ruptured old
beliefs. The crisis of the Left, inspired not only by neo-liberal politics
but Margaret Thatcher — a female Prime Minister — produced radical reshaping of the welfare state, gay and lesbian rights and the uneasy

link between the labour and feminist movements. Unfortunately for the British Labour Party, if any person claimed the adjectival description of *revolutionary* then it would be Margaret Thatcher. When mines closed, Body Shops opened. Nationalised industries made way for a share-holding citizenry. The Labour Party held caveats on social democratic rhetoric but was defending class allegiances that increasingly had little popular support. As in Australia through the late 1990s, the Left had to be defensive, rather than innovative, in policy formations.

The New Times project, instigated in the pages of *Marxism Today*, aimed to decentre class-based unities in favour of feminist, gay, postcolonial and youth-based struggles. It was left to Stuart Hall, cofounder of the New Times project (with Martin Jacques), to articulate the dilemma for progressives:

> A tiny bit of all of us is also somewhere inside the Thatcherite project. Of course, we're all one hundred per cent committed. But every now and then — Saturday mornings, perhaps, just before the demonstration — we go to Sainsbury's and we're just a tiny bit of a Thatcherite subject ...[2]

This chapter builds on Hall's disclosure, questioning the role of clothes and bodily inscriptions within the formulation of post-1980s feminism. I am interested in how understandings of radicalism and revolution have changed for young women and feminist researchers. Has the Left finally erased the border between the trivial and the serious, clothes and change — frocks and politics?[3]

Many of these identity affinities and cultural practices have been dismissed as a denial of politics. For example, Negrin worried that the:

> ... danger with the postmodern celebration of rebellion through fashion is that of substituting revolution in dress for real social change. In the postmodern era, rebellion has primarily taken the form of projecting a certain image through the clothes one wears, rather than engaging with the economic and political structures which produce social inequality.[4]

This is a cheap shot at frocks (and postmodernism).[5] Fabrics are woven with meanings that allow space for play and difference. Negrin's dismissal of the 'revolution in dress' suggests that much work needs to be conducted by the Australian Left on style. By waiting for a repetition of the Maoist 'big change', there is a reticence to explore more affective transformations.

It is not simply 'clever clever' cultural studies to affirm the importance of style to politics. Thatcher's success was built as much on her high heels and carefully groomed hair as her policies. In constructing a new dreaming for a declining Britain, she represented the greatest change possible: a female Prime Minister who was 'the best man for the job'. The mistake so often made by Labo(u)r leaders is an underestimation of style in the process and formulation of change.[6]

FROCKING UP

Fashion is the most complex of social systems. It is constantly changing, spatially specific, but also socially damaging. Clothes are markers of gender and sexuality: fabric signifies (in)subordination. Fashion imposes order, categories, standards and values. As the ultimate hegemonic mask, it permits the expression of individuality and creativity, while actually reinforcing conformity and collectivity.[7] With each item of clothing locked into a semiotic system, space is inscribed for bodily action. Aerobics wear or a swimsuit occupies space differently from a ball gown or dinner suit. Knowing and reading these differences allows us to negotiate social relationships in the workplace, bar or street.

For the suffragettes, fashion performed women's subservience and desire for change. The high starched collars, straw hats and the purple, white and green of the Women's Social and Political Union (WSPU) members were integral to the construction of a suffragette identity and the public demonstration of their dissatisfaction.[8] The corporeality of their protest offered an intervention in the exclusion of women from the modernist public sphere. Their clothes were disruptive and provocative. While the post-Enlightenment period has been sceptical of non-textual resistance, the WSPU tackled this notion through their slogan 'Deeds not words'. These women agitated conventional political labels of allegiance. While seeming liberal, they became increasingly militant, using both firebombing and window-breaking tactics. They mobilised their status as fashionable middle-class consumers to allay the fears of shopkeepers and politicians, only to activate and actualise a potent threat to the status quo. Hammers and rocks were hidden, and later revealed, in muffs and handbags.

The reasons for the trivialisation of fashion are historical and political. Linked with both women and the domestic sphere, fashion is part of a wide-ranging denunciation of the feminine aesthetic. Sparke powerfully asserts that the authority and status women gain from clothes and style has demonstrated long-term and destructive ideological consequences:

> The freedom that women have gained through their relationship with material culture is a politically powerless liberation — and indeed not even necessarily consciously recognized.[9]

Fashion has a bad name in academia and even in cultural studies, but it does form an evocative way to explore the relationship between politics and a way of life. Fashion is not about fabric: there is a network of cultural industries that generate meanings from the cloth. Style exhibits the potential to reinscribe clichéd emotions and visual constitutive elements with innovation and freshness. As the meeting point of class, gender, generation, sexuality and race, a style changes the meanings granted to cultural codes.[10] Fashion is not respectful of wearability. It does not aim to satisfy *real* women or men, to make ordinary people feel better about themselves or contented that they are carrying five extra kilograms, all of which seemed to have lodged in their protruding stomach or flabby thighs. Style intends to make people feel inadequate, incomplete, in need of one more accessory to complete the self. Obsessions with clothing verify the contradictory and ridiculous nature of capitalism. While Marx argued that class is the articulatory nexus of economic and political relations, style embodies a belief that different shirt colours, skirt lengths and attention to accessorising actually matter. Thorstein Veblen's theory of vicarious consumption showed that the aristocracy used clothing to display conspicuous spending.[11] For women in particular, style plays a part in the construction and symbolic expression of social position, being oppositional, subversive or conservative. That is why women's fashion is frequently uncomfortable. It shows evidence that women are economically dependent on men. A corseted, high-heeled, over-painted woman with large bouffant will not find breathing easy, let alone an 18-hour work day. While the rights and role of women have changed, it is important to track the continuities: the nineteenth-century corset enacted a discipline enforced from without. The whalebone and fastenings have given way to the twentieth-century corset of muscle, a discipline enforced from within. Fashion, though, is not only a negative force in society. It is also a node for play, resistance and struggle. It is slippery to analyse, being both excessive and ambivalent. Therefore, fashion remains the canary of culture: an early warning system of change.

Susan Faludi in *Backlash* revealed the most spectacular demonstration of this canary effect. Nineteen eighty-seven was proclaimed the year of the dress, following the 40 per cent cut in the annual production of women's suits the preceding season. The bubble skirt was not an adequate replacement for the waist-tucked two-piece suit. Yet from this time, the sale of clothes declined, with women buying a wider array of merchandise — including homeware, audio-visual products and leisure goods. Therefore, when the fashion was not suitable personally, politically or socially, it was not purchased. Faludi argued that 'the more confident and independent women became, the less they liked to shop; and the more they enjoyed their work, the less they cared about their clothes'.[12] While her premise is debatable, she does show that women are literate in the fashion discourse. They are not duped consumers, satisfied to wear a knotted tea towel or a potato sack with a label.

DRESSING DOWN

The closer a garment is to the skin, the more it reveals about societal movements. While designers tried unsuccessfully in the 1980s to replace the linen suit with a lace teddy, the bra has quietly undergone a revolution, accurately shadowing the multiplicity of women's current roles. The bra is a highly complex garment. Comprising fifty individual parts, it must also be washable, soft and cheap. As women's leisure and work-based practices have diversified, so has the bra. As Pauline Swain reveals:

> We live in the age of the specialist bra; support styles for sport; flash, lacy numbers for dressing up; then there's the 'invisible' look. Sometimes called T-shirt bras, these garments are moulded and seamless ... Others, smooth in contour and slightly padded, don't show the outline of nipples. Lingerie saleswomen report that women who teach in boys' schools are keen on them.[13]

The wonderbra, pegged as the ultimate 1990s invention, was actually patented by Gossard in Britain in the 1960s. Yet this earlier era found little use for it. The ideologies of breasts have, throughout the century, changed the way we think about clothing and corsetry. Consider how the century's corsetieres have pumped and prodded the protrusions:

A breasted history

1920s	Flattened flapper
1930s	Enhanced Harlow
1940s	Missile mammaries
1950s	Monroe monsters
1960s	Twiggy steamroll
1970s	Feminist floppy
1980s	No-bounce sports bra
1990s	Pre-implant push up
2000s	Pre-diet minimiser

The bra packages the body, revealing some parts and restricting particular movements. It remains fascinating to see how a piece of flesh can connote a moulding of femininity. Similarly, underpants (also referred to as knickers, smalls, briefs, pantaloons, bloomers or drawers) are a new intervention in women's fashion history. Only 200 years ago, women began sporting this male garment. While the current fashion is more decorative than functional, it is in the realm of intimate apparel that women first started 'wearing the pants'.[14] Underwear demonstrates that fashion is not functional. A G-string brief has no clear social purpose, except to conceal a visible panty line. This line would not occur if women were not wearing underwear, as has occurred through-out much of history. Men's items remain positively drab when com-pared to women's lace and satin inserts. The aim is to affirm masculine difference from women's apparel. For men to cross-dress involves a major transgression. While women may dress like men, men may not dress like women. Clothing serves a pivotal function for men, granting them both status and dignity. Men require a wide array of masculine props, which cannot be encased within a pair of Y-fronts or boxers. For men to claim power, they need their body covered. The man's suit is able to speak both the language of power and distinction from women. It inscribes space and imposes a demeanour.

These social demarcations are of course arbitrary. All fashion is con-sciously irrational, maintaining a knowingness about its own perfor-mance. Most purchases make perfect sense at the time. Only in retrospect, when glancing through old family photo albums, do we ask, 'what was I thinking?'. Cultural systems are produced around clothing that normalise even the most ridiculous excesses. Think of platform shoes, body shirts and polyester flares. To dress is to address the view-er. Social rules function through appearance. Indeed, the consensus of our society is based on the ability to quickly judge others by a glance. The differences of class and gender in particular are performed exces-sively through fashion. Simone de Beauvoir revealed that:

> Women … know that when she is looked at she is not considered apart from her appearance; she is judged, respected, desired by and through her toilet. Her clothes were originally intended to con-sign her to impotence, and they have remained unserviceable, eas-ily ruined: stockings get runs, shoes get down at the heel, light coloured blouses and frocks get soiled, pleats get unpleated.[15]

Fashion attempts to render political — contestable — matters as nor-mal. Supposedly *natural* differences of biology are layered with cloth-based distinctions. Therefore, fashion allows the naturalisation of differences. Clothing restrictions on both men and women are used to justify distinct domestic and public roles.

RIDING PILLION IN A PENCIL SKIRT

For cultural theorists, most research into style and fashion springs from the spectacular youth subcultures walking along the streets. Feminist research on style has critiqued this narrow focus and has broadened the nodes of inquiry to link Marxist economics, Freudian theory and ethnography. The generation has been transformed into a genderation. For the few women working in the Birmingham Centre for Contemporary Cultural Studies during its influential years in the 1970s, women's studies was more than 'a fashionable academic fetish'.[16] The 'gender issue' was in fact a minor consideration in the early Working Papers in Cultural Studies formulated within the Centre. Women ride pillion on the back of this subcultural theory. The confrontation between Marxism and feminism required a shift in Leftist thought, so that the means of production referred to more than men's activities in the public sphere. Fashion is not only an embodiment of economic forces; it allows the public performance of private desires.

Angela McRobbie is the most influential commentator on the question of gender/youth.[17] She critiqued the absence of young women from sociological accounts of youth, yet did not tackle the major epistemological question: if women were squashed into the already bulging class/youth package, would the contents of the parcel explode? Such a class/gender/age bundle would not be recognisable: understandings of politics, sexuality and deviance would have to be radically reconfigured. McRobbie has provided a major theoretical legacy to researchers of fashion and style. The dilemma remains the choice of methodology through which to find effective traces and sources of textile memories. Do we construct a chronicle of 'great women', such as Thatcher, Cathy Freeman, Julie Burchill or Drew Barrymore, or do we rely on the experiences of young women who left only a few traces of their lives within ethnographic accounts?[18] While recovery feminism alerts us to the gaps in our knowledge of young women, the rupture seems unbreachable between Lucy Lu's leatherwear and the uniforms of Brisbane schoolgirls. The contradictory nature of studying young women is locked into this manner of methodological paradox: overwritten and overread popular cultural texts alongside spaces of blandness and invisibility. As postmodern simulation and post-coital stimulation intertwine, it is obvious that there will be no clear victory for feminism or the Left in the resultant embrace.

Those who have the least space for ideological manoeuvrability are working-class young women. During the 1980s and 1990s, young women were caught in a mesh of recreational shopping, cheap bourbon, low paid work, training schemes and minimal employment advancement. What role did fashion and pleasure play in this history? Julie Burchill, with an unerring ability to grasp the contradictory lives of young working-class women, tied drinking, dancing, pop songs and attitudes toward men:

> Nikki was sipping her mould-breaking cocktail and watching the dancers abstractly while her friends talked intensely. They were at that stage of extreme drunkenness which is unique to pretty and semi-smart working-class girls and is marked by monologues, quotes from Tina Turner songs, physical contact verging on the Sapphic and analysis of the male sex which is three parts banal to one part genius.[19]

Being a working-class woman is not merely a question of social positioning in response to material or sexual oppressions. It involves a language and physicality that transcend the boundaries of a feminist or Marxist sexual/political subject. It is a style of dressing, friendship, drinking and speaking.

There is an outside to this structure of exclusion that trivialises 'the feminine sphere' and semantically derogates women's linguistic practices. A rarely cited article, written by a London Comprehensive teacher, quietly reconfigured the paradigmatic possibilities of 'resistance'. She monitored the behaviour and conversations of young girls sitting near a heater before school. Offering alternatives in a highly conservative era, Anne Krisman suggested that her 'Radiator Girls' 'had developed their own survival strategy ... not work[ing] against school but alongside it'.[20] The politics of adjacent ambivalence hints at a resistance *that is not one*, a resistance generated during an era with no alternatives. Here, we begin to discover a resonance with the *Marxism Today* slogan, a world where wearing the right clothes is a constituent part of a revolution.

While young men were (and are) attempting to (violently) reconcile the contradictions of their lives, the Radiator Girls continued to exist alongside, rather than in opposition to, the structures of power. Resistance, for Krisman's Radiator Girls, was not adversarial and did not involve assuming a political position, but, actually avoiding one. While Thompson 'gave' the working class a history,[21] Krisman granted the girls some space, without overreading their activities. This generation offered a challenging problem for feminist critics. The girls' affront to authority was radically different from the 'tough' subcultures analysed by sociologists during the 1970s. The calmness of Krisman's article conveyed the even-tempered conversations of girls sitting by a radiator. Were these young women engaging in resistance? They were not so much anti-school or anti-authority, but actually occupied their time with clothes, make-up, boys and music.

The dilemmas and problems of young women are trivial and, at times, pathetic. That is not a theoretical put-down. Ideally, these concerns are examined in a way that grants them meaning, not credibility. While textual sites and political issues such as Madonna or HIV are used as the fodder to articulate a sexual revolution, female sexuality is rarely played out on this scale. Lynda Measor, like Anne Krisman, presented some of these small conflicts. Measor related numerous stories that remain sobering reminders of feminism's limited relevance to young women. These failings were embodied in the problems associated with wearing a pencil skirt:

Sally: Sylvia, well I hope you don't mind me saying so, she's a bit of a tart as well.

Interviewer: Is she? Why?

Sally:	Well she comes to school in that pencil skirt. She wears nothing but that stupid pencil skirt.
Jenny:	She wears ever such low tops.
Sally:	Yes.
Jenny:	She wears spotted tights with great big heels to school.
Sally:	And she wears quite a bit of make-up.[22]

Jenny, who expressed a desire to wear the garment, continued the problems with the pencil skirt:

Jenny:	You get those names, though. I am scared to wear my pencil skirt. I have a navy blue one. It is nice but I don't wear it at school, really, because of getting called names.[23]

While Jenny, in the presence of Sally, discussed everything *except* Sylvia's pencil skirt (her 'low tops', 'spotted tights' and 'great big heels'), she avoided the main topic of discussion as she may have been implicated in the label of 'tart'.

If there is ever a political need to justify theoretical attention to clothing and sexuality, then testimony like that of Jenny and Sally shows the realness of this link, particularly for young women. Young women are ruthlessly aware of their body politics. Their breasts pop out of low tops, their legs are revealed through pencil skirts and faces can show the trace of too much make-up. When reading the testimony of young women, I am struck by the vulnerability of their bodies. While the history of groping is yet to be written, it would make a fascinating ethnographic study, being conducted in the backseats of cars, at the beach and in lounge rooms. The 'testing' of women in the sexual domain is a profoundly physical examination. There is a (black) humour derived from the sexual 'rules' of adolescence. As Joyce Canaan described:

> If young women fail the 'test' [and have sex with young men] they will be labelled 'slags' and thus considered sex objects to be used instrumentally by males. If they pass the 'test,' at this point in their lives their male partners are likely to drop them for a 'slag,' or 'sexually easy' young women.[24]

The socialisation of these rules, which naturalise this sexual order as 'the way of the world', means that young women have to negotiate coping mechanisms that may not appear revolutionary, but are profoundly revelatory. As one of Bhavnani's interviewees distinguished:

> I don't see why they [men] should be able to go with girls and get

called good and the girls do it and get called bad. That's like inequality, ain't it?[25]

Women have small victories of consciousness. Young men are also implicated in this growing awareness:

> You find the girls go out with the harder ones. They get a reputation when they go out with the girls, no matter how they look. Like you'll find a girl will go out with them … [T]he girls go with them to look good being seen with them. They think it's good to be seen with a hard person.[26]

It is an obvious repercussion of the sexual pressures placed on women that men, too, are monitoring the social rules. The need to be seen as hard makes 'soft' men profoundly unpopular. The 'hard man' becomes a handbag to be paraded, to make young women 'look good'. If she is to be called a slag, then she may as well be viewed as a slag with a hard boyfriend.

'The girl' is a paradigm that needs to be resurrected from its subservient, binarised status. Both illusionary and real, the girl is available for reclamation and recycling. The girl is, indeed, a site of political opportunity and value. Cixous suggested that 'if women were to set themselves to transform History, it can … be said that every aspect of History would be completely altered'.[27] New topics and interests — like pencil skirts, make-up, shoes and jewellery — alter the status of serious, scholarly work on youth culture. Notions of evidence, politics and methodology instigate a feminist challenge that can no longer be appended as a footnote or special chapter. Feminist scholars of fashion, working against cultural populist tendencies in cultural studies, have strayed too frequently into what Jean Duruz terms 'the tales of victims, of depressing and oppressing powers of the market and of male authority'.[28] Fashion offers a way to speak knowledges about status: too frequently analyses have been split between the destructive capacity of clothes and the playful performativity of style. Ethnographers invariably discover disquieting testimony about the costs and pains of fashion. To simplify the connection between desire and consumption is to ignore the implementation of styles as a tactic for reverse surveillance.

The body is more than a coathanger for fashion: it is a spatio-temporal map that is dressed and undressed, hidden and revealed. While fashion remains caught in the feminine web, we must consider its liberatory possibilities. It is difficult to discover the nature of oppositional styles for young women because of the research interests of feminist ethnographers and the impact of mainstream fashion. Yet the potential for representational protests provides a negotiation of the clear division between men and women, class and gender. As part of a visual challenge that questions the boundaries of the beautiful and the tasteful, fashion is a part of popular culture. It is the syntax of social relations. Fashion, sex and gender write upon each other and collapse into one other.

To claim the revolutionary/revelatory nature of frocks is to trace far more than the transformation from modernist workers to post-modern consumers. Women have used this volatile, trivial site to grasp space and change social rules:

> There was this great big girl, Linda. She must be six feet. She wears a pair of Doctor Martens. This geezer who was pissed tried to grab her. She gave him a right hard punch.[29]

The figure of Linda is a resistive metaphor that shows how young women not only infiltrate the testimony of young men, but the paradigm of male youth culture. If the shoe fits, then buy it. This relationship between revolution and revelation is continued in the next chapter, moving the object of study from fashion to cosmetics. Perhaps between big Linda's Doctor Martens and the Radiator Girls' tacit conversations by the heater, an analysis can be commenced that assesses young women and their fashion as constituent elements, rather than inconvenient adjuncts, to the study of social change.

BUFF PUFFING
AN EMPIRE

THE BODY SHOP, AND COLONISATION BY OTHER MEANS

At the beginning of *Colonialism's Culture*, Nicholas Thomas tells of washing coffee cups while listening to a broadcast that detailed racism against indigenes. The self-righteous horror and disgust of white commentators at nineteenth-century injustices provokes ambivalence, confusion and disquiet in Thomas.[1] I understand his uneasiness. I have been thinking about The Body Shop for the last three years. I have written letters, visited websites, collected advertisements and *kept thinking*. Intellectual and personal concerns have not surfaced while doing dishes, but in more private spaces: rolling my tired foot arches over wood implements 'made in India for The Body Shop, London', moisturising my legs with the Cocoa Butter Body Lotion that uses 'Cocoa beans from Ghana made for The Body Shop, London', or washing my hair with Brazil Nut Conditioner — harvested by the Kayapo Indians of the Amazon rainforest, but again supplied to me from The Body Shop, London.

Certainly I have made this research process troubling for myself. I buy products from the Community Trade programme, then use them on my body. This is colonialism (and capitalism) at its most intimate and distressing. How do I feel about using cocoa beans from Ghana? My cultural studies critique is too easily replaced with squishy liberalism. The exoticism can add interest to the banal acts of beautifying, but it is a process of economic, social and intellectual appropriation — taking the goods, services and ideas of the other, for my self-improvement and, yes, vanity. That the masculine act of colonisation survives through the feminine practices of cleansing, toning, exfoliating and moisturising demonstrates how past truths are rubbed into the skin of contemporary culture.

It is no accident, nor an act of awkward assonance, that has triggered the title of this chapter. The buff puff, as both noun and metaphor, exfoliates our old (ugly?) pelt and reveals a young and glowing facial surface — putting the best skin forward. The buff puff is also an indicator of a New British Empire of business, cosmetics and self-indulgence. The success of The Body Shop is remarkable. The first shop opened in Brighton, England during 1976, selling a range of twenty-five products. Currently, 580 products — with a similar number of accessories — are sold in the worldwide outlets. This growth is made even more remarkable when considering the Small Business Association statistics that show that nearly 80 per cent of new businesses fail.[2] Every two seconds, someone in the world buys a product from the firm. Every 2-and-a-half days, a new Body Shop Store opens.[3] The Body Shop is an economic and social phenomenon. Anita Roddick, to poach *The Economist*'s description, remains 'the best publicised of the new self-made successes'.[4] While it is easy to situate The Body Shop in the era of shoulder pads, filofaxes and sundried tomatoes, the origin of Anita Roddick's ideology (or — as she phrases it — 'what I really think') is based on a book that was published nearly 140 years ago.

WHAT I REALLY THINK: WHY ANITA RODDICK IS THE NEW SAMUEL SMILES

My idea of shopping hell is to be trapped in a Laura Ashley showroom for an entire afternoon.[5] The delicate floral muesli bowls and tastefully puckered tablecloths leave me screaming for release. Body Shop feminism is much like being trapped in a Laura Ashley detention centre. Everything is natural, maternal, nurturing and soothing. The Dunedin Body Shop even has frolicking dolphins painted over its exterior walls. When aromatherapy is a solution to society's problems, the world becomes — as Burchill inferred — 'a green and pleasant land full of anti-racist, non-sexist vegetarians … dancing round may-poles, weaving corn dollies and reading the books of George Orwell'.[6] While Orwell's politics is in affinity with Anita Roddick's, her (self) management style is derived from an earlier, more conservative writer.

Samuel Smiles published *Self-Help* in 1859, the same year as John Stuart Mill's *Essay on Liberty* and Charles Darwin's *Origin of Species*. As one of the canonical texts of the contemporary self-help movement, it was a publishing triumph of the era, selling 250 000 copies by the end of the nineteenth century. The treatise stresses the building of character, with little faith in either governmental directives or collective societal change. Rather, extraordinary achievements are accomplished through 'ordinary people' demonstrating commitment and hard work. Just as Oprah and her 'Change your life TV' co-hosts rebutted charges of self-absorption and selfishness, so did Smiles defend his movement towards personal improvement:

> The title of the book ... has led some, who have judged it merely by the title, to suppose that it consists of a eulogy of selfishness: the very opposite of what it really is, — or at least of what the author intended it to be ... its chief object unquestionably is to stimulate youths to apply themselves diligently to right pursuits ... and to rely upon their own efforts in life rather than depend upon the help or patronage of others.[7]

In this way, the help of self becomes the help of community, nation and world. To discuss the inequalities of class or rank becomes an excuse to avoid being industrious. As expected, belief in hard work, dedication, energy, resilience and honesty coalesce in *Self-Help*. What is so odd is the unerring similarities and resonances between Anita Roddick's customary cries of 'What I really think' and the thought of Samuel Smiles. To fathom this connection is to understand much of The Body Shop's world view. Compare these two statements, separated by 130 years:

> The path of success in business is usually the path of common-sense.[8]

> My mother once said that I ran my shop the way she ran her household during the Second World War. Then, she wasn't being environmental. She was simply a good housekeeper. I was doing the same. And it worked. Commonsense usually does.[9]

These notions of commonsense are both taken for granted and assumed to be of benefit to 'society', broadly and ambiguously defined. The aim of this chapter is to unpick this seamless fabric(ation) and demonstrate the repercussions of these hegemonic negotiations for both women and disempowered, frequently formerly colonised, communities.

Roddick's theory of enlightened capitalism is, as *The Economist* described it, 'an alternative revolution'.[10] While she affirms an anti-marketing marketing, her strategy is a logical response to the risks present in the contemporary cosmetics and beauty industry. Because her packaging and advertising overheads are low, products can be trialled, improved or removed from the list as necessary. Although the bulk of the company's 1500 outlets — trading in twenty-three languages in forty-six countries — are franchise operations, every outlet sells the same products in the same packaging and organised on the shelves with remarkable standardisation. This means that wherever we are, a familiar shop layout welcomes us. We enter a McDonald's and know — on arrival — that we can order a chocolate thickshake and sundae. Similarly, we wander into The Body Shop in Singapore's Raffles Complex, or London's Covent Garden, or Dunedin's Central Mall or Perth's Booragoon Shopping Centre and know that we can find lip scuff, buff puffs and mango body butter. While there is a clear branding of the organisation, Roddick seems proud that 'we have no marketing department and no advertising department'.[11] Obviously, her notion of marketing and advertising is narrow, reliant on exposure through newspapers, magazines, television and radio. For example, Roddick determines a difference between The Body Shop and Benetton.[12] She obviously forgets that shop fronts, catalogues, postcards, websites and mail order services all deploy very effective marketing strategies.

Although Roddick affirms the value of diversity in local and indigenous communities, there is a rigid uniformity in business practice. This contradiction has remained unnoticed in the literature on The Body Shop. The reason for this absence is clear: the firm needs to perform a global diversity of practices and productions within a uniform, generic package. As Paul Brown has affirmed:

> Many of Anita's ideas were generated by her trips to meet the different communities with which she dealt — she listened to their traditional remedies and recipes. On her return, she passed variations of these ideas onto the chemists who worked in the company's laboratories.[13]

The unabashed trafficking in ideas is breathtaking. This statement emerges not from a hard-edged critique of her business principles, but from a celebratory biography. She is not only unflinching about the power relations involved, but actually re-affirmed her 'discovery' of distant lands:

> I wanted to be Christobel Columbus, going into little villages in Mexico or Guatemala or Nepal and seeing what they had to trade instead of going to those boring old trade fairs where everyone buys the same mediocre products year after year.[14]

Her *Body and Soul*, which is a combination of autobiography and business manual, is written with such confidence and self-belief that her hand seems almost shadowed by that of Samuel Smiles. She described her customers as 'generally classless, mostly female and mostly under thirty-five'.[15] While Roddick describes her customers as classless, she is one of the five richest women in England and holds an Order of the

British Empire. Business and First Class passengers on British Airways flights receive a free Body Shop pack. Packaged differently for men and women, it features a small pamphlet describing the products and the reasons for the BA/Body Shop affiliation:

> What makes an idea take flight? A few miles above terra firma is the perfect place to think about an answer. Take The Body Shop as an example. Whoever would have thought that a little shop selling naturally-based skin and hair care products on a Brighton back street 20 years ago would have grown into a huge global business with over 1,400 stores in 46 countries. The Body Shop's approach was innovative unconventional and common-sensical. It still is, over two decades later ... That's why we can celebrate a partnership with British Airways — together seeking new ways to nurture the soul and help the world celebrate its individuality.[16]

With this product only given to elite passengers, 'the world' is not celebrating individuality with The Body Shop. Once more class, wealth and status are unmentioned and displaced nodes of difference.

The Body Shop is best known for two political commitments: its reuse–refill–recycle approach and an antagonism towards animal testing. These two beliefs are major challenges to the conventional truths of the cosmetic industry, which is founded on generating large quantities of packaging and waste. By maintaining a commitment to minimal wrapping and public disclosure of environmental performance, The Body Shop has changed the way business is conducted.[17] As its maxim affirms: 'we've always believed that profits and principles can and should go hand in hand'.[18] The consequence of this premise can result in odd products and strange objects, like the animals-in-danger soaps launched in 1991. My question is not only *who* buys a dolphin soap with a giant strawberry sponge, but *where* do they put this stuff?

The Body Shop's stance in favour of natural, herbal and botanical products has, in the last three years, become an industry standard. Clairol's Herbal Essences sexualised the new age through orgasmic television commercials. Coty released The Healing Garden range of products, which are available through K-Mart. As Bittar has suggested:

> It was only a matter of time before its [The Body Shop's] 'natural' position became appropriated by a raft of would-be heirs, from boutique brands to mass, from traditional products like soaps and shampoos to arcane new categories such as aromatherapy ... For all the well-meaning promises of the Body Shop, Roddick's refusal to play the game with the big boys, to actively market her eco- and socially-friendly message, allowed her high-concept point-of-difference to, as it were, fade into the woodwork.[19]

Bittar is aware of The Body Shop's success, but demonstrates that this success has been copied and deflated. The Australian firm, The Body Collection, more overtly and embarrassingly demonstrates this mimicry. Below the green and beige marketing badge is the maxim 'not tested on animals'. This Australian business has generated an almost exact replication of The Body Shops strategies. With the natural becoming fashionable, The Body Shop is also exposed to the risk of losing market share. While natural ingredients will remain a staple of the cosmetics industry, their future as a marketing tool is more doubtful. Bittar also hints at the difficulties faced by The Body Shop in the United States.

The Body Shop's movement into the United States has not generated the expected success. Indeed, of all The Body Shop publicity brochures and pamphlets I received from the franchise operations around the world, the American material was the least polished, cohesive and convincing.[20] The American contribution to worldwide sales is only 16 per cent of the total.[21] While continuing many of the initiatives in other areas of the business, such as opening a community store in Harlem during 1992, the US franchise's positioning in the market seems uncomfortable and inappropriate. Certainly the Canadian franchise, one of the first international franchises to open in 1979, is working well. It has operated within the global template, but affirmed distinctions:

> The Body Shop is in the business of trade. Its unique difference lies in the philosophy that trade should be in more than just material goods. The Body Shop trades in knowledge, in experience, in ideas and community action.[22]

This ideology is more overtly revealed in Canada than in the documents emerging from London. The Body Shop Canada affirms transparency in its social and environmental activities and a strong feminist directive through programmes to stop violence against women. It is also the only franchise that goes into detail about the Community Trade Programme. The Canadian Body Shop's materials are pedagogic, teaching consumers why this trading process is important and how it is activated. There is, as the Canadian Body Shop affirms, 'a message in every bottle'.[23] However, its success renders the moderate success in the United States even more ponderous.

The Body Shop affirms a high standard of excellence in the protection of animals and the environment. Its first Values report was released in 1995 and was available on the Internet in 1997.[24] While it is easy to be dismissive of such actions, there is a continual rhetorical restatement that:

> One vital ingredient goes into every product from The Body Shop: our values. Our values are what we care about and why we are in business. We want to think, act and change things for the better.[25]

Such pronouncements that come from a cosmetics company are extraordinary and should be welcomed. Scrooge journalists and theorists may bark 'humbug', but there is a desire to do business differently. As the American publicity suggests, 'her [Roddick's] goal was to make her business the antithesis of the mainstream'.[26] The problem is that The Body Shop restates many nineteenth-century colonial relationships, with a denial of class and race-based inequalities and an affirmation of a very narrow mode of feminism. How such a business is challenging and critiquing hegemonic notions of profit, industry and beauty, is a worthy topic. For example, in 1998 the Australian and New Zealand Body Shop conducted a Social Audit, asking customers to contribute to a social and ethical review of its operations. Roddick described the audit as 'social accounting which looks at how our business practices affect our stakeholders'.[27] We must contemplate how a business that affirms natural products also naturalises profit, enterprise and personal achievement. It is fascinating, for example, to read a Body Shop Shareholders' report. Not only is there the customary review of share prices and profit margins, but also sections about employee activities, franchisees' concerns and the challenges of the Aid not Trade programme.[28] A new relationship is being formed between the human pelt and profit.

SKIN, HAIR AND ATTITUDE

> Make no mistake about it — I'm doing this for me.
> Anita Roddick[29]

The Body Shop is an easy target for critique but there is no doubt that Roddick has offered a voice and presence for women in business. She presents a fascinating antithesis to Margaret Thatcher, Jenny Shipley or Hillary Clinton, performing an alternative model of feminine success. That such a presence arose from the beauty industry is no surprise. Selling beauty has been a way for women to attain financial independence throughout the twentieth century. Helena Rubenstein, Elizabeth Arden and Estée Lauder have all made their fortunes through cosmetics. These women traded on self-doubt and fear of ageing. Selling beauty — youth — success — romance — love — in a jar, the desire remains the same: for personal change. What makes Roddick distinct from these powerful women is that her opinions were and are tempered by second wave feminism. Roddick's mode of business is not part of the current vogue of 'the Darth Vader School of Management'.[30] Born in 1942, Anita Roddick is the archetypal baby boomer. With great flair and courage, she stated: 'I think all business practices would improve immeasurably if they were guided by "feminine" principles — qualities like love and care and intuition'.[31] This attitude feeds into the firm's human resource principles. The Body Shop staff in shops around the world spend half a day each month on company time involved in local projects.[32] Yet while promoting community values, gendered truths and inequalities survive. Roddick was named Businesswoman of the Year in 1985, but her firm still exhibits a gendered bias in upper management. Although women are 65 per cent of The Body Shop's employees, they represent only 43 per cent of the top four salary bands.[33]

Through this management contradiction, the status and role of men and masculinity in The Body Shop discourse is highly contradictory. The 'For Men' range commenced with two major product lines: the provocatively titled Activist and No Debate. Interestingly, there is no Activist line for women. Moisturisers for men are termed the delightfully obscure 'face protector'. While the entirety of the women's range aims to 'smooth and soften' the skin, the men's products are 'woody', 'spicy' and 'dynamic'.[34] These differences in description serve to naturalise distinctions in acceptable feminine and masculine attributes.

These gendered differentiations only serve to reinforce the key problem for The Body Shop products. If they are not 'hope in a jar', if they do not possess magical anti-ageing properties, then why should customers buy them? The answer to this question is explained in *Full Voice*. This brochure is framed as a magazine about self-esteem, asserting that 'we have a greater obligation to our customers than simply tending to their looks'.[35] In this way, the purchase of goods can be justified not because they are derived from the well of youth, but because they build self-esteem. Recently, The Body Shop increased the promotion of its Colourings range, created in 1986, moving away from the body lotions, creams and essential oils that had been their base goods. This was a risky shift in emphasis, as the disparity between The Body Shop and conventional cosmetic houses became more problematic to discern. What is the difference between a Revlon black mascara and the Body Shop's version? Again, the answer to this question is derived from the fount of self-esteem. As the Colourings catalogue pronounced, 'make-up makes you look more together, more alive. Makes you feel good about yourself. And that's no bad thing!'.[36] The launch of this change in marketing focus — from environmentalism and animal protection — was signalled by the famous image of a naked, Rubenesque woman reclining on a sofa. The caption — 'there are 3 billion women who don't look like supermodels and only 8 who do'[37] — signalled a desire to 'get real' and connect 'self-esteem and democracy'.[38] This directive was built upon through 1998 and accelerated in 1999, the United Nations Year of Older Persons.[39]

The problem derived from this self-esteem marketing is obvious. Most women who use The Body Shop range will never run a corporation or travel to the Amazon rainforest. Indeed, while the 1980s is frequently framed as a difficult decade for feminism and women, the 1990s was actually far worse. This realisation places The Body Shop creams — which soften and smooth — in a clear context. Similarly, the aromatherapy range becomes one more bandaid to cover the scab of women's exhaustion:

> Bergamot is one of the best essential oils to use if you're feeling down or just worn out. It's a refreshing fragrance that helps you uplift your body and mind and it is claimed to boost your self-confidence and help clarify your goals.[40]

Hope in a jar returns once more.

Roddick's anti-marketing marketing affirms that 'Our products won't make you ten years younger or irresistible to the opposite sex. What they will do is cleanse, polish and moisturise'.[41] The Body Shop has also moved beyond the conventional beauty rituals into publishing. *Mind body soul: The Body Shop book of wellbeing* traverses the terrain of qi gong, shiatsu, crystals and aromatherapy. Roddick describes the text as 'presenting a formula for wellbeing that integrates the pragmatic concerns of the flesh with the spiritual yearnings of the soul'.[42] It is here that holistic notions of beauty feed into New Age practices and access the wider self-help movement.

The profound contradiction of The Body Shop is the use of beauty products to further global causes. In one of the most famous — and vitriolic — attacks on the business, *The Independent* wrote in 1992:

> They represent causes attractive to the liberal conscience. Yet this goodness is used, remorselessly, to sell vanity products. You wash your hair in global concern. And it is debatable whether the wizened peasants on the wall are dignified or patronised.[43]

It is in the midst of this attack that cultural studies frameworks are at their most effective. Fashion has been a site of politicised interest for some time. Notions of beauty must not be dismissed as uncontested, as *The Independent* piece has done. However, where the piece is accurate is the concern about the Community Trade programme. The condescension of 'the wizened peasants' is a marinade of all The Body Shop's publicity material. The process through which dominant positions are maintained, constituted and reproduced is reliant on how the topography of difference is mapped on the body.

EMPIRE BY OTHER MEANS

> One of the most strongly-marked features of the English people is
> their spirit of industry … It is this spirit, displayed by the commons of England,
> which has laid the foundations and built up the industrial greatness of the empire.[44]
> Samuel Smiles

> We British don't have the culture of enterprise.[45]
> Anita Roddick

If British colonialism had been a purely political structure, then the anger and hostility toward it would have faded with the retraction of the governors and troops. It is the ambiguity of Englishness that has lead to a continual concern and watchful disquiet. Colonisation is not a historical category, vacuum-sealed in the nineteenth century. To demonise the practices of the past is a way to relinquish and decentre the racism and injustices of the present. To focus on the barbarism rather than the civilising rhetoric of the past allows us to ignore the remarkable similarities of contemporary marketing directives. As Thomas has suggested, 'in the bourgeois living room, this culture evidently offers a spiritual palliative to our overheated, overconsuming, unnatural, postindustrial world'.[46] Most clearly, this tendency may be termed modern primitivism, which illustrates the affinity with the fetishised and beautifying practices that were framed as part of primitivism. Local practices become infinitely transferable through global movements of capital. Modern primitivism is diffused through consumer culture, resulting in colonised peoples being framed as culturally stable and unable to survive modernity without help from former colonisers.

Whenever theorists discuss globalisation, they are actually discussing some other issue. Globalisation may be an awkward synonym for modernism, postmodernism, colonialism, postcolonialism, imperialism or capitalism. It is a term that prioritises Western power structures and strategies. However, there is a need to move from macro-theoretical configurations, to investigate the heterogeneous, particular and specific. As Ann Cvetkovich and Douglas Kellner have suggested, the key to theorising local and global is 'to divest them of normative baggage, especially conceptualisations that would positively valorise one side of the equation and denigrate the other'.[47]

The Body Shop is based in Littlehampton, England. A total of 1300 staff are employed at this venue and they produce 8600 tonnes of product. A London office controls the press, design, development and video productions.[48] In 1988 a (neo)colonial relationship with the Celtic Fringe was (once more) fostered, with a soap-making plant being established in Easterhouse, Glasgow, an area of high unemployment in Scotland. Once more, the benign English appeared to be caring for their Celtic neighbours. The grasps at the outer reaches of

Empire continued in April 1994 with a 100 000 square feet site being opened in Melbourne. This site in Mulgrave is a warehouse, production, mail order and retail support facility.

The first branch of The Body Shop Australia was opened ten years before the Mulgrave site, in July 1983. Barry Thomas and Graeme Wise own the franchise for Australia and New Zealand. Both these nations, as with all franchise operations, import almost all their products from England. However, unlike most of the other Body Shop businesses, twelve globally distributed products were actually developed in Australia. Known as the Mulgrave Twelve, these products have included Chamomile Shampoo, Dewberry Body Shampoo, Bath Oil and the Tea Tree Oil range. This last product is integral to understanding the Australian role in the worldwide Body Shop. The leaves of the *Melaleuca alternifolia* occur naturally in New South Wales. The indigenous use of Tea Tree grants these products both longevity and credibility and is mobilised to publicise these goods worldwide. For example, a brochure distributed in the Singapore Body Shop (published in London), described tea tree oil as 'a little treasure from Down Under. A proven natural anti-bacterial cleanser — it has been used by Aborigines for over 40 000 years'.[49] This is nostalgia for simple products, consumerism with a conscience. Indigeneity becomes a marketable ideology, yet the colonial relationship is both uncritiqued and restated.

While the colonial conversation continues, The Body Shop's Australian and New Zealand operations are quite significant to the global structure of the business. Roddick seems particularly impressed by the service she has witnessed in this region, revealing that 'I've never met an Australian shop assistant who isn't perfect'.[50] Financially too, they are profitable and efficient. In 1997 Australia and New Zealand operated seventy-one of the 1491 worldwide stores (4.8 per cent), but contributed 8 per cent to the retail sales figures of the business.[51] What is perhaps most interesting is the unification of Australia and New Zealand into one entity: the Antipodes is indeed back. It is always interesting that an unerring similarity is pressed on the region from outside, while obvious distinctions and differences emerge from within. There are major distinctions between The Body Shop's operations in Australia and New Zealand. Australia does much more than produce raw materials for manufacturing into finished products within England, or even the United Kingdom. The Mulgrave site produces and bottles a range of products for the global Body Shop stores. The contradictions emerge in the ways these products are labelled and marked. The Tea Tree range — which is based on an indigenous Australian plant — is marke(te)d with remarkable inconsistencies. Colonisation is continued through packaging rather than product. While The Facial Wash and Tea Tree Oil are labelled 'Product of

Australia', the soap is simply 'Made in Scotland'. In British shops, all Tea Tree products are (surprisingly) labelled 'Made in London'. This appropriation of ideas is rendered small in scale when compared with the New Zealand shops. Aotearoa supplies no goods, ideas or products to the global Body Shop. Instead, New Zealand becomes a State of Australia, part of the franchise operation managed from Victoria. The Antipodes therefore masks the subtle movements in meaning between Australia, New Zealand and Britain.

Notions of 'home' and 'abroad' are maintained throughout the official documents of The Body Shop, with non-British spheres termed 'international markets'.[52] Australian and New Zealand Body Shops are therefore allowing the memories of past colonial relationships to survive in the present. As Healy argues, 'ruins are never simply gone or in the past; ruins are enduring traces; spaces of romantic fancies and forgetfulness'.[53] These spaces and traces remain in the Body Shop's Antipodean operations.

Roddick stated that 'we live in a society that makes no values at all of anything south of the equator and I was brought up to think science and technology was the answer'.[54] While Roddick may have sympathy for those of us living south of the equator, her treatment of Antipodean distinctions maintains a long-worn path of inaccuracy, simplicity and reification. Under a close-up photograph of an ageing indigenous woman, Roddick wrote the caption: 'to a young Aborigine male in Australia, a seasoned old woman represents more than wisdom and experience — she is also an object of desire'.[55] This woman — like indigenous peoples discussed throughout the publication — is granted a visual presence, but denied a voice. There is a remarkable confluence between the mode of photography in The Body Shop's publications and that in *National Geographic*. Anne Cranny-Francis described the latter as 'a particularly striking example of this kind of cultural imperialism, whereby peoples from regions geographically or culturally "remote" are primitivised by the camera, which give[s] them a bodily presence but never a voice'.[56] The possibility of sexism, inequality and injustice within indigenous communities is not a permissible or debatable question.[57] Instead, the 'seasoned old woman' becomes a signifier for 'our' way forward, as desirability by men remains the clear determiner of feminine success. The subjectivity of the colonised always escapes analysis. It is not surprising, considering the history of the academic discipline, that The Body Shop became the first cosmetics company to employ an anthropologist. The fetishisation of difference, exhibited through the Body Shop's obsession with the bodily practices and rituals of every other region, nation and place *except England*, implicitly hints at a bankruptcy of ideas.

There are enormous gains, in terms of credibility and authenticating frameworks, in suggesting that 'we combine modern technology with ancient ideas'.[58] Travel is framed as moving to something new and different, which challenges and questions the truths of 'the West'. Continually, Roddick states that 'traditional' practices will be lost unless she can rescue communities by making them economically viable:

> Because The Body Shop is a huge company with a great need for raw materials, it's easy to see how useful it would be if we could satisfy that need by building trading relationships with groups who would otherwise have no secure livelihood.[59]

The Trade not Aid commitments of The Body Shop are both ambiguous and contradictory. The basis of the programme is the idea that a special purchasing relationship is necessary between The Body Shop and already existing community organisations. The aim is to generate long-term sustainable trading affiliations. What is noteworthy about this link is that The Body Shop publicity focuses not on the community organisations themselves, but the rights and roles of consumers.

> Community Trade products provide customers with an opportunity to use their purchasing power in ways that support these communities while receiving a good quality product. At the same time, they become informed about the source of the ingredients in the products on the shelves and the accessories available.[60]

This description neglects to reveal what the English-based business gains from the relationship.

These problems are exemplified by the relationship between The Body Shop and the Kayapo Indians of the Brazillian rainforest. Roddick believed that conservation and husbandry of the rainforest were principles that would 'reward the Kayapo, as primary producers,' while not 'disrupt[ing] their culture or their environment'.[61] While her desire for economic sustainability is justifiable, The Body Shop is perpetuating a trade relationship between primary producers and the manufacturing sector, or Imperial periphery and core.[62] The Shareholders' report for 1997 reported the Community Trade programme in carefully couched terms:

> We see our relationship with our Community Trade suppliers in a slightly different way to our other suppliers. These trading relationships are a reality check for us in the West. Trading with communities in need constantly helps us to remember how the majority of the world live. It helps us to remain thoughtful of our business ... Another important measure for us is how they help us to retain the human element in our trading.[63]

It is this aura of charity that remains most disturbing. With overt phil-
anthropy replaced with phrases like 'the human·element in trading',
saving the world becomes as easy as opening our wallets and purses. It
is important that my meaning is clearly understood here. I am not
denying the possibility of indigenous agency and resistance. Instead, I
am suggesting that indigenous communities have their values squeezed
into the cookie cutter of The Body Shop's values, economic imperatives and needs. Roddick outlined the basis on which the trading with
the Kayapo was to take place:

> I was convinced that there must be a way of making the rainforest
> economically viable with a trading strategy that was based on con-
> servation and good husbandry. If the controlled extraction of sus-
> tainably-managed plant materials could provide a livelihood for
> the rainforest people, I felt it was up to them how much change
> they wanted to accept or how far they should be 'civilised'.[64]

The problems in this strategy are clear. The Kayapo and The Body
Shop are not dialoguing as equals. The degree of choice, autonomy
and decision-making within this 'business relationship' will always be
highly restricted. While the Kayapo leaders wished to be paid in cash
for their goods, Roddick admitted that 'I was not at all sure that hand-
ing over money was the right solution ... I wanted to be able to reward
them as primary producers, but I didn't want to jeopardise their culture'.[65] Significantly, this 'protection' renders indigenous peoples
childlike, but also restricts the framework in which they may make
'autonomous' decisions. The characteristic of exploitation in the postcolonial era is not ruthless removal of trees from a rainforest, or dump-
ing of waste in the Amazon. It is a saturation of the space between
producer and consumer with ambivalence, ideological hand-wringing
and the looping of political and economic goals.

While The Body Shop is a better mode of capitalism, it is feeding
off the ideas, rather than the bodies, of colonised women. That is why
the role of Anita Roddick is so pivotal. Gender has a primary role in the
operating principles of colonisation. There is, as Meyda Yegenoglu has
shown, a 'complicity between imperial subject constitution and feminist representation'.[66] Roddick and The Body Shop lift the metaphoric veil that swathes the truths and realities of the Orient and its women.
Liberation and resistance are highly context-specific. British colonisation was a modernising, masculine enterprise, but the process has been
continued — and widened — by cosmetic firms such as The Body
Shop. This method is presented overtly and without apology:[67]

> Before I opened the first shop in 1976, I'd been around the world
> and seen how women in other cultures cared for themselves. The

skin of Tahitian women looked pretty good for all their regular cocoa butter massages. And fresh pineapple seemed to get skin clean and clear in Sri Lanka. Why not use the successful traditions of other peoples to develop new products back home in England?[68]

The answer to Roddick's 'Why not?' is found in the realm of power, colonisation and profit. For example, some Body Shop hair accessories are produced by a rural women's organisation in the Philippines. But while the fund for their goods is used for welfare programmes, there is no public discussion of the money made by The Body Shop for these goods. The 'Trade not Aid' slogan actually involves the firm gifting disempowered and frequently colonised peoples with the right to trade rather than the right to a voice. This maxim focuses attention on the disempowered and deflects attention away from what the Body Shop gains from this relationship. Governments give aid, but businesses instigate trade.

My aim has been to neither demonise nor celebrate The Body Shop, or to chastise or applaud Anita Roddick's role as its founder and spokesperson. The business provides a living, thriving example of Stuart Hall's maxim that:

> Empires come and go. But the imagery of the British Empire seems destined to go on forever. The imperial flag has been hauled down in a hundred different corners of the globe. But it is still flying in the collective unconscious.[69]

What is remarkable is that the imperial trade relationship is still saturated with the aura of charity, civilisation and culture. The New Empire of profit, self-esteem and personal growth allows the imperial flag to keep on flying. While we rub peppermint foot balm into the 'podes, the politics of this personal profit still eludes us.

BIT BLOKEY, EH?
LES MILLS AND THE
MASCULINISATION OF
AEROBICS

Two stories activate the action in this chapter. The first occurred on 3 January 2000 — a public holiday Monday — when Les Mills' Body Combat arrived in Western Australia. As I walked around the calico bags framing the door, the sounds of sirens and bombs whirred from the speakers. The stage was surrounded by (hopefully) unarmed missiles and backed by an unfurled parachute. A windsock fluttered from the air vent. Two men, both wearing khaki fatigues, paced rigorously around the room. One was oiled up and muscled. The other looked like a (slightly more toned) Sergeant Schultz. After this sensory assault, my attention turned to the participants: the room was split evenly between men and women. The soundtrack encouraged men to behave badly: not one, but *two* Queen songs are enough for any aerobics room. In fact, it is too much for *any room*. Another one bites the dust — another feminine sphere is lost. With the men now back at aerobics after relinquishing the space fifteen years ago to leotards and lycra, the resultant class was quiet, uncomfortable, unco-ordinated and far more aggressive than was necessary. Without looking or thinking, clumsy men kicked women without considering where flying feet may have landed. This was not a good experience.

Story two: whispering women throughout the ensuing week asked each other whether or not they would try Body Combat again. The usual 9:30 am Friday class had been given over to the new aerobics phenomenon. The consensus was that we would give it one more go. I was on holidays, so I joined the mums, retired women and others on leave for another combative experience. With a female instructor leading us, there was not a single man in the room.

The resultant class was brilliant, capturing an essence of aerobics. With much laughter, silliness and giggling, it was one of the best hours I have ever spent in a gym. After the instructor told us to 'think about kicking and killing someone in particular, as it always improves your form', the class fought imagined husbands, partners and bosses for sixty minutes. Indeed the form did improve. The knees and elbows were sharply jolted into imagined foes. During a moment of silliness within the pre-choreographed cool-down — involving a Dungeons-and-Dragons-like scenario where the good guy (that is, the participant) holds an imagined sword/light sabre and kills a dragon/Darth Maul — the instructor looked at us with a grin and said: 'a bit blokey, eh?'.

This chapter investigates the Les Mills 'phenomenon' and its two main advertising motifs — evolution and revolution. I investigate the history of aerobics, while granting particular attention to the gendered nature of its formation. In other words, I connect women moving with the women's movement. I also contemplate the importance of the Les Mills palate of classes to the long-term survival of aerobics. Such a study is important. Aerobics is a highly under-researched pursuit, as it is situated at the boundary of leisure, fitness, exercise and sport. To study aerobics requires distinct methodologies, poaching paradigms from fashion theory,[1] popular music studies, cultural studies, feminism and men's studies. It also conflates with histories of bodybuilding and weight-lifting.

Aerobics, by number of participants, has been in the top three sports in Australia for the last five years.[2] What makes aerobics a pivotal topic of study in women's culture is the fact that men exhibit a much higher general involvement in sports than women, but women dominate aerobics. Further, aerobics participation rates are well distributed over all the age groups in the national study, particularly when compared with netball, rugby union, soccer and softball.[3] The other powerful difference is that most attend more than once a week. The only comparable pursuit in terms of regular involvement is lawn bowls.[4]

Australian participation in aerobics

Year of assessment	% of Australian population involved in aerobics
1996/7	4.1
1997/8	10.4
1998/9	11.4

Statistics derived and compiled from the Australian Bureau of Statistics, *Participation in Sport and physical activity*, 1996/7, 1997/8, 1998/9, number 4177.0.

The point of this chapter is to show that disempowered groups (such as women) use disempowered sites (such as aerobics) to renegotiate their social position. Obviously this is a hegemonic struggle, which gleans indefinite results. Aerobics is the McDonald's of sport: fast, ubiquitous and cheap. As an activity that is often framed as fitness for women, aerobics is overlooked, trivialised or condemned by both sports journalists and sports scholars. Yet these (literal) ladies who lunge deserve attention, inside and outside a feminist framework.

MAKE IT BURN

While sports aerobics is a description, sports football is a tautology. To add a 'corrective' noun to aerobics serves to demean the 'mass participation' activity. Considering the breadth of behaviours loaded into the word 'aerobics', it remains difficult to write about, historically or socially. The small entry in *The Oxford Companion to Australian Sport*[5] mentioned both popular and elite participation. This continuum approach to the history of aerobics is beneficial, problematising the elite/sport and mass participation/fitness binary oppositions. The presentation of aerobics as both exercise and sport also performs the shift from trivial to serious and feminine to masculine spheres. While aerobics is framed as something that women do 'to stay in shape', at the elite level such as the world championships, there are frequently more men than women in each national team.

Aerobics, in its current form, has multiple origins. Derived from gymnastic traditions, dance culture, the martial arts, yoga and weight training, it bleeds beyond boundaries. Writers frequently remain loyal to their moment in aerobics history. As Dennis Hemphill disclosed:

> The fitness classes that I taught were co-ed and involved a lot of group exercise, partner exercise, circuits, fitness games and the like. While these activities were largely non-competitive, there were usually more women than men in the classes. However, aerobics was then 'colonised' by the dancers, who brought in the choreography, leotards, mirrors, etc. It was at this stage that more women began participating, but many men left.[6]

Hemphill is obviously authenticating a particular period in the aerobics narrative, attacking the late 1970s and 1980s 'colonisation' by the dancers. He frames men's departure from aerobics as a problem, rather than a time of feminine autonomy and space. Confluent with this change was the arrival of competitive, performance-based aerobics, resulting in FIG incorporating sports aerobics as one of its four disciplines.[7] While Hemphill's melancholy at a loss of general (insert masculine) participation is understandable, he did not infer that the feminine modality of aerobics has an alternative history to reveal. As David Rowe has suggested:

> There is a powerfully resilient association between sport and masculinity that obstructs equality of access, participation and reward for women. Sport has been one of the major means by which masculinity is constructed against femininity in a manner that presents a clear hierarchy of cultural power.[8]

While Rowe focuses on 'the deep inequalities within sport itself',[9] he does not address how his definitional matrix, which actually determines sport, is also an act of critical disempowerment. To explore the role of women involves distilling and separating the masculinity that saturates notions of sport. Women are not excluded through 'mainstream' investigations of sport because of supposed biological difference/inferiority. Instead, it is the ideologies that encircle feminine corporeality that renders women's sport less worthy of attention. That is why aerobics is integral to this modified rendering of sport. As it occupies the space between sport, leisure, fitness and exercise, it is an ideal case study.

Sports Aerobics — like elite, competitive gymnastics — has clear rules and marking criteria. Each routine is sixty-five seconds in length and must exhibit a balanced movement between floor, upright and airborne positionings. The participant must move aerobically over a 7-metre by 7-metre stage, mobilising steps appropriate to the set music. There are rewards for rhythmic variations, with scores determined through difficulty, execution, artistic acuity and originality. Outside of this elite activity, a distinct meaning system permeates the semiosphere.

Aerobics is an intrinsic activity that gains meaning of and for itself. It involves a combination of cardiovascular, strength and flexibility exercises to music over a 40-minute to 60-minute period. As a fitness practice activating large muscle groups, it is expected to produce benefits such as improved heart and lung function, increased muscle tone as well as fat reduction. Aerobics, as a term and format for exercise, was 'invented' by Kenneth H Cooper, a US Air Force surgeon. His concept of aerobics was presented in a 1968 book that revealed the benefits of exercise and the importance of cardiovascular activity. From this American base, there is now a far greater diversity of classes. While Jane Fonda and Richard Simmons are ghost-like phantoms in contemporary aerobics halls, much has changed since the 'make it burn' days of striped leotards and leg warmers. Aerobics remains a promiscuous paradigm, poaching rhythms and movements from martial arts, ballroom dancing, funk and salsa rhythms. Depending on the level of the participant's fitness, there are barbell classes, toning classes, rebounding classes, cross-training classes, stationary-based cycling classes,[10] high-impact classes, martial-arts fitness classes, yoga-based stretching/flexibility classes and step. Aquarobics is available for those wanting a gentler programme. During a lifetime, participants may move between different modes and movements to suit their lifestyle or goals. Also, new hybrid classes are continually being formed, of which Tae Bo is the most obvious example.

Aerobics, by the literal definition of the word, refers to the presence of oxygen. The point of the activity is to train the heart, lungs and cardiovascular system to deliver oxygen to the body. Such a practice becomes increasingly important in an era where many Australians and New Zealanders engage in no physical exercise.[11] Aerobics is important because it provides a site for women to enter a highly masculine sphere, the gym. Yet how women handle the (metaphoric and literal) weights is more difficult to determine.

DISCIPLINING THE BODY POLITIC

The aim of exercise, and particularly weight-bearing activity, is to create micro-trauma in the muscles. When the muscles repair, they become stronger. Weight-bearing exercise allows the maintenance of lean muscle tissue and the loss of fat, particularly for women attempting to lose weight, which has become the most popular feminine hobby of our times.[12] Therefore, fitness, health and slimming magazines have been recommending that women use weights.[13] Aerobic and anaerobic movements combine to build both muscular strength and endurance. The Les Mills suite of programmes actualises these concerns, while forming new relationships between aerobics and adjoining fitness activities.

Bodybuilding, like aerobics, incorporates a wide array of practices and behaviours. The desire to improve musculature through weight training has triggered a fetishisation and fragmentation of the body. As Kenneth Dutton and Ronald Laura have shown, photography has a clear role in the history of bodybuilding.[14] Therefore, it is not surprising that debates about representations of gender have a place in the analysis of both weight training and bodybuilding. The practices serve to critique, question and perhaps rupture accepted notions of masculinity and femininity. In the last ten years, the level of acceptable musculature on a female body has changed radically, resulting in shifting configurations of both fitness and beauty.

Not surprisingly, feminist theorists have been drawn to the physique of female weight trainers and bodybuilders. These women have been described as occupying a 'contested terrain [of] technological interventions and bodily manipulation'.[15] Women who build their bodies occupy a space outside of Wolf's 'female weakness, asexuality and hunger'.[16] Weight training is particularly important for older women. Margie Sheedy, for example, explained the life of her fifty-something mother who had played tennis and walked regularly through most of her adult life:

> Now Carmel and her friend Patty have decided they want to improve their fitness levels, not by increasing the kilometres they walk or the number of balls they hit, but by going to pump aerobics once a week. For some people this mightn't seem like much, but Mum is on the other side of 50, and she has probably only done aerobics a couple of times in her life. After her first class, she was thrilled because she had done something different to improve how she feels about herself, and she had kept up with women half her age.[17]

Such activities, although recently bundled up into the Les Mills programme of Body Pump, are obviously part of a longer narrative of callisthenics. Importantly, weight training brings inactive women and men to a point where they can become more active. The research conducted by Miriam Nelson at the USDA Human Nutrition Research Centre on Ageing at Tufts University confirmed that strengthening-exercise prevents muscle and bone loss from older women and also increases the effectiveness of weight loss.[18] This research into weight training dialogues awkwardly with feminist theory and sports historiography. Lifting weights is a volatile intervention, but does demonstrate that the old aerobics — of high impact, high energy movements conducted to a bridge-free soundtrack — has changed to incorporate these new ideologies. Aerobics has never been static and has always been fashionable, ephemeral and fickle. The difficulty is determining how these new notions of acceptable body image and behaviour have impacted on contemporary notions of fit femininity.

Weight training is too often folded into histories of weight control. Weight watching is a disciplining of the body into a managed self, pushing and prodding flesh into an ideal, normative package. Organisations like Jenny Craig utilise surveillance through the use of scales and measures. Weight is involved in the management of the self. Weight regulation becomes a public activity. Measurements through the pinch test, dress sizes and height/weight tables order the body politic. Jane Ussher has documented that 'this obsession with food, with shape, with firm-fleshed thighs, is not just about health — it is about control of female sexuality'.[19] Individuals are targeted as objects of discipline, with the line between normal/excess weight being patrolled. A woman's fat content is pathologised. For men, size can signify success. As Gordon Campbell suggested, 'American dreams do run to fat. Genius starts out thin and plumps up. Elvis Presley, Orson Welles, Marlon Brando'.[20] Conversely, most women at different life stages have a Karen Carpenter moment, a desire to enact a drive-by fruiting of their own bodies.

DORA GRAY

The young body, taut and sexualised, holds a solipsistic mirror to a Dorian Graying society that, through the surgical knife or the aerobics class, attempts to stave off the wrinkles in the mirror.[21] Slicing through this vanity is the community-building component of aerobics. Throughout Australia and New Zealand, women gather at 9 am and 10 am classes, place their children in crèches and — for one hour — have a jump and laugh with their friends. Studies have found positive physical and psychological outcomes from this practice:

> The findings from the present study suggest that aerobics might have the capacity to liberate women by enhancing their physical self-perceptions. Therefore, although differentiating tasks may intensify the culture of gender, the results from the present study indicate that aerobics may be an activity through which young women can attain positive psychological outcomes.[22]

This study, which focussed on 113 women between the ages of fifteen and sixteen, emphasises both the feminine and non-competitive elements of the practice. Similarly, Annette Farnsworth found that 100 per cent of 645 women polled, aged between twenty-five and forty-nine, affirmed the great importance of being fit and healthy.[23] With the 1970s being the decade of tough fitness (no pain no gain) and the 1980s a time of superwomen, stress reduction and diet, the 1990s was bound to be a calmer era of aromatherapy and yoga. With sport and leisure configured by understandings of work, women's incorporation into physical culture is relationally formed by their immersion in the workforce. It is no coincidence that the Les Mills franchise has implemented a more ordered, rigid and predictable pattern for aerobics classes, which accompanies the increasing demands of women's contribution to the public sphere.

Aerobics has a pedagogical function, teaching physical co-ordination, balance, fitness and also intricate and complicated affiliations between goals and desires of individuals and those of the group. It is not a reification of femininity, but one of the few places where women of different ages, classes, ethnicities and educational levels can meet, mingle and talk. This 'new style women's club'[24] accesses narratives of femininity through the changes of marriage, pregnancy, divorce, illness and ageing. As Reed has suggested, these classes are 'one of the last places that women regularly gather without men around'.[25] As most women work in male-dominated environments, aerobics can offer feminine space, a (transitory) movement away from men and masculinity. Well, sometimes.

I should have known something was wrong when forty-something women, squeezed uncomfortably into lycra bike pants, started to giggle. I should have known this was not the usual aerobics class when thirty-five steps were already in place ten minutes before the commencement of a 4:30 pm step aerobics session. I should have known I was in deep trouble when one of the giggling forty-somethings offered me ten dollars for my spot in front of the instructor.

Then Warren entered the room.

Sharp intake of breath. A six-foot, muscular but slender, blonde aerobics instructor delicately shaped a contoured lycra unitard. This man was perfect. His quads protruded seductively under the garishly patterned fabric: the veins in his arms portrayed strength and stamina. There was no gut, no flab — just tight sinew topped by golden hair. My athletic self was completely overcome by the erotic self. I kept on thinking, why am I sweating, why am I wearing this T-Shirt with the slogan 'My next husband will be normal' and why-why-why wasn't I more careful shaving my legs this morning?

I was self-conscious and clumsy during the entire class. I could not look Warren in the face. I was embarrassed to be exercising before such a syntagm of masculine sensualness. I did not want to be this close to such a beautiful man.

Such an encounter could easily trigger a Harlequin Romance. An under-confident woman brought to sexual poise and passion through the charms of Warren, the aerobics instructor. We would, of course, end the tale as lovers and aerobics partners, explaining to *New Woman* magazine how we combine our busy working schedule as Australia's mixed double sports aerobics champions with our intensely physical private life.

Sadly, the female erotic gaze must always be tempered by masochism. For women to gain pleasure it must be a bi-product, an accident that is attained while doing something else.

Aerobics may seem to present women in their natural state, but it is a highly vulnerable space. Devoid of make-up, squeezed into lycra and facing an enormous mirror, the female body is rarely presented with such fragility. However, Moya Lloyd has been critical of aerobics' role in changing the aesthetics of the female body. She described aerobics as the 'one area of activity that engages many women in search of slenderness [that] has escaped sustained scrutiny'.[26] For Lloyd, aerobics is affiliated with eating disorders. Other readings are lost. I agree that the health industry has been professionalised, transforming participants into consumers of exercise. But Lloyd simplifies this process, by arguing that 'the discourse of health and fitness is no less discipli-nary or regulatory than the discourse surrounding aesthetics; and although it may appear more benign, that is all it is — an appear-ance'.[27] The time has come for us to grant attention to appearances, representations, surfaces and superficialities.

Where research needs to be conducted is in the connection between aerobics and personal control. Bordo, quoting Aimee Liu, stated that 'I will be master of my own body, if nothing else, I vow'.[28] Locked in a pumping panopticon, the good body is thin, toned and streamlined. Aerobics is not so easily framed as a symptom of disor-dered eating. These women are not ensconced in the home, counting calories and monitoring fat content. Certainly, they are transforming the self into a project. But it is a negotiated self, a site of both anxiety and display. It is ironic that for men exercise and sport are naturalised, while women's fitness practices are pathologised. Judith Rodin has pre-sented this problem best, instructing her readers that 'You must over-come the notion that how hard you work is the measure of what kind of person you are'.[29] These studies do not explore the construction of aerobics-based communities as a positive force. Instead, the old ide-ologies of narcissism, beauty and youth re-clothe fitness participants.[30] Defiantly though, women are re-writing femininity and building a new type of feminism.

Many narratives — of strength, flexibility and competency — wash across the mobile body. Each adds potential and problems to under-standing the relationship between sport and women. For feminists such as Naomi Wolf, fitness and exercise are synonymous with bodily management.[31] While high-profile feminists have attacked aerobics for its retrograde politics, it is apparent that the power encircling the aer-obicising body is hegemonic rather than coercive. Aerobics is not only, or even mainly, a negative force in contemporary society. Rather, it pro-vides a site of negotiation by women and an interrogative space for crit-ical debates in feminism. By aligning aerobics and anorexia, the positive social (and political) benefits of the former are overlooked or displaced. Put another way, when aerobics participants turn to face the mirror, myriad ambiguous — if not contradictory — gazes are reflected back. The critical eye, which compares, critiques and attacks the self, is con-currently paired with the challenging 'I' of empowerment, community and fitness. Women moving into the masculine zones of gyms and weight training centres are framed as 'a problem'. Ironically, it is the feminists who first determined this *problem*. The analytical tragedy of this work is that aerobics has been trivialised, demeaned and made vul-nerable to a masculine (re)colonisation. Oddly, but perhaps not, this reclamation of lost territory has been sourced from the most Antipodean nations of the old Empire.

START THE REVOLUTION TODAY

By the mid-1990s, burned out on grapevines and step aerobics, 'the signs of aerobics demise ... [could not] be denied'.[32] The irony is that the next 'revolution' in aerobics did not come from the United States: it was not a Tae Bo-led recovery. The 'evolution' commenced in Auckland. Aerobics, as the most American of fitness pursuits, has triggered the most Antipodean of grafts. Therese Iknoian reported in 1993 that:

> Aerobics has come full circle. A quarter of a century ago, it started as a fitness activity for the US masses. Fifteen years later, that activity spawned elite competition in the US which, through the magic of television, sparked grass-root classes around the world. Next came national competitions in many countries.[33]

Clearly, this 'full circle' extended further than Iknoian's imagining. By the 1997 World Sports Aerobics Championships, held in Perth, there were no American winners in the male and female singles, duo or trio competitions. In all, forty nations have registered for the international Sports Aerobics competition. From within this global expansion, innovation emerged. The surprise was that it was derived from Aotearoa/New Zealand.

Les Mills is famous in Auckland. Holder of an MBE and a four-times New Zealand Olympic field athlete, he was also a controversial mayor of the city from 1990 to 1998. He formed the first Les Mills World of Fitness in 1968 and, although he retired from the fitness industry, his family continues to run and expand the chain of clubs. One of the Auckland gyms has 10 000 members. It features an inordinate number of classes (144 per week), with many participants. The overall quality of the sessions is high, with an English-based instructor describing the classes of Mike McSweeney (Director of Body Pump choreography at Les Mills Auckland) as 'something normally only experienced at fitness conventions — yet for these New Zealanders, this was a "regular time-tabled" session!'.[34] The key is that all instructors perform the same pre-choreographed routines for three months. Then, a new Les Mills audio and video tape, notes and choreography are released.[35] Therefore, each of the programmes release four distinct routines a year. Quality control, like all Fordist enterprises, is high. Because of the set chorography, consistency is elevated, but there are many problems, both for instructors and participants. Although based in Auckland, Les Mills International sells franchise rights to fitness centres and provides the chorography, music, clothes and instruction.

When Body Pump arrived in Australia, under the banner of 'Start the revolution today', a potent mix of politics and sport was revealed. The accompanying poster utilised a Darwin-like evolution chart.

Instead of developing from apes to modern man, a man squatting under a bar and weights slowly reached full extension. The rationale for the connection of evolution and revolution was clear. The income from aerobics had declined, replaced by both personal training and home exercise equipment and videos. A way to increase participation was to make aerobics — with its intense feminine modality — male-compliant. The addition of weights along with simple, repetitive movements and minimal choreography, was the strategy used to fulfill this goal.[36] Body Pump was the first Les Mills programme to be internationalised. It arrived in Australia during 1996. It is an 'aerobics workout' that uses a bar and weights. It was discovered that the use of a bar, rather than barbells, improved the form and posture of participants. It is a user-friendly weights package. The successful launch of this programme has been enhanced through the arrival of Body Step, Body Attack (the high-intensity workout), RPM (the cycling programme) and Bodybalance (the yoga and stretching session) — all from Les Mills. Besides the combative exercise formats and the more masculine language of 'pump' and 'attack', what distinguishes these sessions from conventional aerobics is the increased emphasis on strength work.

By 2001, there were 455 centres across Australia using the Les Mills body training systems, growing at a rate of fourteen new licensees a week.[37] The Les Mills package of classes has instigated two major changes to the conventional aerobics. Firstly, the musical soundtrack has breaks. For non-aerobics readers, this change may seem minor. However, so much of aerobics through the 1980s and 1990s was based on dance choreography and a soundtrack resembling a disco-club mix of continual beats between and through songs. Les Mills separated the tracks, which also distinguished between the muscle groups and exercises used for each song.[38] In this way, a high repetition of movement and action could be layered, learnt and remembered. This innovation removes a major definitional component of aerobics: classes based on a bridge-free soundtrack.[39] The aim is to minimise the number of stops and starts. This leads to the second major innovation of the package — the rigid choreography. Instructors attend intense workshops and obtain videos and tapes to learn the precise movements to accompany the specific phrasing of the music. There is no diversity of steps between instructors and little creativity from the fitness leaders. Put simply, the participants complete the same class, sometimes two and three times a week until a new tape, music and choreography arrive.

Newson noticed that 'pre-choreographed classes take away the creativity of the teacher'.[40] The fitness leaders move from moments of high stress — having to deliver a perfectly formed new choreography every three months — to the boring repetition of the same class at the end of that period. Every instructor I have asked has mentioned the lack of initiative and interest at the closing stages of the three months. There is even a formal recognition of this problem on the website:

> At the end of the day, we can only do so much. We provide world class training and programs for instructors. We take the hard work out of it by providing all the music and movements. If instructors don't have the personal drive and commitment, the rest can fall down.[41]

In an ironic reversal, the creative energy has been removed from instructors, but if they fail to perform the script correctly, it must be blamed on a lack of personal commitment. When I asked Rod Harvey, General Manager of Les Mills Australia, about this problem, his reply was staunchly critical of other modes of aerobics leadership:

TB: There has been discussion in some of the fitness industry magazines that the Les Mills training systems reduce the innovation and creativity of individual instructors, because of the pre-choreographed style. I am sure you have heard this criticism as well. How do you counter it?

RH: The issue of restriction of creativity does not come up very often as the industry fell into a big black hole in the late 80s as a result of the freestyle instructors complicating their programmes to the extent that people were not able to follow them. It has only been in the last 3–4 years that there has been a resurgence in the group fitness industry and we find it extremely coincidental that since the pre-choreography of Aerobics the numbers and quality of instruction has lifted. This in turn has ensured that most gyms have followed suit in simplifying their programmes.[42]

Mr Harvey's comments could be re-written to acknowledge the link between dance and aerobics, which allowed female participants to challenge themselves to learn new movements. The desire for new steps is still observed in participants waiting for the arrival of new choreography — or 'the launch'. Completing the identical class, at the identical time, with the identical instructor for three months can be quite debilitating for a workout. This is most obviously a problem for Body Step programmes. Steppers are generally the most experienced of aerobics participants, with the highest capacity to manage choreography and quick transitions.[43] Therefore, the movements are mastered quickly, rendering much of the three-month period repetitive and dull. The only way this paradox has been addressed is that, through Body Step 40, the speed of the music was increased to 135 beats per minute, compared to the usual 124 beats per minute. This is a method to access the fitness of experienced steppers, but makes the situation even more difficult for those new to this mode of movement. The Les Mills programme is based on the premise that aerobics became too complicated, thereby eroding the participant base. They therefore wanted to form an 'interesting, yet easily repeatable workout'.[44] The conflicts of the past and present history of aerobics are revealed in the presentation of Body Step. This was exemplified by the club I attend in suburban Perth. A new Body Step tape emerged in October 1999, but was not replaced until February 2000. By the end of the period, most participants were groaning at the opening bars of the tape. Other steppers stopped attending — until the next launch.

While there are difficulties, it is obvious that Les Mills International has instigated a major change in the fitness industry. By January 1999 there were 11 157 instructors trained in the choreography worldwide, with 40 per cent of the fitness club market in Australia featuring a Les Mills programme. The choreography has spread to forty-three countries.[45] This means that the Body Pump class attended in Auckland should be the same as that conducted in London or Perth. The movements, music and directions are the same. This has been confirmed as being of a great advantage to instructors:

> Dear Bodypump team, I am a bodypump instructor from Dunedin, now working in Dublin, Ireland at the West Wood Club. I thought that I would like to pass on a thankyou to whoever it is out there that has made Bodypump such an international fitness craze. What I mean to say is what other job can you travel to another country on the other side of the world and have a class from home going just as strong. Hands up for New Zealand made.[46]

While utilising an international mode of music, generally sung in English, there has been only one overt New Zealand reference in the soundtracks. Pump 32 featured a haka squat track. However, no other Maori or Pacific Islander interventions have been used. Certainly, the success of these programmes with participants is high. The website features an array of testimonials for each of the choreography styles.[47]

The desire to increase the testosterone in the aerobics hall has been the trigger for the 'innovations' mobilised by Les Mills training systems. Aeroboxing, circuit training and Pump make weights part of the fitness experience. The Les Mills Franchise, aware of the intense femininity attached to aerobics, instigated a change to the name of the practice. This re-languaging transformed aerobics timetables into group fitness timetables. Other masculinist interventions have also taken place:

The aim of Body Pump by Les Mills is to increase participation levels in aerobic studios world-wide by providing a memorable, results oriented workout.[48]

A sport without winners, losers or finishing lines has been transformed into a site of clearly specified results. Similarly, the slogan for Body Combat is 'Go hard or go home'. Combat-style moves allow for the strengthening of both heart and body through self-defence chops and kicks. Its simple, athletic movements work at the anaerobic threshold, thereby improving stamina. However, the marketing slogans used to advertise the programme are laughable:

> We call it bodycombat for a reason. You're fighting for your life, for the fitness you deserve and the total body wellness you must have. You want to stay in shape? Put your hands up and start defending yourself.[49]

The happy collectivity of aerobics is diffused. Improving fitness and having fun with friends has been distorted into 'you're fighting for your life'. However, the Master Instructors in Auckland would be horrified to see how suburban women play with the choreography at their 9 am and 10 am classes. The staunch maleness of 'defending yourself' has resulted in giggling and mocking of the hyper-masculinity of the movements. Much to their displeasure, men have been pushed out of these 'aerobics classes' once more, not through the complexity of the choreography, but through women's laughter. Continuities remain between the history of aerobics and the revolution of Les Mills.

Aerobics classes — even in the free-style mode — have become structured. The Les Mills training systems merely intensify this principle. When American-styled aerobics arrived in Australia during the late 1970s, it was not overtly choreographed and exhibited little musical phrasing. Being repetitious and high impact, its leisure life was short lived, to be replaced by the 1980s mainstream boom in aerobics. However, in the desire for innovation, new steps and movements became more specialised, resulting in niche marketing of myriad aerobics activities. Certainly, step aerobics, for the first-time participant, is both daunting and embarrassing. Through the 1990s, those who were comfortable with aerobics were also comfortable with co-ordinated movements and themselves. This simultaneously created a group belonging in a non-competitive structure. The professionalisation of aerobics instructors resulted in these fitness leaders attaining greater skills and accreditation.

While the Les Mills Franchise wished to frame its practice as both a revolution and evolution, it was actually far more embedded in aerobics history than imagined. Like all previous revolutions — for hi lo,

step, circuit training, XTC, shape, grid, aqua and aeroboxing, the Les
Mills classes will be replaced by the next trend. For example, CS, from
Western Australia, recorded on the website:

> I am a regular user of your programs. I do Bodypump,
> Bodybalance and Bodystep. I wanted to write to you and tell you
> how much I am enjoying them from the normal aerobics. I am
> especially enjoying Bodybalance, as it is quite new over here.[50]

The key is that CS, like all aerobics participants, is a neophyte, a lover
of the new. Intriguingly, Les Mills is the alternative to 'normal aerobics'. But like all *others*, they actually mould and change the centre, *the
normal*. Glancing at the current Group Fitness Timetable for my suburban club, I see that, of the thirty-six classes in the weekly timetable,
twenty-one are part of the Les Mills suite. That is, they have become
the normal choreography for contemporary aerobics participants. All
the theoretical/political problems of earlier aerobic modes have
recurred: from the desire for weight loss ('RPM is my calorie killer …
I have lost seven pounds in the last three months'[51]) to the difficulty
women have of finding time to exercise ('They give you the muscle
tone and fitness if you don't have much time you get an excellent
workout'[52]).

It will only be a matter of time before the next revolution emerges.
However, like all previous interventions in the history of aerobics, this
Les Mills moment will be carried forward. Body Pump will remain,
alongside perhaps Body Balance, but the others will be replaced with
distinct modes of collective exercise. Problems are already surfacing.
The aerobics co-ordinator at the Body Club Bullcreek released the following message:

> I know a lot of you are concerned about the timetable going total-
> ly Les Mills programmes, I want to assure you that if a freestyle
> class is popular it will stay that way. You have to admit though, that
> all of the Les Mills programmes cater for the beginner right
> through to the advanced all at the same time.[53]

The only class that successfully caters for all beginner and advanced
users is Body Pump, because a variety of weights can be added.
However, Body Step requires a high level of fitness and low level of
skill. I have seen new participants slink out of classes in puffing embarrassment. Similarly, I have seen experienced steppers walk away in boredom. Body Combat is quirky, fashionable and funny, but it will be
replaced. Body Balance offers a solid, effective integration of simple
yoga poses, while dynamically connecting the moves.

Les Mills has mobilised myriad ideologies of our age. The desire
for muscle tautness and fitness, when matched with a lack of time and

a need for visible results, has created a successful programme. However, as with all texts, the audience responses are not within the control of the creator, even with such a high level of choreographic standardisation. Throughout suburban aerobics classes, Les Mills has slotted into familiar patterns. Women may have their 'guard up', their 'bar up', or place their arms in 'body step position', but the older histories flood the floor. While the increasing use of weights will have a long-term impact on aerobics movements, the other revolutions will pass. In the end, aerobics is not about fitness, fat or finesse. It is about community, conversation and catharsis. These attributes cannot be pre-choreographed, but are an embedded presence in femininity.

PART 2

MOVING WOMEN

FASTEN YOUR SEATBELTS, BUT NOT THE HIGHCHAIR: BETTE DAVIS AND SPINSTERHOOD

ONCE UPON A TIME

Every now and again — generally during the question time of a conference or lecture — I feel like an extra in a 1940s melodrama. Dashing men combat dastardly (and generally dead) theorists. Vixens give good leg while Doris Days and Deborah Kerrs keep honour and integrity intact by seething, not speaking. Recently, I delivered a seminar with three of my postgraduates that discussed the relationship between female staff and students in a supervisory situation. I expected — and received — a solid female audience. It was an unusual meeting of supervisor and postgraduates. At the time, all four of us were aged between twenty-four and thirty. I knew that this situation would not return and wanted to mark its oddity and specialness, while ensuring that my students were thinking actively about age, feminism and teaching.

During the question time for this paper, the assembled audience expressed extreme anger. Unfortunately, it was directed at me. One questioner had her arms crossed, voice raised and defences up. She accused me of creating 'clones' of myself and over-emphasising the continual patriarchal ideologies within the supervisory structure. After all, she had a male supervisor 'and he was a darling'. Thanks for sharing. Unfortunately, the vixen was only winding up, rather than down. Experience can be a brutal weapon when viciously wielded by the wounded. She explained that I had no knowledge of children or childcare and would therefore discriminate against women who made a decision during their candidature to postpone their studies for a time to 'create a family'. She told the assembled gathering that her male supervisor had been so understanding of her pregnancy, while a friend of hers (there is always a friend, eh?) had been supervised by a (recoiling horror) childless woman who had shown no empathy for her plight. As a result, the friend later withdrew from the Doctoral programme. After the denouement of this tale, much sighing and tittering tumbled from the mouths of the attentive collective. Single women without children are dangerous: even men are better women than those dried-up drag queens.

I remained silent, having no desire to justify my life choices. It has never been my political or theoretical position to be anti-children or against families. My mistake was to not mention childcare and relationships during the seminar. There was a reason for this absence. None of the female speakers, including myself, have children or a husband. We are single and childless, and that was a problem for the audience. I did not realise that — no matter what the context — women must *always* mention progeny and partners. Instead, I had discussed the workplace and the challenges of balancing teaching and research. Obviously, we now live in an age where all women must — always — possess not only a womb with a view, but also a womb *on view*.

My thoughts tumbled awkwardly and incoherently. At this seminar — and for the first time in my life — I felt ashamed of being 'alone'. I was a social failure, left on the shelf. Cinematic scenes cascaded before me: Orlando running through the maze — a spinster and alone — as she hurtled from the Georgian to the Victorian era. She was so rash that she actually had sex with Billy Zane — the very definition of desperation. No — I do not feel like Tilda Swinton. I have not got the hair. I am Captain Kathryn Janeway, of 'Star Trek: Voyager', boldly going where no spinster had gone before. That is not right either. I do not have the voice or the power to mistress a mighty starship. Then, the pain of realisation hit me.

I am Bette Davis in *Now, Voyager*: the maiden aunt, the dutiful daughter, the social failure and the sexual incompetent. And I did not smoke, which ruined the whole effect of her seduction. Without the nicotine emerging from two smoking barrels, I was doomed to be alone — forever.

I'D LUV TO KISS YA, BUT I JUST WASHED MY HAIR[1]

> They had style, they had grace
> Rita Hayworth gave good face
> Lauren, Katharine, Lana too
> Bette Davis — We love you[2]
>
> Madonna, 'Vogue'

Raised in Boston's industrial city of Lowell, Massachusetts, Bette Davis was born in the shadow of one war and worked through the next. She performed for six decades through 112 films, winning two academy awards and being nominated a further eight times. Her roles moved from ingenue to slut and from spinster to 'the first lady of fright'.[3] Her career and life survived four husbands,[4] a child with mental challenges, a financially demanding mother and sister, breast cancer, a radical mastectomy, a disloyal daughter and a stroke.[5] Despite these social dislocations, she is ranked among the ten greatest stars of all time.[6]

Bette Davis, although possessing moments of glamour and great beauty, played roles that required sensible shoes. Her face and body were padded and rouged; her costumes were neck-to-knee nightmares. Moving from the ageing Queen Elizabeth to the eyebrow-challenged Charlotte Vale in *Now, Voyager* and to the vain Mrs Skeffington, her 1940s films presented marriage as a state to be avoided, a complicated entanglement of emotions. She took enormous risks on film, including shaving her head and plastering her face with powder. When asked at an award ceremony if she regretted not being a coveted and adored movie star, she replied, 'wouldn't it be a rather meagre ambition if that was all one strived for?'.[7] Her body became a tool to be deployed. She possessed the most recognisable eyes of the century[8] and a rhythmic walk enhanced by wet-nail-polish gestures. Her remarkable vocal projection was necessary for a Hollywood that needed recordable voices for the new talking pictures. Bette Davis was loud; she had character and stamina.

Robert Wagner described her onscreen performances as doing 'things that people didn't even begin to imagine'. Her first[10] remarkable role was Mildred Rogers in the 1934 RKO production *Of Human Bondage*. It was the rawest, most brutal performance yet recorded on film. It was also one of a small number of filmic texts of the time devoid of any romance. Playing a woman with few redeemable characteristics, she utters — in a manic spin — the greatest filmic putdown:

> Me? I disgust you? You're too fine. You cad. You dirty swine! I never cared for you, not once … It made me sick to have to kiss ya. I only did it because you begged me. You hounded me! You drove me crazy! And afterwards, I wiped my mouth. Wiped my mouth.[11]

This was the first of many roles where Bette Davis enlarged the parameters of acceptable female behaviour. As she aged she found it difficult to obtain work, but never 'retired'. To make the fight even more difficult, her private life was a mess. Beaten by all four of her husbands, it is no surprise that Bette Davis, when reviewing her life, believed it would have been easier to remain single. Her first husband, during divorce proceedings, proved mental cruelty because of Davis's attention to her career:

Attorney Flannagan: In what respect was your wife cruel
                          to you?

Nelson:	I expect it was as a result of her career ... She thought her career more important than marriage.
Flannagan:	Did she tell you that?
Nelson:	Yes, she did.[12]

The divorce was granted. The difficulties in managing public success with a disastrous private life resulted in her judging men and masculinity in narrow terms. As she admitted to her dominating mother in *Now, Voyager*, 'I am not afraid'. She was prepared to be independent[13] and to manage with less. Through the years of staunch fighting, Davis provided clear challenges for contemporary women and feminism.

I WAS THINKING OF MY MOTHER[14]

To state my position clearly, I am *over* the discussion of second and third wave feminism.[15] I am bored by the stiff proselytising of the former and embarrassed to be the same age as the whining, petulant latter.[16] By separating the waves, the experiences and struggles of thousands of women are discredited and denied, including our mothers and grandmothers. They were frequently not interested in reform, but in survival. Greer's portrayal of these women's lives is hardly recognisable:

> The working girl who marries, works for a period after her marriage and retires to breed, is hardly equipped for the isolation of the nuclear household. Regardless of whether she enjoyed the menial work of typing or selling or waitressing or clerking, she at least had freedom of movement to a degree. Her horizon shrinks to the house, the shopping centre and the telly.[17]

Whatever the value of Greer's vitriol, there is no need to ridicule a group of women born during the Great Depression, who survived appeasement and grew up through the war. To reduce the intelligence and consciousness of remarkable women to 'the house, the shopping centre and the telly' is unforgivable, even for the purpose of inflaming feminism. To discover another reading of these women's lives, Bette Davis's films can provide a corrective database. Greer has rarely worked well with films or popular culture. This (increasingly) problematic absence can explain her lack of empathy and understanding of working women's lives through the twentieth century. Hollywood films have not only sold celluloid: they have advertised a social and economic system. Indeed, it is difficult to assess our current age without a consideration of these pervasive, punctuating images.

Critical attention placed on Bette Davis, Katharine Hepburn or even

Sharon Stone may be dismissed as teabag-weak, liberal feminism. However, I do not write in celebration of individual success and autonomy. What interests me is that these women affirmed work as the integral definer of their identities. Their honest articulation of an inability to manage family and career seems refreshing and powerful.[18] We live in an era of self-help nightmares like *Supercouple Syndrome: How Overworked Couples Can Beat Stress Together*[19] and *Are you tired of being tired?*.[20] Feminism, at its most potent and gutsy, offers alternatives, consciousness and options. To term the actions of difficult women as liberal feminism is demeaning. The place of these non-traditional constructions in feminine consciousness is spiky and tortuous. However, effective feminist analysis must open out these (filmic) paradoxes.[21]

A great irony of this supposedly postfeminist era is that there were actually more roles for older women in the 1940s, 1950s and 1960s than in the current age. The normalised pairing of Jack Nicholson with Helen Hunt, Pierce Brosnan with Denise Richards, or Sean Connery with any woman with a pulse under thirty, leaves few representational opportunities for women in their forties and fifties. Bette Davis kept working by moving into television and back to the stage. Bette Davis was never 'beautiful', even in her thirties. There remains a fear of the ageing, experienced woman who will not be silenced or erased because she does not fulfill masculine notions of attractiveness. The role and place of Margo Channing, Norma Desmond and Mrs Robinson in filmic memories have constructed an archetype of inter-generational relationships. However, contemporary films have not built upon or critiqued this earlier legacy.[22] Therefore, some feminists have moved back in time.

Judith Mayne recoiled from a desire to victimise the representation of femininity in the cinema. She theorised that:

> Given classical cinema's obsession with sexual hierarchy, feminist film critics could choose the somewhat obvious task of amassing more and more evidence of women's exclusion and victimisation, or they could undertake the more complex and challenging project of examining the contradictions in classical films, that is, what is repressed or unresolved, and potentially threatening to the patriarchal status quo.[23]

For Mayne, Bette Davis films are particularly notable in this regard. *Now, Voyager* offers spaces between patriarchal directives and feminine investments in the narrative. While the text can be read as a medicalisation of feminine aberrance, with a male doctor leading the woman to emotional contentment, there are other readings. The strength of Davis's films, and also those of Crawford and Hepburn, is that they value experience and personal transformation. The key is to assess how feminist theory and politics can mobilise these changes.

FASTEN YOUR SEATBELTS[24]

We live in an era that valorises a particular mode of motherhood. The women who 'have it all' — husbands, children and careers — are the feminist heroes of the era.[25] The profound difficulty of managing — let alone enjoying — the complexities of the workplace and the home are rarely discussed. Rhona Mahony believed that women are *Kidding ourselves*.[26] She asserted that women make decisions at high school and in their twenties with profound consequences that they never anticipate or consider. There is little recognition of the difficulties involved in negotiating who does the dishes, who takes the clothes off the line and who scrubs the kitchen floor. Bargaining these tasks does not occur within a framework of equality. Most women marry men who are further advanced in their career, older and earning more. It makes obvious economic (rationalist) sense that the partner on higher wages will perform less home duties. Female hypergamy — or women 'marrying up' — is the characteristic of most societies. This disparity is only increased through divorce. While divorced men remarry more quickly than women, they also increase the age gap between the husband and wife. Therefore, the power inequality intensifies with subsequent remarriages.[27] When children are added to the union, the rupture in women's lives amplifies. Having children reduces the average women's income, but men's wages increase with the responsibilities of a family.[28] Therefore, children swell a woman's reliance on a man.

Too often there is an assumed dependence of women on men. For example, both my brother and I are Dr Brabazon. We laugh that our mail may be confused, with him receiving my historical journals and me confronting an illustrated proctology report. However, the paths of a medical doctor and historian rarely cross. One day, I was ordering a cake from a patisserie, leaving my name with the sales assistant. She immediately looked up and asked if I was Mrs Brabazon. I looked quizzical, like I heard an alternate refrain in my name. She continued, 'is Dr Brabazon your husband?'. Still not catching on, I said, 'no, *I'm* Dr Brabazon'. Her chance to look quizzical. 'But my grandmother was seeing a Dr Brabazon in Mandurah. I had assumed …' Pennies drop. 'Oh, *that* Dr Brabazon is my *brother*, not my *husband*'. It was a real *Return of the Jedi* moment. Luke, Leia and Han giggled around my shoulders. This story would not be so disturbing, except that my brother is fifteen years older than I am. It is indeed intriguing that I am old enough to be a doctor's wife, but not mature enough to be a doctor. There is great humour to be derived from being — even implicitly — viewed as outside of conventional social allegiances. It creates a space for confusion, fun and freedom. Being nobody's 'Mrs' is refreshingly disturbing.

Not surprisingly, theorists are starting to chart alternative modes of social organisation. The economic and social productivity of the unmarried is under-researched. Jocelynne Scutt claimed that 'Spinsters have frequently been the breakers of barriers, achieved "firsts", created or expanded institutions, established career paths for others'.[29] Spinsters embody atypical social trajectories. These alternative lives are frequently invisible. The social circles of the single and partnered rarely conflate. For example, Leonie Still, Deputy Vice Chancellor of Edith Cowan University, stated that 'If I ventured out alone I was usually met with embarrassment from couples'.[30] There are few role models of singleness, of vaulting the glory box, and little discussion of the practicalities of singleness. Language signifies unfulfilled potential: childless, child-free, without issue and nullipara.

Bette Davis never managed this potpourri of women's identity. She juggled (and dropped) the balls of men, children, career, ageing, weight, fashion, sex and celibacy. For some, Davis is the great anti-feminist flare for women who over-emphasise a career — 'she got what she wanted and paid for it: four stormy marriages of her own, an estranged daughter, a lonely life'.[31] It is important that journalists are not allowed to rewrite her historical significance through the 'loneliness' of her later years. Bette Davis was the first — and finest — presentation of an independent woman on celluloid. Watching these old films with a feminist eye is a highly rewarding and disturbing experience.[32] It is remarkable to view women creating new visual languages and dodging patriarchal codings.

Writing about women on film is always contingent and subjective. Feminism has accompanied much of cinematic history. If early American cinema has a unifying trope, it is an exploration of women and how their sexuality could be controlled. As Janet Staiger revealed, 'Woman and woman's sexuality were not taboo as topics but were a focal point for understanding a changing social order'.[33] What I find intriguing about the biographical treatment of Bette Davis is the preponderance of camp and queer interpretations. While not suggesting that these modalities are inappropriate or incorrect,[34] I am interested in their rationale. Daniel Harris disclosed that:

> ... for me and for other gay men growing up before the gay-rights movement, our love of Hollywood was an expression not of flamboyant effeminacy but, in a very literal sense, of swaggering machismo ... Quite by accident the diva provided the psychological model of gay militancy.[35]

Gay politics seems able to use flamboyant excess and paradoxical performances in a way that is not needed within feminism. By leaving these feminine performances un(der)considered, journalists have been able to ask 'are they strong women or just macho guys in drag?'.[36] Also, the poor quality of Davis biographies, almost invariably written by men who possessed a minor acquaintance with her, expressed naïve and dangerous political frameworks:

> Bette was sometimes accused of being a fag hag, particularly by her husband Gary Merrill. The problem was that because she was such a strong and dominating personality, she often made hetero-sexual men feel threatened. Gay men posed no threat to her, and were quite willing to let her think she dominated them. It was also interesting that she was so attractive to strong women. When we were discussing the subject of lesbianism once she thought about it for a while and said; 'If I woke up to find two big boobs in bed beside me, I would die'.[37]

The conflation of strength and lesbianism, weakness and fag-haggery, is highly destructive to feminist theory and politics. Masculine labelling of feminine behaviour often results in awkward contradictions and bizarre couplings of sexuality and identity. While gay men who identi-fy with female stars have generated important work, feminist theorists have offerings to this debate that do not enfold into the tropes of queerness.

Misogyny is founded on the separation of femininity and masculin-ity and the marginalisation and ridicule of women. The women who have been framed as a threat in our culture — like the Sirens, Cleopatra, Mae West and Sharon Stone — are therefore used by misogynists to patrol distinctions in the gender order. While homo-phobia and misogyny foreground and naturalise heterosexuality, it can-not be inferred that homosexuality and misogyny are mutually exclusive. The worship and desire for the bevelled diva, the ageing cin-ema star, also convey a mocking humour for the lapsed glamour of the ageing woman. The key now is to reclaim the woman from the diva and to investigate the feminism that does not speak its name.

SLOW CURTAIN, OR THE EPISTEMOLOGY OF THE SHELF

All about Eve is one of the very few pictures that become more dis-turbing as the viewer ages. A horror film without a bloodied hook for a hand or Freddy Krueger fingernails, it tells the tale of the ambitious understudy trying to destroy the life and career of a 40-year-old actress. It has been described as 'a movie about ambition and backbiting'.[38] The role of Margo Channing is arguably Bette Davis's finest perfor-mance. Yet Margo's war is not with the evil Eve. Instead it is with wrin-kles, the corset and clock. Her vulnerability has maintained a cult following for the film.[39]

It is odd that feminist theorists are rarely drawn to *All about Eve*.

Exploring a woman confronting the costs of her career and the price of personal happiness, *All About Eve* presents a highly volatile exploration of femininity, away from domesticity and compliant motherhood:

> Funny business, a woman's career. The things you drop on the way up the ladder so that you can move faster. You forget that you'll need them again when you go back to being a woman. There is one career all females have in common whether we like it or not: it's being a woman. Sooner or later we've got to work at it. No matter how many other careers we've had or wanted. And in the last analysis, nothing's any good unless you can look up just before dinner or turn around in bed and there he is. Without that, you're not a woman. You're something with a French Provincial Office or a book full of clippings. But you're not a woman. Slow curtain. The end.[40]

Margo's remarkable monologue — which presents the awkward confluences of female, woman, femininity and sexuality — reminded 1950s viewers and current theorists that *it takes work* to be a woman. So few writers identify the importance of this speech — and its ending. Suzanne Fields asks us to 'compare Ally's [McBeal] sexual sensibility to that of Bette Davis as Margo Channing in the movie *All About Eve*, whose great insight is that a career woman is nothing without a man'.[41] Perhaps such a reading of the major speech is possible while completely ignoring 'Slow curtain. The end.'. The narrative being outlined is tough, demoralising but — in the end — profoundly ironic. Margo is Hamlet's mother, encased in a fur coat, guzzling a large martini. Compare this complexity to an Ally McBeal comment from the first episode:

> All I ever wanted was to be rich and to be successful and to have three kids and a husband who was waiting at home for me at night to tickle my feet.[42]

Ally's unproblematic acceptance of husband *and* children *and* career is a poor shadow of Margo. This tough woman, reliant on the martini marinade, is a corsetted Judith Butler, embodying the danger of the feminine subject being the only concern of feminist politics. It is 'women's common subjugated experience', not *being a woman*, that actually demands attention.[43] What makes Davis so significant to this alternative story is that she does not wallow in her sacrifice. Instead, she gains consciousness, confidence and the capacity to change. *All about Eve* revels in the difficulties of being an ageing woman. Margo Channing's corset is a metonym for Bette Davis's performance of femininity. She simply does not fit within the laced-up confines of the 1950s.

Quite importantly, the legacy of *All about Eve* has survived. There is more than a trace of Margo in Jules, the lying, desperate marriage-wrecker of *My Best Friend's Wedding*. Julia Roberts placed herself in an elite and small list of actresses satisfied to perform the role of difficult women and bitches, rather than victims or selfless mothers.[44] At the end of the film, much like Charlotte Vale nearly fifty years earlier, Jules did not snare her groom. Instead, she ends up dancing — in a lavender gown no less — with a gay man, her 'new' best friend:

> You think, what the hell. Life goes on. Maybe there won't be marriage. Maybe there won't be sex. But, by God, there will be dancing.[45]

This was no Hallmark moment. While sixty years ago the cinema was filled with Crawfords, Hepburns, Johnsons and Stanwycks, we live in an era of the action movie. *The First Wives' Club* — and any film with Sharon Stone — are caveats to the contract, but we have lost 'the ladies who lunge'.[46] While female stars had similar drawing power to men through the 1930s and 1940s, the Rambo decade has sated our lives with masculine iconography. This era was described by Morris as 'placing increasing pressure on that solitary individual, the middle-aged single woman'.[47] These solitary figures are placed in a conflictual representational field. As dangerous women, moving outside of the responsibilities of families and husbands, they are, within both conservative and new labo(u)r ideologies, not serving the national interest.

A 1992 parliamentary report surmised that 20–30 per cent of Australian women will never have children. Similarly, the marriage rate in 1996 was the lowest since 1900, with a predicted 22 per cent of women remaining unmarried at the age of thirty-five. This last figure, the highest level in Australia's history, indicates that the number of men and women who will never marry has doubled over the past twenty-five years.[48] Single women are therefore quietly changing and challenging the face of contemporary feminism. Perhaps such women are part of Greer's 'reaction ... not revolution'.[49] Perhaps such women are what Greer described as 'like the white man's black man, the professional nigger'.[50] *Perhaps* single, childless women moving through patriarchal structures have found a path distinct from Greer's imagining. While the baby boomers critiqued the feminine destiny of women, Michele Patenaude affirmed that 'my generation wanted to do its own thing but ended up doing the usual thing'.[51]

Women in my family have always worked outside the home and have always been dragged into motherhood. My great-grandmother built a house and shot kangaroos for food. My grandmother was a real-life Minnie Bannister, managing a corner shop through the war. My mother held a remarkable variety of jobs through post-war rural and urban Western Australia. All these women had children, but they were not terribly keen on the prospect.[52] They appreciated the end results of reproduction, but not the inconvenience.

Married in 1950, my mother waited four years for the first child and another fifteen for the second. My mother remained rake-thin during her first pregnancy. When I asked her why an eight-month expectant woman was allowed to fly from Broome to Perth on an old DC3, my father replied, 'No one noticed she was pregnant. She just looked like she'd eaten a slice of pizza'. Similarly, my mother desperately tried to keep as slender as possible during her second pregnancy. In 1969 married women were still seen to be risky employees, because they would (obviously) become pregnant. My mother, at forty, was seen to be 'past it' and therefore 'safe'. So when the shock of her late pregnancy eased, Doris was desperate to hide it from her boss. She did not want to jeopardise other married women's chances to gain jobs and promotions.[53] At the end of the second trimester, my mother was still wearing size ten skirts and high-heeled shoes. She remains a tough woman, who fought feminist wars through her body and the fashion that encased it.

Not having children seems a mark of respect to the women in my family. Dodging pregnancy is *not* a sacrifice, but a logical response to the context of contemporary women. It is tough to be alone. It is tough to be single. It would be foolish to assume that feminist politics and theory would make this life choice easier. I am savvy enough to know that no political movement can be representative of all its factions. However, to naturalise motherhood, childbirth and child rearing is to reinforce and replay patriarchal truths. Replacing the 1950s housewife with the 1990s superwoman was not a social revolution. We must monitor ourselves at every opportunity to ensure that we do not restate John Gray's mantra of Venusian/women as nurturing, caring and loving. This pseudo-sexual revolution is a hegemonic device to prevent women from seeing alternative lives and opportunities. Some have stated overtly that 'feminism has betrayed childless women'.[54] Even Ann Snitow remained shocked and bemused when 'a feminist theorist tells me she is more proud of her new baby than of all her books'.[55] What is intriguing is that children and the workplace are being ranked in this way. Childless women are feeling pathologised. They are also asserting that feminists are not supporting their nullipara sisters.

Intriguingly, when Marilyn Lake listed the five feminist reforms instigated by the activism of second-wavers, three of these relate to children and childcare.[56] Yet with great clarity, she inferred that there are political problems with the feminist commitment to childcare. Firstly, it (implicitly) terms children a hindrance to attaining equality with men.[57] Most importantly, she accepted that while 'childcare came to be seen by the women's movement as the working woman's basic right ... the rising voice of economic rationalism supported it as the means to move women off welfare benefits'.[58] Because of the structural addition of childcare, the full-time workplace has only minimally altered its organisation to the feminine rhythms of domestic responsibilities. In other words, childcare facilities are a bandaid that has not triggered more wide-ranging structural changes in the workplace. At the conclusion of her book, Lake fathomed that:

> One symptom of the contradictions involved for women seeking freedom in a man-made world is the rapidly declining birth-rate; it has been estimated that around one third of women now in their twenties will not bear children.[59]

Ironically, she has performed this contradiction through her text. While there is a new, emergent social challenge to motherhood and reproduction through the bodies of young women, the body of her text is spent dealing with the legislation encircling motherhood.

The issue of reproduction does not allow for a restatement of the banal division between second and third wavers or the interests of heterosexual women versus lesbians. Instead, I argue that it is pivotal that the contemporary women's movement — both inside and outside universities — disengages the commonsensical relationship of motherhood, childcare and feminism. If feminism is mainly about maternal motivations, then it will continue to exclude some of its most visible, stoic, vulnerable and complicated representatives. Also, there will be a long-term and destructive impact on the movement if these changing societal structures are not considered. Quentin Bryce, for example, compared her life to that of her family. While she had five children by the age of thirty, her adult daughters are yet to become pregnant. Unfortunately, she contended that 'I think that young women and young men are on pretty much of an equal footing as they embark on their careers now. It's when maternity intervenes that the picture changes'.[60] The consequences of her statement are worrying. Is motherhood the only structure that has blocked women from power? If that was the case, then the signifier 'spinster' and the attendant adjective of 'barren' would be terms of celebration, rather than abuse.

Unless feminists visualise and mark the other sites of oppression under patriarchy, then the movement will be threatened.

I have not — and will not — have children. I have been told, like most little girls, that I will inevitably give birth. My protestations against the unavoidability of this action are now being treated more seriously. The lavender scent of spinsterhood is settling around my shoulders. It suits me well. It does, however, place me in a generationally-awkward position. As all my female colleagues — literally every woman on my floor of the building — have children, I cannot share their baby stories. I have no photographs or mementos in my handbag. I shop and cook for one. I hold my remote control and — yes — I can programme my video recorder. There is not one Metallica compact disc in the house. Yoghurt, rather than VB, reclines on my refrigerator shelves. It is a peaceful, solitary and subtle existence. I may have denied my *sacred calling*, but I have — in comparison to Adrienne Rich's memories of 'anxiety, physical weariness, anger, self-blame, boredom, and division within myself'[61] — discovered much joy and excitement. It has not been a sacrifice. It has not been a 'cruel choice'.[62]

I ask of my feminist colleagues that the assumptions of parenthood and children are removed from the shoulders of all women. I am not asking that women choose between public success and private happiness. Anyone who assumes that single living is easy or streamlined should attempt moving alone through contemporary life. Our culture is a bicycle built for two, with two kiddie seats. Magazines, such as *She*'s October 2001 edition, feature breathtaking headlines such as 'Alright, I admit it, I want a husband'.[63] Is feminism actively critiquing these truths? For all the teachers reading my words, examine your curriculum, readings and pedagogy. Are there spaces for the difficult women, the witches and bitches, the quizzical spinster and relieved divorcee, who have shunned motherhood and attempted a new way of living, speaking, writing and being?

Certainly, all women share an experience of motherhood. We are, as Adrienne Rich articulated, of women born.[64] While feminist theorists focus on the space between the institution of motherhood and women's experience of it, there is still an assumption of reproduction. Popular culture has frequently reinforced this ideology of femininity. Ponder this question from a women's magazine: 'Are you too old to have a baby?'.[65] This inquiry is particularly inflammatory, considering that the average age that Australian women are having their first child is 29.5 years. The antagonistic treatment of childless women and couples is even more overt in the core magazine of conservative femininity, *Family Circle*:

> These are the couples who make the decision not to have kids, not now, not ever. Their reasons on the surface seem incredibly selfish

— they want a better lifestyle, they don't want their careers to suffer, they want to spend more time with each other, travelling, reading and enjoying life ... Most parents are outraged when they hear of this group ... I know I was. I got quite worked up about it for a few days ... I just couldn't understand how you couldn't want children — don't they have any idea of what they are missing out on?[66]

This editorial allows no space for alternative renderings of femininity. Such an ostrich–head–sand attitude ignores women's disquiet and resistance towards the narratives of a happy family life. Such 'outrage' only adds to the difficulties facing women who live new models of femininity. We need to move beyond a system where sacrificing women are validated, while others who claim autonomy and separateness are selfish. Not having children is a legitimate decision. Other women in particular must not traffic in guilt and shame. There are profound personal consequences for this anger:

When my husband and I reached the agonising decision not to have a baby, we were accused of being a multitude of things — including selfish, immature, irresponsible, thoughtless, heartless, cheap, and heading for the biggest mistake of our lives. The sexes reacted differently to our decision. Our women friends were much more judgmental than the men.[67]

The time has come to stop this judgment. Couples who make this 'agonising' determination are certainly not irresponsible. They have clearly assessed and measured the consequences of their actions.

It is not surprising that, in a desperate search for women operating outside of marriage and motherhood, there is a retraction to classic cinema. By transforming 'the fat lady with the heavy brows and all the hair'[68] into an articulate woman able to make choices, *Now, Voyager* is justifiably a classic of cinema. As Stanley Cavell has determined:

Here is this woman retracing the reigning concepts of her life — what a mother is, what a child, a home, a husband are, what happiness is — and yet this man stupefyingly asks her whether she will be happy.[69]

What would the contemporary women's movement ask of Charlotte Vale? Questioning films such as *Now, Voyager* serve to inscribe, re-write and interpret a feminist history. We need to return to Bette Davis. A new theory of femininity can emerge when we look at — and through — those eyes.

ON NOT ASKING FOR THE MOON

As self-styled 'young feminists' are wont to say, they must refurbish
the house of feminism to suit themselves.[70]

Marilyn Lake

What a dump.[71]

Bette Davis

At the conclusion of *Now, Voyager*, Charlotte Vale does not ask for the moon, but remains satisfied with the stars. Contemporary feminism needs a Bette Davis, a firebrand woman who is tough, resolute and passionate. She worked hard, thought deeply and spoke out while post-war masculinity congealed around her. Shadows of men were cast in relief through her light. Leaming has missed the point of both Bette Davis's life and post-war feminism when she asserts that 'whereas [Orson] Welles was always fighting *for* something, Davis only knew how to fight *against* — and therein lay all the difference'.[72] Feminism, at its best, fights against patriarchy, against colonialism, against ageism, against economic rationalism. Only by waging the good fight against the powerful, can feminism and contemporary resistive politics combat *for* social justice.

My words have followed Bette Davis through her bumpy night. Such biographies of the self are integrated into the project of building a sexualised body. This chapter is also fighting for something. While feminism must be socially responsible and contextually appropriate, it must also have political goals to make others uncomfortable. Through this discomfort, consciousness is generated and perhaps change activated. However, too much of contemporary feminist politics assumes motherhood as the natural state of women, because of the economic threats to childcare. I am well aware that a Bette Davis will not provide a solution to the problems confronting women. Collective troubles require collective solutions. My goals cannot be contained in self-help manuals or nine steps to success.[73] Women share *something*: that something is not children, husbands or family values. It is a shared subjugation within patriarchal structures. These inequalities manifest themselves differently, dependent on race, class and age. Perhaps feminism teaches us that, like Charlotte Vale, we need not accept the crumbs off the table, an empty bottle of perfume or a crumbling Camellia. Indeed, we may even learn to light our own, metaphoric, cigarette.

NOT A HAPPY ENDING

This chapter commenced with an attacking questioner during an acidic question time. It seems appropriate to conclude with a similar response to another public presentation, delivered a year later. I presented some of the ideas expressed in this chapter at an International Women in

Leadership Conference. I received an incredible audience reaction, with many women expressing gratitude that this difficult issue was finally being raised. The next day, I received the following envelope:

Ms Tara Brabazon — *speaker*
% International Women in Leadership Conference
via The Esplanade Hotel
Marine Terrace
Fremantle   6 1 6 0

Encased in the envelope was the following, roughly torn document. There was no covering letter, no business card, no sense of who sent the correspondence:

LONDON, Nov. 21, 00 (CWNews.com) - The Archbishop of Westminster has announced a new teaching document on sex that warns that promiscuity is destabilizing society.

Speaking at a press conference yesterday, Archbishop Cormac Murphy-O'Connor said people should respect "the sanctity" of sex in the context of marriage and producing children. And he called for changing attitudes to sex to become "a priority."

"We need to address the trivialization of sex," he said. "It is a terrible thing in our country that people are being urged to use sex without any real meaning." He said the new document-- which has yet to be published-- will challenge the increasing "individualism" in a society in which people do not share a common sense of morality.

The archbishop said: "Unfettered individualism is damaging. People think what is good for me and my truth is the only one that matters. Core values should be held by everyone."

My presentation did not promote a particular mode of sexuality. That is not my place as a writer or feminist. Obviously, this viewer of my presentation had assumed that any woman who denies the single destiny of children and a husband must be promiscuous and selfish. That is not the case. It is both rude and improper for a woman to address another in this way, particularly without having the pluck to include her name. My only goal is to create a space for women to think consciously about their life choices. Women share so many experiences, but reproduction is not one of those community-building strategies. It is to men's advantage to name and claim women as mothers and housewives. It is to women's benefit to aim for more autonomy and a diversity of roles.

There is obviously a problem emerging between particular religious beliefs and feminism. These paradoxes have been performed by Kirsten Birkett's book *The Essence of Feminism*.[74] The text is an anti-feminist tirade. It is reactionary and nostalgic, suggesting that Christianity provides a greater empowerment than the women's movement. She is certainly correct to suggest that the liberation of women has been accompanied by social problems. However, to glorify the wife and mother role as being without difficulty or trauma is naïve and foolish. The feminist movement is one answer to the uncertainties in women's lives. It is not *the* solution to all questions. But neither is Christianity. Have courage to discuss different world views. Have courage to argue a position. Have courage to justify a case. Have courage to not hide behind God, or even an Anglican Archbishop.

BRITAIN'S LAST LINE OF DEFENCE: MISS MONEYPENNY AND FILMIC FEMINISM

I'm a bitch
I'm a lover
I'm a child
I'm a mother
I'm a sinner
I'm a saint
I do not feel ashamed
I'm your hell
I'm your dream
I'm nothing in between
You know you wouldn't want it any other way.[1]
Meredith Brooks, 'Bitch'

Good old Moneypenny. Britain's last line of defence.[2]
James Bond, *On Her Majesty's Secret Service*

The fracturing of femininity is a strength of, as well as a problem for, contemporary feminism. No political label can encompass the plurality of women. The representational politics of subjectivity has been a central topic for theorists since suffragettes chained themselves to the gate of Number 10 Downing Street. Without a metaphoric Boadicea to embody strength, the political applications of contemporary feminism seem tenuous and unresolved.[3] In response to these larger concerns, this chapter explores a minor character from a long-running film series and demonstrates that even in the midst of saturating sexism, a voice of social justice and responsibility can speak. It is timely to evaluate a superspy's supersecretary.

Miss Moneypenny has featured in more James Bond films than any figure except the title role.[4] She is the assistant to M, head of the British Secret Service. All agents, administrators, technicians and scientists must pass through Moneypenny's office and antechamber to reach the Imperial core. She is, as the Lazenby-Bond described her, 'Britain's last line of defence'. Three actors have played the character: Lois Maxwell,[5] Caroline Bliss and Samantha Bond. Moneypenny's scenes with James Bond have become a generic characteristic of the series.[6] The sexual politics enacted through these semiotic snippets of footage provide an insight into the desperations of filmic feminism. This chapter introduces the character of Moneypenny, following the changes to her body, politics and framing, disclosing the spaces of *textual* harassment and seduction.

Filmic feminism may seem a clumsy or awkward phrase, yet it acknowledges a political framework that stands for and against specific discourses, world views and values. A politically astute identification is made of who speaks, who is spoken for and how subjectivity is constituted. As Judith Butler has stated:

> Politics and representation are controversial terms. On the one hand, representation serves as the operative term within a political process that seeks to extend visibility and legitimacy to women as political subjects; on the other hand, representation is the normative function of a language which is said either to reveal or to distort what is assumed to be true about the category of women.[7]

The relationship between feminist theory and politics is particularly convoluted and ambiguous when invoking desires for social justice in the cinema. There is a necessity to concede that the label of 'woman' expresses confusion and anxiety. While statements about the fragmentation of the sisterhood are common, it is rare to watch the workings of feminine desperation within a film's frame. Very few historical or semiotic spheres have persisted as long as the Bond phenomenon. The character of Moneypenny dwells in the crevices of patriarchy and normative categories.

Feminist readings of Bond films are frequently negative and generalised. As Lindsey has (over)stated:

> The James Bond films ... depict women enjoying rape, especially since Bond is the 'good guy' and the supposed fantasy of every woman. Once raped they are then ignored by the male star. Rapes and murders are likely alternatives to women in token roles.[8]

Although Moneypenny is the token woman in the masculinist, colonial project of the British Secret Service, she has never been raped or murdered. Instead, the muffled eroticism of Moneypenny and Bond has survived for over thirty years, forming the longest unconsummated screen relationship. Wearing suggested that 'women need to be depicted in situations in which they are active and autonomous, assertive and able'.[9] Miss Moneypenny performs a mode of femininity outside of marriage, fidelity and the private sphere. Certainly the character is framed by her attachment to men. Yet all forms of gender organisation are historically specific and mobile, particularly in film. When strong binaries are presented, like an aggressive, powerful, financially secure heterosexual man, or a woman who is a home-maker, wife and mother, the ideologies of these formations are subsumed: they have become normalised. Only through the presence of anxious or contradictory binaries, such as a woman active in the public domain or a politically active gay man, can the oppressive structures that determine the limits of acceptable behaviour be revealed. Moneypenny is liminally placed: as a white woman, she evokes a convoluted position in the colonial framework. While not holding power, she handles its signifiers at all times. Bond is a primary representative of strongly heteronormative masculinist ideologies. Moneypenny's office is encased not only by the proverbial glass ceiling, but also glass walls. She can view power, but wields little. Moneypenny remains the woman behind the man (M) behind the legend (Bond).

Moneypenny is not a static figure: sexual politics and Bond films have changed markedly since 1962. The workings of ideologies are difficult to trace and document without analysing the behaviours, institutions and texts that circulate in society. Bennett and Woollacott described Bond as 'a moving sign of the times',[10] yet this description is far more appropriately applied to the superspy's supersecretary. As Bennett and Woollacott have suggested:

> 'The Bond girl' of the 1960s disconnected female sexuality from traditional female gender identities, reserving the latter virtually intact ... whilst articulating the former in male defined norms of genital sexuality.[11]

The obvious rupture in this reinscribed femininity is Moneypenny. She is neither a safely sexual, nor predictably patriarchal, performer. She remains a bitch,[12] a demanding woman who cannot be trusted.

From the first Bond film, *Dr No*, Moneypenny and Bond display a flirtatious but good-willed attachment:

Bond:	Moneypenny, what gives?
Moneypenny:	Me, given an ounce of encouragement. You never take me to dinner looking like this, James. You never take me to dinner period.

Bond: I would you know, but M would have me court marshalled for illegal use of government property.

Moneypenny: Flattery will get you nowhere, but don't stop trying.[13]

The acknowledgment of flattery, rather than sexual harassment, renders Bond's comments benign and banal. In 1962 terming Moneypenny 'government property' was not framed as offensive. The consensual nature of the liaison allows for the negotiation of (in)dependencies. Pivotally, James Bond has a flexibility and freedom not possible within the limits of Moneypenny's office. In *From Russia with Love*, Bond is sent to fetch an encryption device. Moneypenny supplies his transportation arrangements:

Moneypenny: One plane ticket. Lucky man, I've never been to Istanbul.

Bond: You've never been to Istanbul? Well, the moonlight on the Bosporus is irresistible.

Moneypenny: Maybe I should get you to take me there some day. I've tried everything else.

Bond: Darling Moneypenny, you know I've never even looked at another woman.

Moneypenny: Really, James?[14]

Here, in the second Bond film, the representation of Moneypenny starts to change. The humour from this scene is generated because the filmic viewer knows that Bond looks at (and touches) many other women. Moneypenny is aware of the joke and doubts his intentions. By *Goldfinger*, Bond is more open to Moneypenny's advances:

Bond: And what do you know about gold, Moneypenny?

Moneypenny: The only gold I know about is the kind you wear on the third finger of your left hand.

Bond: One of these days we really must look into that.

Moneypenny: You could come around for dinner and I'll cook you a beautiful angel cake.

Bond: Nothing would give me greater pleasure, but unfortunately I do have a business appointment.

Moneypenny: That's the flimsiest excuse you've ever given me. Well some girls have all the luck. Who is she, James?

M: She is me, Miss Moneypenny, and kindly omit the customary byplay with 007. He's dining with me and I don't want him to be late.[15]

The *Miss* in Miss Moneypenny is significant. Operating outside of the roles of wife and mother, the character challenges customary feminine narratives. Still, her desperation for a golden wedding ring is clear. Doyle and Paludi described marriage as 'a rite de passage, an entrance into the world of adults'.[16] Moneypenny maintains a job with considerable responsibility. Operating in the liminal social space between youth and old age, without the attendant adjective of *married*, is an awkward semiotic site for women. The spectre of the old maid, although never mentioned in the films, hovers uncomfortably around her desk. By maintaining her singleness, Moneypenny does not allow the male/female, active/passive binary to stand. While she is helplessly romantic, she also actively pursues her quarry.

The ambivalence of the Bond/Moneypenny relationship not only adds raillery to their scenes, but inserts soap opera elements into the action film series. The banter continues in the next Bond film, *You Only Live Twice*:

M: Moneypenny, give 007 the password we've fixed up with SIS.
Moneypenny: We tried to think of something you wouldn't forget.
Bond: And that is?
Moneypenny: 'I love you.' Please repeat it to make sure you've got it.
Bond: Don't worry. I've got it.[17]

The 'romance' between Moneypenny and 007 in these early Bond films is humorous, but relatively innocuous. This reading is inculcated through the choice of actors: Sean Connery and Lois Maxwell were the same age and therefore able to engage in a more equitable exchange of ideologies and innuendoes. Moneypenny remains a semiotic suffragette: probing and questioning the limits of women's sexual and societal roles. As with the suffragettes however, the political effectiveness of her words in the long term is difficult to assess and is easily undermined.

George Lazenby replaced Connery in the Bond role, making Moneypenny's part even more pivotal to the survival of Bond. Moneypenny, along with M and Q, allowed for a continuity of plot and character development:

Moneypenny: Where have you been?
Bond: Much too far from you, darling.
Moneypenny: Same old James, only more so. Heartless brute, letting me pine away without even a postcard.
Bond: Pine no more. Cocktails at my place — just the two of us.

Moneypenny: Oh, I'd adore that, if only I could trust myself.
Bond: Same old Moneypenny. Britain's last line of defence.[18]

This new Bond, who is the 'same old James, only more so', claims both a similarity and difference with the past by maintaining the Moneypenny moment. Significantly, on this occasion it is Moneypenny who rejected Bond's advances. Once more, an equitable jousting is established. However, as Roger Moore assumed the Bond role, major changes in the gender order took place.

During *Live and Let Die*, the relationship became iniquitous. Moneypenny complicitly withholds from M the details of a sexual encounter between Bond and an Italian spy hiding in his closet:

M: Now come along, Miss Moneypenny. Morning, Bond.
Bond: Sir. Thankyou *(to Moneypenny)*.
Moneypenny: Goodbye, James, or should I say Ciao bello?[19]

Similarly, in *The Man with the Golden Gun*, Moneypenny is de-eroticised, while Bond mocks her knowledge and ability:

Bond: Moneypenny, you are better than a computer.
Moneypenny: In all sorts of ways, but you never take advantage of them.[20]

Through the Moore years, Moneypenny's role was reduced. She became an instrument of the plot. This tendency is clearly shown in *Moonraker*:

Bond: Good morning, Moneypenny.
Moneypenny: But why are you so late?
Bond: I fell out of an aeroplane without a parachute. Who's in there?
Moneypenny: Q and the Minister for Defence.
Bond: You don't believe me.
Moneypenny: No, and you should go right in.
Bond: Yes, Moneypenny.[21]

From this banality, the framing of Moneypenny became twisted and negative. Although Maxwell is the same age as Moore, she was aged through make-up and costuming. The Moneypenny scene is at its most destructive in *For Your Eyes Only*:

Moneypenny: James …
Bond: A feast for my eyes.

Moneypenny:	What about the rest of you?
Bond:	I was just going to get around to that.[22]

Her facade is ragged, over-painted and old, compared to a youthful, muscular and tanned Bond. The age difference, rendered through performance rather than chronology, makes Moneypenny a figure of ridicule. Her vanity is confirmed though the on-screen application of make-up. Her 'weakness', judged by the value of face rather than face value, allowed a fatiguing Roger Moore to be propped up as an ideal man. This archetype is a socially constructed image and permits the proto-feminism of Moneypenny to be depicted as a desperate visual joke.

By *Octopussy*, the ageing Moneypenny no longer has control over her own office. A younger, blonder woman was hired as her assistant:

Bond:	Well I must say you've become more beautiful every day.
Moneypenny:	I'm over here.
Bond:	Well of course you are.
Moneypenny:	And this is my assistant, Penelope Smallbone.
Bond	What can I say, Moneypenny, except that she is as beautiful and charming.
Moneypenny:	As I used to be.
Bond:	I didn't say that.
Moneypenny:	You're such a flatterer, James.
Bond:	You know there never has been and never will be anyone but you.
Moneypenny:	So you've told me.

The indignity and condescension by which the older Moneypenny is represented is to the detriment of the character and the films. Germaine Greer stated that 'the sight of women talking together has always made men uneasy'.[23] Such discomfort is not witnessed by Bond as he attempts to trigger jealous competition between Smallbone and Moneypenny. By the final Moore motion picture, *A View to a Kill*, Moneypenny is adorned in a floral frock for a day at the races. In response, Bond simply asks, 'Don't you think it's a little bit over the top for the office?'. As an excessive site, she becomes a camp figure, an aged aunt, rather than sexualised partner to Bond. Through her clothing, Moneypenny, like all women, suggests how her body is to be read and treated. By making fashion a site for humour, her sexuality is muffled or perhaps even extinguished.

It is significant that when the feminist movement was radical and active in the public domain, the representations of Moneypenny were at their most repressive and disapproving. Framing Moneypenny as the tortured spinster who no longer had a right to pine for the dashing hero transformed the supersecretary into a warning beacon for ageing women. The commencement of Susan Faludi's *Backlash*[24] is witnessed in these Bond films from the 1970s and 1980s. Second wave feminism aimed to formulate connections between women, but during this era Moneypenny remained isolated in her office.

Not surprisingly, when the Bond role moved from Roger Moore to Timothy Dalton, Lois Maxwell was replaced by a younger, blonder version, more suited to a Duran Duran video than a 007 film. She arrives as Q is briefing 007 for his next assignment:

Q: Her methods of killing include strangulation between the thighs.
Moneypenny: Just your type, James.
Bond: No, Moneypenny, you are.
Moneypenny: I'll file that with the other secret information around here.[25]

As during the Connery years, humour re-entered the relationship. However, for 'equality' to be constructed, Moneypenny had to be young and beautiful. The decline of Moneypenny's role signalled a loss of the plural representation of femininity within the Bond discourse. Through the Roger Moore and Timothy Dalton years, the Bond gender order becomes rigid and binarised.

Only with the arrival of Pierce Brosnan is the Moneypenny character revived:

Bond: Good evening, Moneypenny.
Moneypenny: Good evening, James. M will meet you in the situation room. I'm to take you straight in.
Bond: I've never seen you after hours, Moneypenny. Lovely.
Moneypenny: Thank you, James.
Bond: Out on some professional assignment — dressed to kill.
Moneypenny: I know you find this crushing, 007, but I don't wait home every night waiting for some international incident, so I can rush down here to impress James Bond. I was on a date, if you must know, with a gentleman. We went to the theatre together.
Bond: Moneypenny, I'm devastated. What would I do without you?
Moneypenny: As far as I can remember, James, you've never had me.

Bond:	Hope springs eternal.
Moneypenny:	You know, this sort of behaviour could qualify as sexual harassment.
Bond:	Really? What's the penalty for that?
Moneypenny:	Some day, you will have to make good on your innuendo.[26]

This film is significant to the Bond series for many reasons. Firstly, Brosnan's performance of masculinity maintains a knowing display of codes and narratives. Importantly, the new Moneypenny is attractive, bright and efficient. Her clothes once more signify a desiring and desirable woman, who is able to demand rights in the workplace. Her availability, yet distance from Bond is reinforced by Moneypenny's recognition that she has never been 'had'.

By rendering Moneypenny sexual yet unattainable, the tension, conflict and humour of their relationship continues with a sharper edge. The power imbalance between them is narrowing. It is Moneypenny who enters the security code into the situation room, not Bond. The importance of hearing the words 'sexual harassment' in a Bond discourse must not be underestimated. As Doyle and Paludi have suggested, 'we need to think of sexual harassment as being not the act of a disturbed man, but rather an act of an over-conforming man'.[27] Bond is a hyper-heteronormative masculinity. Moneypenny reminding Bond of his responsibilities and limitations curtails the textual harassment of the character.

The gender order of the Bond world view was changed radically through *Goldeneye*. The film offers remarkable potential for feminist viewers. Not only is Moneypenny renewed, but the remarkable occurred: M is played by a woman. The office dynamics change radically. Suddenly, Moneypenny is no longer isolated in her office, but part of a feminist stronghold. M becomes an ally, a powerful boss who made her displeasure (and feminism) clear:

M:	You don't like me, Bond. You don't like my methods. You think I am an accountant, more interested in my numbers than your instincts.
Bond:	The thought had crossed my mind.
M:	Good, because I think you're a sexist, misogynist dinosaur, a relic of the cold war, whose boyish charms although wasted on me obviously appealed to that young woman I sent to evaluate you.
Bond:	Point taken.[28]

The presentation of a female head of the British Secret Service radically reframes the Bond character. A subordinated masculinity, particularly if the character is heterosexual, Anglo-Celtic and able bodied, is an odd vision in a patriarchal culture. It shakes (but does not stir) what Tolson has termed 'a masculine aura of competence'.[29] A successful masculine performance means that superiority to women must be affirmed in a myriad of contexts. With Bond possessing a female boss and an assistant discussing sexual harassment, filmic feminism does mark the textual frame.

By viewing the Bond films in chronological order, it is clear that feminism has had an impact on filmic representations. A backlash may continue, but the hegemonic reconfiguration of masculinity and femininity in *Goldeneye*, *Tomorrow Never Dies* and *The World is Not Enough* demonstrates that significant changes are being made. Sommers may claim that 'I am a feminist who does not like what feminism has become',[30] but few would dispute what Moneypenny has become. Even Bond has been labelled a 'sexist, misogynist dinosaur'. Such a categorisation is completely appropriate and a justifiable payback for the ideological wars fought over Moneypenny during the Roger Moore years (1973–1984). It seems that the point has indeed been taken.

Patriarchal structures have the capacity to silence alternative stories, enacting an active and passive subordination of women and homosexual men in the workplace, leisure spaces, the home and streets. All these oppressions are made possible by evading discussion of men's power and domination. The feminist potentials from the past require an attention to popular cultural texts, such as film, television and fashion. Clearly, Moneypenny's representation during the Roger Moore years configured ageing women as invisible and inept. Yet the potential of the character to move and build on this weakness permits the remaking of an unmarried woman. Instead of the doting, embarrassing spinster, Moneypenny is an active, intelligent and demanding woman, claiming her rights and reminding Bond that he is accountable for his actions.

It would be straightforward to saturate Moneypenny with the excesses of patriarchy. Actually, the role has demonstrated much alteration, subtlety and disquiet. Importantly, she has served to reshape and refocus the limitations of Bond's power. Women who seduce men summon the spectre of the shrew, who is independent, demanding and wilful. However, unlike bad women from daytime soap opera, Moneypenny has not been punished for her autonomy. Instead, the language of feminism ('sexual harassment') and the changes to societal structures (M is currently a female) have altered both her demands and rights. Neither Bond nor Moneypenny is committed to the other: no rings have been exchanged and they never consummated their conversations. As with the Nescafe couple,[31] talking substitutes for sex. Their desires permit the competent performance of sexual differences. At times, these exchanges are dirty, dangerous and disturbing. Cinematic representations of seduction are what Sharon Willis has termed 'part of film's allure: as we read it, it also reads us'.[32] Film is a contestable sphere. It does not reflect its time or society: instead it reinforces, moulds, twists and subverts many truths of a culture.

Moneypenny moved beyond the home and lived outside marriage throughout much of the post-war period. She remains a figure of strength and commitment during an era of changing social and political structures. Lindsey stated that 'Movies are creations of male fantasies. Women need to invent their own fantasies and portray these as well'.[33] Such a statement undermines feminist theorists' recycling and reworking of filmic texts from the past. Even the most repressive of sites, like the action adventures of James Bond, offer a Moneypenny moment of humour, discomfort and rejection for 007. She provides a transgressive reinscription of the masculine, colonising project while allowing the superspy to maintain a heterosexual performance. As the bitch, rather than the love, of Bond's life, she is not only Britain's last line of defence, but feminism's first foothold for attack.

I'D RATHER BE IN CHYNA: WRESTLING (WITH) FEMININITY

Never date a woman who can beat you up.[1]

Nate Penn and Lawrence LaRose

Professional wrestling is the Dead Sea Scrolls of contemporary sport. Its excess, performativity, scripting and sexuality unearth the syntax of our era. It performs the problems and inequalities in the realm of both sport and sports theory. If Socrates was walking through New York rather than Athens, he would be asking questions about wrestling. The contradictions, theatrics and playfulness of the World Wrestling Federation would be too seductive for the great thinker to ignore.

Wrestling, as a sport to think with, offers much to feminist scholarship. To focus on ring rats or breast implants not only misses the point of the pursuit, but ignores the rapid shifts in its history. In the last five years it has changed, and swiftly. This alteration has many triggers, but one under-theorised origin is a woman who most appropriately claims the title of lunging lady. Chyna, known as the ninth wonder of the world, has transformed the level of acceptable musculature in women and taken on the men — literally — at their own game. Originally treated as a physical freak, accompanied to the ring with fans holding placards reading 'Chyna is a man', she has challenged the place of women and men in wrestling. This chapter enters the ring of sports entertainment to claim a feminist icon in the making.

WRESTLING 3:16

Wrestling has been in existence for 5000 years. The basic holds of the modern sport still convey a trace of the grappling represented in the tombs of Beni Hassan in Egypt. Book 23 of *The Iliad* presents the epic wrestling match between Odysseus and Ajax.[2] With competition and rules added through the Greco-Roman participation in the sport, it was the European intervention in wrestling, tempered by industrialisation and colonisation in the nineteenth century, that brought the practice into the modern age. The catch as catch can (CACC) style that became popular in the United States by the mid-nineteenth century mobilised a combination of the Lancashire style and jujitsu holds.

Wrestling as a spectator sport evolved throughout the late nineteenth century. During the second industrial revolution, life altered with great rapidity. Notions of culture, work and leisure were whisked into starchy new realities. The expansion of middle-class consumerism and urbanisation, along with the rise of working-class consciousness, granted wrestling an evocative, fiery context. Emulsifying the volatile notions of masculinity, nationalism, corporeality and technology, physical culture was integral to the industrial project. While no sport is older than wrestling, no sport has been more active in moving into the new media with innovative modes of spectatorship.

The role of the paying customer has been greater in the history of wrestling than in any other modern sport. The rivalry between Frank Gotch and George Hackenschmidt exhibited the popularity of freestyle wresting in both the United States and Europe. Their matches in 1908 and 1911 were reported through front-page coverage in European and American newspapers. Chicago's Dexter Park Pavilion and Comiskey Park were filled with mat enthusiasts. The attention granted to these matches embodies the intense popularity and international inflection of pre-war wrestling. Such nationalist rivalries appeared dangerous after the war, with the United States' strict immigration laws blocking the entry of foreign competitors.

With the reduced emphasis on genuine international competition, there was a desire to make the matches faster and more exiting. To enact these changes, scripting was necessary. Promoters, particularly through the 1920s and 1930s, were ridiculed for their deceit. As Grantland Rice, a 1930s commentator, observed:

> The wrestling public wanted to eat its cake and have it too. It wanted all the excitement and action of a faked match, carefully rehearsed, but it also wanted all the action to be on the level when perhaps the situation would not justify a continued offence on both sides.[3]

The notions of deception and play forged the relationship between wrestling and the public. This orchestration allowed particular holds and finishing moves to become associated with particular wrestlers. From Bret Hart's sharpshooter and The Undertaker's Last Ride, athletes transformed into physically powerful entertainers.

There is a notion that sport cannot be scripted. This is a naïve real-isation, as all sport is emersed in national narratives of triumph, despair and success over incredible odds. Before a cricket match is played between Australia and England, a century of Ashes conquests instigates a momentum to the play.[4] The endless revelation of statistics, replays and commentators' anecdotes all transform the simple act of a bat hit-ting a ball into a monumental struggle between the mother country and her talented, wayward, wild colonial boys. Anyone who thinks that the All Blacks are simply a rugby team needs to live in New Zealand for a time. National narratives of triumph, desolation and Kiwi ingenuity run on with the team whenever they enter Dunedin's House of Pain. While the outcome of a cricket match or a rugby tournament may not be scripted (or should not be), the framework in which these competi-tions take place — and the way the results may be understood later — are soaked in national scripts of success and failure.

The repositioning and reframing of wrestling as sports entertain-ment rather than sport had an economic rather than ideological trigger. By demonstrating that 'choreography' and results were predetermined, tax would not be payable to state-based athletic commissions who wanted a portion of pay-per-view subscriptions. Therefore, the decep-tion of the sport has fed the reality of its entertainment. The more that religious commentators, sports journalists and politicians attack wrestling, the more popular it has become. As Neal Gabler has shown, 'the perception of disreputability ... has helped make it not only an expression of transgression but a way for millions of fans to exercise their own transgressive impulses'.[5] Obviously, wrestling is a theatrical representation, but through its excess it serves to reveal the brutal aspects of all sport.

Because of the close tie between audience and action, professional wrestling initiates an incisive conveyance of the desires, hopes, humili-ations and concerns of the age. Chris Heath found that 'real life is ... heartlessly cannibalised'.[6] Foreign threats to American industries and security — from the Japanese to the Russians to the Iraqis — are ridiculed with relish and passion. As John Rickard intimated, wrestling 'offered all sorts of possibilities for dramatising and enlarging con-flict'.[7] The WWF is a metonymy for the world. The canvas cannot con-tain the conflicts, spilling into dressing rooms, boiler rooms, parking lots and international televisual networks. When 93 000 people attend-ed the second Wrestlemania at the Pontiac Silverdome in Detroit to watch Hulk Hogan defeat Andre the Giant, it was clear that wider struggles and conflicts were being revealed in and through the grap-pling of titans in tights. Even the corporatisation of the current age becomes wrestling fodder. Triple H, the mythical wrestling heel, stat-ed that 'to the average person, the real-life enemy now is their boss'.[8]

Even considering the huge live audiences, more spectators watch wrestling on television. To understand wrestling is to move through multiple mediations from wrestlers, promoters, referees, photographers, fans, historians and journalists. Feminists, though, have rarely entered wrestling, even though female fans, particularly through television, are as numerous as men.

GORGEOUS GEORGE ON THE BOX

Wrestling and television are the Bogart and Bacall of sport. Television transformed wrestling from a series of local franchises into an international phenomenon. Gorgeous George in the 1950s, with a sequined robe and blonde curls, enhanced the visual spectacle. He began the emphasis on costumed gimmickry and outrageous personas. Such interventions only increased through the excessive entry rituals of Goldust, the Undertaker and Kane. There is an ideal symbiosis between the low production costs of wrestling and the incessant desire for cable-based product. Currently, four of America's top ten cable television programmes are wrestling shows. It is now possible to watch wrestling five nights a week. Nine hours of wrestling are featured every week on Australia's cable stations, augmented by monthly pay-per-view cablecasts. Therefore, the notion that wrestling only attracts a working-class audience is inaccurate. The movement onto cable opened out the sport to middle-class viewers and confirmed its popularity. Without reruns or repeats and airing through the Christmas period, professional wrestling has demonstrated a commitment to the televisual media. The WWF programming goes into 120 countries, mobilising eleven languages.

Within a two-hour wrestling spectacle, only forty minutes of actual wrestling is presented. The need to develop the storyline creates a weekly televisual gala, a Jerry Springer with a sleeper hold, or soap opera with a testosterone spritzer. Large men in lycra, grabbing and throwing each other, probe the realm of both the camp and carnivalesque. But wrestling is no longer divided between good and evil, baby faces and heels. As Laura Bryson, the managing editor of the *World Wrestling Federation Magazine*, has stated:

> I'm a chick who's not afraid of change, and I demand to be entertained when I devote five hours of television viewing a week to the World Wrestling Federation. I love the tragedy of Kane, the energy and mystique of the Hardy Boyz, and the power struggles amongst the McMahon family. And while times have changed, in essence much has stayed the same ... it's just that sports entertainment has finally caught up to the fact — because we, the people, demanded it.[9]

The success of Stone Cold Steve Austin served to move wrestling out of these binary oppositions of good and evil and away from the Cold War bluster of Hulk Hogan.[10] Certainly there are standard motifs that accompany the wrestling drama. The metal chair, carelessly left near the stage, and the Spanish announcer's table, which is broken through aerial manoeuvres in every pay-per-view, are recurrent tracks through the narrative.

Importantly, professional wrestling has also claimed a strong presence on the World Wide Web. The WWF website, wwf.com, was one of the first outlets to create a profit from streaming video. While professional wrestling has been successful in the older visual media, it is clear that the future of the business will be found on the web. Shane McMahon, president of the WWF's new media, worked with Microsoft Corporation to customise a format for the WWF to be viewed online.[11] Therefore, the media convergence has created new relationships between sport and popular culture.

Professional wrestling is currently undergoing a moment of extraordinary popularity. The risks of the enterprise — through live events, broadcast and cable television, pay-per-view programming and licensed merchandise — make it the archetypal risky business. In May 1999 the 34-year-old wrestler Owen Hart fell to his death while being lowered into the arena. Suddenly the carnage was injected into the simulacra. Cameras were diverted from the tragedy. Within a year, the WWF was more successful than it had ever been. Sports journalists and critics forget the intense physicality and trauma of large men fighting and performing every week of the year. Wrestling must be fake: if the aerial manoeuvres, the bleeding and the falls were all performed without premeditation, far more wrestlers would be injured, many very seriously. By placing the focus on narration rather than authenticity, higher truths can be revealed. It is, as Jeff Archer suggests, 'the Shakespeare of Sports'.[12]

To complain about the scripting and performance of wrestling is like whining about the depressing ending of *Romeo and Juliet*. It misses the point. Michael Ball has described professional wrestling as the 'ritual drama in American popular culture'.[13] As a hegemonic mode of social control, wrestling is important not for its competition, choreography or soap opera, but for it symbolism. Throughout the last 150 years, wrestling has performed the tension between social and technological change. As June Senyard documented:

Spectator sport ... enfranchised the urban masses into consumerism and authorized their pleasure in the public sphere. It also broke conventional understandings of the urban masses as merely subsisting with the occasional festival to relieve the daily grind.[14]

Wrestling is creating new myths and feeding into old ones. It is a highly American spectacle of the American age. The emotional intensity of wrestling is gripping. If we try to 'read' it using methodologies from sports history, then it will appear ludicrous. However, notions of civilisation are being probed and questioned by both the live and virtual crowd. Through these rituals, social bonds and dislocations are observed. Michael Ball showed that:

> Wrestling is a sport with a long tradition of ritual activity. Early societies used wrestling or some related form of physical combat to settle disputes between tribes and other groups. The individual wrestlers participated in ritual activities in which they became the symbols of their group's strength and power.[15]

Wrestling remains important because it occupies the space between sport and entertainment, reflexively commenting on both. It also grants competition secondary importance, with the narrative before and after the wrestling actually being of greater magnitude. Through these legends, wrestling maintains a semiotic intimacy with American life. The relationship between wrestling and politics has been shown most clearly by the election of Jesse 'the Body' Ventura in November 1999 as the Governor of Minnesota. There is a clear connection: both wrestling and politics express difference and disillusionment.

D-VON, GET THE TABLE

Tag team champions Buh-Buh Ray and D-Von Dudley started their careers as villains, crashing old women and 'helpless' victims through tables. After these acts, Buh-Buh Ray would enter a euphoric state. The crowd hated the duo, booing their evilness. Slowly though, Buh-Buh Ray started to crash men through tables. Their career changed when they fought a much-hated team. The 'Right to Censor' mouthed all the right-wing criticism of wrestling, fixating on the violence, sexism and the impact on children. RTC wrestled in white shirts, black ties and black trousers that never seemed to cover their white socks. Buh-Buh Ray and D-Von became bored with the RTC's rhetoric and 'got wood' by cracking them through a table. From that point, Buh-Buh and D-Von have been two of the most popular performers. Throughout their matches, the crowd chants for wood. The spectacle reaches an exhilarating moment when Buh-Buh Ray screams to his partner, 'D-Von, get the table'. Announcers' comments cannot be heard over the crowd's explosive enthusiasm. Certainly, wrestling is aggressive and sexual, but it is of a distinct order to that encountered in the rest of television. As the Chairman of the WWF, Vince McMahon, has confirmed:

Anyone who says we're about violence ... I say 'Hello?' Violence is about guns, rape and burglary. You're not going to see Uzis, knives and guns on our show ... We're not teaching you to blow people up ... Let's talk about sex: look at 'Beverly Hills 90210.' We're very tame compared to that.[16]

Throughout its modern history, wrestling has been critiqued for its violence, sexism, racism and homophobia. If there is a disgraced 'ism' of the era, then wrestling contains it. John Hartley believed that 'the creation of the audience as a paedocratic "other" often says more about the critic than it does about the audience'.[17] Viewers of television are not innocent, God-fearing children who never leave the shelter of their mother's protection. They are thinking, critical, laughing, dancing homespun theorists who cruise through the truths of a time. Are the male fans of wrestling sexist? Probably. But they are doing nothing that the rest of the culture does not reward and encourage. Wrestling is not the problem. It is not the performance of the problem. It has the honesty to admit that ideologies have to be contested. If a value is important, then fight over it. Being horrified at the oppression of women simply pushes the problem into squishy tittering around a cheese platter. Wrestling starts its fight in the home and never promises clean starts or conclusive endings. The one–two–three on the mat is only the start of the conflict; the trigger for the next outrage.

DEAD MEN WALKING

Sports theory, at its best, must detail a greater complexity than the notation of scores, winners and losers. It must trace cultural significance. While boxing is interposed with narratives of excellence and accuracy, wrestling's tales always appear grander and more potent. Revenge and justice, pain and pleasure are captured through the externalised torture of suspension holds and the athletic springs off the top rope. The function of the carnival, as a transitory liberation, remains as Roland Barthes described it — a 'spectacle of excess'.[18] Wrestling triggers more shrill screams, jutted gasps and voluptuous vitriol that the conventions of a culture should allow. Women's spectatorship remains naïvely framed. John Kobler stated in the 1950s that:

It is not necessarily the sexual appeal of the good-looking wrestling hero that attracts women to the sport. Many of the less attractive wrestlers receive fan letters from women and are mobbed by women at arenas. At least one writer believed this to be due to women comparing the ugly stereotype with their husbands or male friends. The familiar male would appear relatively more desirable.[19]

This is obviously wish fulfilment from Kobler. Female fans adore the loudest, biggest, strongest wrestlers. The 10-year obsession of female fans with The Undertaker is the clearest example of this tendency.

> My interest/obsession with wrestling is devotional. I become completely immersed in the narrative. I upset my best friend's sensibilities by not being interested in any other competition but the WWF. My heart is already — and always — given to one wrestler, a 7-feet, 300-pound titan.
>
> The object of my desire is The Undertaker. I have a coat like his and for a time actually set aside my fear of a smashed skull to ponder riding a Harley Davidson like his. Not that I have ever been on a motor cycle, or worn leather, or considered getting a tattoo. But this man from the dark side has been a constant companion through wrestling.
>
> The fact that he chews tobacco, engages in human sacrifice and has the entire length of his arms stencilled with Gothic torture symbols is not terribly off-putting. Any man who can walk the ropes of the squared circle and then give their opponent the Last Ride is a worthy object of desire.
>
> Other women agree. Lady Takers pepper the net. Female fans go into great detail about his muscular development, long, textured jackets and relationship with his tortured brother named (of course) Kane. I quite like him too. Also seven feet tall and 300 pounds, Kane is masked because of a tragic house-burning incident. The Undertaker still holds himself responsible for the savage maiming of his younger brother. This truly is the fodder of life.
>
> My point though, is obvious. The realness of wrestling is not remotely the point of this activity. Wrestling is about ritual, soap opera and enormous men throwing each other onto tables. If this is patriarchy, then at least it is encased in lycra. It is flexible, dexterous and accepts the drops and holds of life. If only men outside the ring were so malleable.

Many 1950s critics of wrestling were worried about the female spectators of wrestling. Rex Lardner related that 'Georgeous Gene Dubuque was walloped on the head with a lady's loaded handbag. Lady spectators sometimes take off their shoes and strike hapless wrestlers within reach'.[20] These male writers were obviously highly disturbed by women's behaviour, of using classic feminine artillery — handbags and high heels — to express their anger. The female fans were having a fine time. Not surprisingly, the voice of masculine control tried to squash the fun:

Wrestling is a mockery of the spectator, and, when many spectators are women, it is women who are mocked ... Moreover, in his
mockery of the demonstrative, vociferous female spectator, the
wrestler, has, in fact, become a woman. The female wrestler com-
pletes the cycle of the farcical feminization of the sport.[21]

We find in Stone's words a desire to protect women from watching
large men pummel other men into vulnerability. Obviously this writer
is allowing a dense misogyny to encase notions of wrestling, competition, pleasure, humour and laughter. He does not even attempt to
understand how or why the 'vociferous female spectator' enjoys watching men hurt each other.

What is so fascinating about the theory encasing wrestling is the
fact that writers are far more comfortable discussing the homoerotic
inflection[22] than offering the possibility of women's desires and viewing practices. It seems that discussing queer moments is preferable to
the horrifying realisation that women adore watching and cheering
300(plus)-pound, 7-feet men. A cursory glance at the *WWF
Magazine*'s letter column reveals frequent articulations of feminine
desire. When D-Generation X dressed as Gangsters, with the full pin-
striped effect, for the cover of a February 2000 wrestling magazine, the
female fans expressed great approval:

> The picture is reason enough for more women to watch
> wrestling.[23]

> I've never been a huge fan of DX ... the 'Fab Four' have never
> looked better than they do in those suits on the front cover.[24]

The complete impossibility of active female attraction means that most
male critics are missing an entirely different reading of the spectacle.
The performance of male injury, suffering and demoralisation is not
considered attractive or appealing for women. Mick Foley, for example,
has suffered concussion, a thrice broken nose, a twice dislocated jaw,
severed right ear, teeth dislodged, a broken wrist and thumb, broken
toe, herniated disks and bone chips in the elbow. As either Cactus Jack,
Dude Love or Mankind, it is no surprise that the most frequent plac-
ard that welcome him to the arena is 'Mick Foley is God.' Sharon
Mazer has realised that 'professional wrestling explicitly and implicitly
makes visible cultural and counter-cultural ideas of masculinity and
sexuality'.[25] The idea that women like watching men being injured,
enacting revenge and triumphing over impossible odds never seems
interesting or important for journalists or theorists of wrestling.
Wrestling is male-centred. But the notion that men are the only audience of these programmes is ludicrous. It is only when reviewing the

1950s moral panics about women watching the spectacle that the fear of women's pleasure, humour and enjoyment is uncovered.[26]

The clearest interpretation of why women, the working class and people of colour find wrestling riveting is derived from John Campbell:

> Wrestling as a sport may not make sense to those who hold the dominant ideology ... other professional sports ideologically value fairness and equality for all the players, respect for the loser and proper celebration of the winner. Some of those who value these sports dismiss wrestling as being a lie or a fake ... Professional wrestling is more of a sow than a sport, but for the aforementioned losers it is a chance to celebrate these differences through the carnival and the spectacle.[27]

A wrestling ending is never a definitive conclusion. A loss is never permanent, but the start of a new fight. New types of resistance are triggered, resistance without a clear start or finish. Wrestling is therefore a part of the argument forwarded within *Ladies who Lunge*. Disempowered groups are using wrestling to renegotiate their social position. Wrestling can appear highly conservative. Yet it is also transgressive and provides innovative, hybrid ways of reading male and female bodies. While being a sport, with the accompanying masculine modality, it uses the generic structure of soap opera, a feminine form. Therefore, highly divergent paths through the narrative are presented.

Women's role in wrestling is underwritten. There are so many entry points. Miss Elizabeth: the baby face ring rat who received physical abuse from 'The Macho Man' Randy Savage, only to have her honour defended by Hulk Hogan. What of Sable, whose career was ended with a sexual harassment case against the WWF that was settled out of court? Women have dexterous histories in wrestling. As Mazer suggested, 'women wrestlers often do cross over from athletic into erotic displays in a variety of ways — from selling photographs of the cheesecake or nude variety to performing in explicitly pornographic videos'.[28] Throughout wrestling's history, women's bodies have been eroticised and sold. Just as wrestling is a pastiche of sport, so is it a pastiche of pornography.

THE NINTH WONDER OF THE WORLD

Don't treat me like a woman
Don't treat me like a man
Don't treat me like you know me
Treat me for just who I am

Chyna's theme music, 2001

The world of professional wrestling is hyper-masculine. It reveals all the images of textured misogyny: women wrestling in mud, overfilled bikini tops and overt competition between 'bitches' for the attention of men. Within this environment, it seems difficult to fathom how a committed, transformational woman can emerge.

It is a radical act to remake the body. While sport is a vehicle for the construction and reconstruction of masculine hegemony, sport does not have to confirm the inferiority of women. The bodybuilding and physical culture movement is the convergence of classicism and modernism. In the early twentieth century, the confusions and inconsistencies of modern life were resolved through (over)disciplining muscle and flesh. It is no coincidence that bodybuilding became popular through the 1920s and 1930s, with a desire to rebuild masculinity and 'reconstruct ... civilisation after the war'.[29] Bodybuilding was therefore seen to be an anti-degenerative function. For women, it offers a distinct path. The strong, muscular and powerful woman is still rare, but has increasing iconic resonance. Gloria Steinem has suggested that:

> Middle-class women are beginning to cultivate fitness and strength. Bodybuilders, everyday joggers, tennis champions, and Olympic athletes have begun to challenge the equation of beauty with weakness.[30]

Men's bodies, particularly when muscular and oiled, connote power. This power is derived from a threat: what he can do to you.[31] For women to possess a consciousness of their physical strength is, as Steinem has termed it, 'a collective revolution'.[32] Obviously, many women possess increasingly complex relationships with their bodies. The magazine of families and femininity, the *Australian Women's Weekly*, reported a survey of 17 000 women, exploring their disquiet about health and wellbeing. The survey revealed that:

> ... many women are crying out for help. For some, weight problems, poor body image and low self-esteem rule their every waking moment.[33]

Of all the women surveyed, 78.2 per cent linked bodily weight with attractiveness. One in four women reported that they have shown disordered eating patterns through their life.[34] What is most startling is that the majority of these women blame 'the media' for their troubles, without actually specifying the process by which this happens. The role of partners and the family are discredited. Further, women's own role in carrying around the (ideological) weight of supermodel slimness is not considered:

Why should I have a bad body image just because the media tells me? The media lumps us into moulds and, if we don't fit, then there has to be something wrong with us.[35]

This woman is a guest star in the drama of her own life. Blaming the media is far easier than actually analysing, questioning and critiquing magazines, television programmes and fashion spreads. Images of Elle Macpherson are not poured into the corporeal vehicle of women, like wine into a glass. A critical function is needed to interpret and negotiate these photographs, shapes and ideas. Also, it is important to confirm that 'the media' does not present a single image of women, men, youth or age. It is up to all women to sort out this cultural material and validate women who perform plurality, difference and distinction.

It has been said that the sculpture is already in the marble. Similarly, the sculpture is already in the woman. That means that there is an important relationship between women and sport. Helen Lenskyj stated that 'I see the physical and the intellectual as two key strands of my feminism'.[36] Sport and physical activity become crucial to women's reclamation of the body. Through yoga or weights, the capacities of the body are extended. While there has been some feminist antipathy to sports research, part of the problem is that women's sport is too often labelled fitness or leisure. Women's bodies are being prodded, disciplined and shaped. Through women's lives, we are taught to keep legs together and not risk bodily damage (careful, you might get hurt). Such limits are challenged by wrestling women.[37]

Women in the WWF are, as Michael Cole has suggested, 'a controversial subject'.[38] These concerns feed into the participation of women in contact sport. Boxing has suffered similar foreboding. Wrestling, as sports entertainment, offers disparate roles for women. One half of the former tag team champions, the Road Dogg, has separated these functions:

As far as wrestling goes, I don't think they have a place. In terms of our show, I think they have an important place.[39]

Many of these contradictions are actualised and negotiated through the Women's Championship Title. Frequently these matches are glorified catfights, involving mud, a strip or ballgowns. In terms of entertainment they are an important 'intermission' in the show. Women such as Trish, Sable, Tori, Terri and Debra have filled this role.[40] There are female wrestlers who are far more involved in the sport rather than entertainment. Jackie and Chyna are the athletes who wrestle with great technique and skill. Therefore, to discuss 'women wrestlers' is an inaccurate generalisation. While they are in a minority, there is increasing athleticism and ability, paralleling the increased acceptance of female bodybuilding. Jackie, for example, is capable in karate, boxing, bodybuilding and wrestling and was the first female to be placed in the men's PWI ranking. She also affirmed her distinction from the 'entertainment' side of the business:

> I wasn't like any other female. I don't stand around the ring and clap and cheer. I'm no cheerleader. I'm a professional wrestler. That's what I have trained to be … I've paid my dues. Working hard for yourself pays off.[41]

First wrestling in the World Championship Wrestling and then the WWF, Jackie claimed her space as a woman, an athlete and a wrestler.

Taking the innovations of Jackie into a politically challenging and socially revelatory realm is Chyna. She rarely wrestles with women, but enters the male competition. With respect, the Big Boss Man has affirmed that:

> It takes a special breed of woman to even want to step into the ring with guys of our size. With Chyna, she may be the toughest woman I've ever seen.[42]

The men in Chyna's workplace are tall, strong and muscular. They are working-class men who use their bodies to wrestle for a living and are paid for their aggression. Chyna has carved out a space of difference that has altered women's mobilisation of physique, sport and wrestling. She was the first and only woman to hold the Intercontinental Belt, beating Jeff Jarrett on 17 October 1999. She was the first competitor to ever deliver a Pedigree move from the top rope.[43] The combination of strength and flexibility has allowed her to perform male-associated grapples and holds with increased resilience and speed. The WWF's writers have difficulties finding a way to describe her new interpretation of old movements.[44]

The story of Chyna is also the tale of Joanie Laurer. Like most wrestlers, Laurer was given a professional name within the narrative. But unlike most of the male wrestlers, Chyna has had the opportunity to reveal the complex relation between the athlete, performer and person.[45] Instead of treating such duality as a lie or personal problem, she has noticed the space and choices that it has provided her:

> I am what I am — a woman of substance, a lady with muscle, and I, Joanie Laurer, can't even stop Chyna … I was meant to be somebody else. And don't let anybody kid you — having two faces for the world to see is a good thing. Getting there? Well that's a longer story.[46]

Through her biography, *If They Only Knew*, she was able to tell that story. It is a powerful testament to a woman struggling with her father, mother, step-parents and violent boyfriends. It is the fights with her own self-image that remain the most powerfully described. While it is a popular biography with a wide readership, she reveals her struggle with bulimia and difficulties in judging and reconciling her differences from other women. She shows that:

> I was always a big, different ... visible girl ... My life is roughly (ha ha) divided into three parts: Being different and hating it. Being different and accepting it. Being different and, well, embracing it.[47]

Her autobiography is a textbook study of a woman reconciling her body image with personal and societal expectations. She participated in three Fitness America Pageants — weighing sixty pounds more than the next-heaviest participant — and finished last each time. Her fitness, strength and muscle development were not inferred as valuable or valued. Similarly, she has been unsuccessful in bodybuilding competitions because she was not thin enough, even for the heavyweight division. She has learned to resolve her height, weight and strength, facing the judgments of others and moderations of herself. Her wrestling identity has carved the space for integrating mind and body, gaze and image. The behaviours and actions of wrestling, the language of throws, falls, brawls and holds, provide ideal metaphors for a woman confronting the complexities of self and body.

While women's roles are being rebuilt within wrestling, Chyna has presented complicated renderings of her own femininity:

> I don't really consider myself one of the women. I consider myself one of the boys. I get along with them extremely well. I interact with them physically and socially. They respect me. I've seen myself evolve into this character ... and now they respect me.[48]

Her language of self-esteem and respect conveys something of her struggles to attain visibility and success. The shape of her body shows a dedication to fitness and training. She has worked on her body for fifteen years, entering a gym and the weights room at a time when few women did so. She conveyed that women possess enormous advantages in bodybuilding, being able to combine endurance with strength work. However, the cost has been enormous:

> I have worked so very hard to get my body to the peak of athleticism, and people rejected it. She's so butch. She's so ugly. She looks like a man. I am not a man. I'm a strong, fit, beautiful woman, and a lot of people are intimidated by that.[49]

Chyna's struggle in confronting the prejudices of other wrestlers, journalists and fans has been rewarded by a reconstitution of acceptable feminine musculature. She has carried wrestling spectators forward politically and socially, accessing a younger audience. Her bodily training enables a focus on corporeality and selfhood. She is not only fit, but has offered a reinterpretation of the meaning of fitness. Chyna is not only 'in shape', but has changed the understanding of a woman's shape. Treating her body as an experiment, she gained the respect of fellow wrestlers and the audience. As she stated:

> When I started, there was an incredible intimidation factor. These guys were going to let a woman beat them up on TV? To get people to accept that I fight men as equal opponents — what a milestone! People don't even look at me as 'the woman' now. They just look at me as Chyna, one of the wrestlers.[50]

She provides a lesson in persistence, self-belief, purpose and commitment. Chyna has moved from being a minor figure in sports entertainment to a major icon of wrestling. She has fought with herself, the WWF and the fans. It has taken time, but she is now among the five most well-known wrestlers, alongside The Rock, Stone Cold Steve Austin, Kane and The Undertaker. She is iconographic and has moulded the way the female body is filmed, photographed and judged.

Chyna's physical commitment to political goals has been at a cost. On a pre-Christmas 2000 edition of 'Raw is War', she was piledriven by Val Venis, of the Right To Censor. Her neck and spine were badly injured and she had to be lifted from the ring. The injury bore similarities to Owen Hart's tombstone on Steven Austin in August 1997. Hart's 220 pounds and Austin's 250 pounds all compressed on the latter's neck. He could not move. Like Chyna, he had suffered a trauma of the spinal chord. On the Christmas Day 2000 edition of 'Raw is War', Chyna was interviewed by the voice of wrestling, Jim Ross:

JR:	What have the doctors told you and what is going through your mind regarding your future in the WWF?
Chyna:	When it first happened in the ring I lost feelings in my arms ... they were showing I had three ruptured discs in my neck. At that point I was basically given two options. The first option was to never wrestle again and um —
JR:	Just take your time.
Chyna:	The second option was surgery where they

	would fuse my neck and then never step into the ring again.
JR:	Your *Playboy* was hugely successful, the book is coming out … movies … At least you have a few things to fall back on.
Chyna:	All the obstacles I've overcome, all the steps of my life has [*sic*] been to be in the ring in the World Wrestling Federation. And I hate what they've done to me and I hate them. They've taken my life from me. Because that is what it is to me. I hate them. I've overcome a lot of obstacles. I'll be damned if I let them get the last of me.[51]

Throughout the time she was injured, Chyna continually referred to the obstacles confronted through her career. Many of these were feminist-inflected traumas, as she operated outside of conventional notions of beauty. The scale of her struggles — physically, socially and personally — warrants respect and critical attention. It is also clear that she has fought the limitations, sickness and illnesses of her body:

> Being a woman and experiencing physical pain because of it is something that's shadowed me almost all my life … All that defined me as a woman in the physical sense just plain hurt. It seemed to just work out that way — I mean, saying the word even hurts. I suffered becoming a woman. Maybe that's why it was so important to become strong.[52]

In great detail, she tells of the challenges faced with both ovarian tumours and breast enlargements. She is honest and detailed in her descriptions of the surgeries inflicted on her body. There is a clinical gaze on her stretched muscles, stitched abdomen and painful implants. Time and again, her biography stresses the separation and confluences between 'me and my body, Joanie and Chyna'.[53]

It is important to ponder why Chyna made a decision to pose for *Playboy*. While such a choice may appear bizarre or backward, it actually confirms her mission. She has treated her body as a project to be discussed, judged and revealed. She has wanted to change the way femininity is understood. At nearly six feet tall and 200 pounds, she is an Irish whip away from the conventional soft, feminine and non-threatening images of the *Playboy* women. It is obvious that, with 14-inch biceps and a bench press lift weight of 365 pounds, she is not a vulnerable, soft image of erotic attraction. Sable, a former wrestler within the WWF, also posed nude for the magazine. But as a short, slim blonde woman, she offered a non-threatening replication of other centrefolds. Chyna is completely different. She reveals flesh stretched over engorged muscles. Most significantly, *Playboy* allowed her to introduce the woman behind the wrestler, preparing her audience for the release of her biography.[54]

In customary *Playboy* fashion, Chyna expresses her interest in 'feminine things',[55] including flowers, make-up and jewellery. The difficulties of her life are also probed. Having left home at sixteen years of age, she 'started using fitness as my identity'.[56] She also attained a degree in Spanish literature. This ability was shown during one of the most impressive moments of Wrestlemania 1999, where HHH and Chyna came out to the commentators' tables, with the latter sitting at the (in)famous Spanish Announcer's Table. Chyna then began a commentary in fluent Spanish, to the amazement and respect of the other viewers at this scene.

Significantly, Chyna was also prepared to countenance the taken-for-granted *Playboy* attitude towards women. She explained her decision in politicised terms:

> It's a powerful statement. There haven't been a lot of woman in *Playboy* who look like I do. I am not the norm for beauty. But this is who I am, and this is beautiful ... I want a husband, and I would love to have a family one day. But I'm not going to be the kind of woman who's at home with the kids. I'd put my baby on my hip and go do a movie. I'm a go-getter and that's what makes my life exciting.[57]

Chyna is prepared to accept her height, weight, career and musculature and remind the viewer that 'this is beautiful'. She is negotiating a new type of feminist hegemony, remarkably in the midst of *Playboy*, a site of feminine disempowerment and occasional humiliation. She has been prepared to confront the tyranny of thinness permeating both television and film. When attending the Emmy Awards in 2000, she towered over the other female guests. Chyna observed of the scene that 'Most of the women here look like they eat every other day ... I'm afraid to shake hands with some of them for fear of tearing off an arm'.[58] Her difference carries a social imperative, as does her capacity to articulate the nature and consequences of that difference. That is why the release of both her autobiography and workout video, *Chyna Fitness*, are important.

For women, politics and movement are aligned. Grace Lichtenstein described 'the Dark Ages before fitness and feminism'.[59] To assume the aligned functionality of this relationship is premature. But in the war over body management, sport and feminism, Chyna is a front-line fighter. The aim must be to enfold the narratives, interpretation and possibilities of Joanie Laurer into Chyna. Few women possess the possibilities of an overt, alternative personality to test the limits of the body. But through the leather costumes, studs and boots, Chyna is more than a minor player in her own corporeality. She is a commentator on women's sporting history. It is no surprise that such an insight is derived from wrestling. As the sport to think with, it is a crunching intercession in discussions of pleasure, femininity, masculinity and desire. When everything is questioned, everything can be renegotiated. With no definitive winners or losers, wrestling offers a future for successful feminist interventions.

At the 2001 Royal Rumble, Chyna challenged for the first time in the Women's Title. In the classic wrestling revenge narrative, she fought Ivory in a payback for the neck injury. Chyna's path to the ring was rapturous. The crowd was filled with signs of support and a Chyna chant filled the stadium. Her performance was impressive, throwing her opponent around the ring like a rag doll. At one point, Chyna lifted Ivory's body into a clean and press, with the limp form hovering above Chyna's head. The crowd exploded in appreciation for the ninth wonder of the world. But Chyna was not victorious, even though Ivory did not win the bout. After a somersault pass, Chyna's previous neck trauma remerged. The ninth wonder of the world defeated herself. Appropriately, on this occasion, she did not win the women's title. She did not need to. From the canvas of misogyny and sexism has bounced back a positive, popular reconstitution of femininity. Chyna is the number one contender to get feminism not only on the mat, but on the wrestling agenda.

BREASTS ON THE BRIDGE: CAPTAIN JANEWAY AND THE FEMINIST ENTERPRISE

CAPTAIN'S PERSONAL LOG, STARDATE 8121.6

It is tough being a female Captain of a starship. I don't really seem to fit in the customised Captain's chair and the Klingons just cannot take me seriously. Vulcans seem to dislike the emotions of human women even more than those of men. Ferengi just want to remove my clothes. My second-in-command even dislikes my choice of music — he just can't stomach Hole. He laughed when Kurt died. I will ignore the insult and control my emotions. I will be tough, like Courtney; straighten up my lipstick and follow Federation officer training.

But every now and again I feel that I am losing control and worry that I will stare emotionally at the camera, proving once again that female Captains just cannot lead in the 'Star Trek' universe.

Computer — delete that last sentence.

Science fiction is a journey through tomorrow. This voyage is conducted through the eyes and ideas of today. As a story-telling form, it trials the future. 'Star Trek', alongside 'Doctor Who', is the longest-running science fictional televisual drama. Trekkie catchphrases have become clichés of the time and the characters are archetypes of loyalty, sacrifice, friendship and leadership. While 'Star Trek' theory has become its own academic industry, there are odd, awkward silences in the intellectual conversation. While there is much material on race and blackness, discussions of gender and feminism remain hidden behind complex, French-inflected psychoanalytic frameworks.[1] 'Star Trek' has moved with the intellectual trends, from 1970s structuralism through 1980s psychoanalysis and 1990s postmodernism. Postcolonial thought is the newest intellectual trend to saturate the programme.[2] This chapter is differently inflected, not only displaying how 'Star Trek' mobilises popular feminism, but demonstrating how theories of feminist leadership jut unexpectedly and rewardingly from this almost too familiar programme.

'Star Trek': the five incarnations

'Star Trek: The Original Series'	1966–1969
'Star Trek: The Next Generation'	1987–1994
'Star Trek: Deep Space Nine'	1993–1999
'Star Trek: Voyager'	1994–2001
'Enterprise'	2001–

TO BOLDLY GO

It's a long way from Shakespeare to Kylie Minogue.[3]

John Hartley

While kilometres of space may separate Lear and Lucky (lucky, lucky), 'Star Trek' always cannibalised the Bard. From Picard's obsession with Hamlet and the Klingon delight in Richard III, Shakespeare remains an uncredited extra throughout the series. The imagining of 'Star Trek' is on such a scale that it colonises cultural myths and grafts them onto its own. The metaphoric Enterprise is big enough to be wandered through, savoured and discussed. It is, as Richards suggests, 'part of the vocabulary of modern culture'.[4] Theorists treat it, like Shakespeare, as a great work of art.[5] Fans affirm it as a virtual world permitting endless frocking up.[6]

'Star Trek' is so well researched by academics because it takes risks, and a stand. Black men and women are featured in positions of leadership. Whoopi Goldberg asked to appear on 'The Next Generation' because 'the only time you ever saw black people in the future was on *Star Trek*'.[7] This critique of a white future was continued with a powerful and controversial instalment of the series.

'Deep Space Nine' is a challenging text: it is a cartography of Trek. While seen in retrospect as the most unpopular of the textual stable,[8] it was also the most exigent. Starfleet had over-extended its Empire-building authority. Captain Sisko explained that he was unable to enforce, or at times justify, Federation Law:

> The trouble is Earth, on Earth there is no poverty, no crime, no war. You look out the window of Starfleet headquarters, and you see paradise. Out there in the Demilitarised Zone, all the problems

have not been solved yet. Out there, there are no saints, just people. Angry scared determined people who are going to do whatever it takes to survive, whether it meets with Federation approval or not.[9]

In 'DS9', the colonisation of other worlds had reached saturation. Starfleet occupied a Cardassian station, which provided a dark, gritty setting and dystopic warnings through obsolete computer systems that were rarely operational. An overworked Constable tried to maintain order. 'DS9' was a (post)colonial Trek. While the adventures and effects were not dazzling, the dialogue was gritty in its honesty. The truths that Starfleet promoted through twenty-five years of televisual history no longer functioned. There was, however, a more considered balance between public and private spheres. 'DS9' was headed by Benjamin Sisko, a black leader. He commanded an authority that did not undermine private success. The Captain's relationship with his son, Jake, is one of the few good fatherhoods in 'Star Trek', distinct from Kirk and David, Spock and Sarek, Worf and Alexander.[10]

When 'Voyager' began, there was a desire to combine the best of 'DS9' and 'The Next Generation'. The combination of Starfleet officers and the rebel Maquis provided early conflict, which settled into the accustomed pattern of coffee, dialogue, staff meetings and compromise. Like Kirk's Enterprise, the series re-established the authority of the Captain. Other writers have pondered the similarity between the womanising Kirk and the woman, Janeway:[11]

> What materialises is a combination of Kirk and actress Katharine Hepburn. What materialises is Kathryn Janeway, captain of the Starship Voyager. This is a wonderful development. Two of my favourite things are Captain Kirk and Katharine Hepburn.[12]

Voyager is lost in space. Being 'lost' initiates both independence and an opportunity for leadership. Janeway cannot wait for orders from Starfleet. This grants her a frontier-like authority. It was no coincidence that 'Dr Quinn: Medicine Woman' and 'Voyager' concurrently featured empowered women negotiating a frontier.

It is Kirk and the 'Original Series' that has most in common with Janeway and 'Voyager'. Both ships provoke an active, colonising mission, 'discovering' new worlds. 'The Next Generation', particularly after the Borg threat emerged, became the conservative, insular managers of the Federation, with Picard being sent on diplomatic missions to rush new worlds into the power block. Both Kirk's and Janeway's crews propel the imperative of discovery and are able to ignore the problems that are left after their departure. The only difference is that Voyager is coming home, rather than heading out.

'Voyager' increases the texture and complexity of the 'Star Trek' paradigm. It is an amalgamation of diverse components of each of the previous series. It is the Trek hybrid, re-telling and reframing the archaeology of the programme. It shows detailed renderings of the workplace and military service. Because the voyage is of such a scale, problems and difficulties must be continually resolved. If not disentangled, the difficulties fester into longer-term disagreements. Picard denies family ties. Kirk left his son to be raised by the mother. 'Voyager' is the only programme that confronts family and homesickness on the extended journey.

FROM JANICE TO JANEWAY

I bring order to chaos.[13]

The Borg Queen

'Star Trek' is a masculine, rationalist universe. What makes 'Voyager' and 'Deep Space Nine' different from the earlier series is that accepted notions of truth and justice are unravelled, critiqued and overturned. Captains Sisko and Janeway write an alternative refrain to the Starfleet melody. Through the Captains' Logs, the viewer is granted insight into the changing modalities of leadership.

Women have always been a part of 'Star Trek'. The pilot episode, 'The Cage', presented a female Number One, the second-in-command. Yeoman Janice Rand had the highest, most captivating bouffant ever to appear on television. Nurse Chapel actively pursued her object of desire, the erotic other, Mr Spock. Lieutenant Uhura was a steadying force on the Bridge, literally the voice of the Enterprise. It is too easy to frame the women of the 'Original Series' as submissive, celibate and loyal. For example, Andrea Juno 'would watch ... a *Star Trek* episode, but was faced with an insurmountable dilemma when I tried to translate the stories to my internal fantasy images'.[14] The Trek women are far more complex than this rendering suggests. Also, we must not forget the crazy females who visited the Enterprise. The man-eaters, salt-suckers, nubile dancers, hysterics and changelings kept Captain Kirk guessing and chasing.

'Star Trek' women have been Chief of Security, counsellors and doctors. In 'The Next Generation', women provide a network of protection for Picard, ironically allowing him to proclaim his self-sufficiency and denial of family. Troi and Crusher are feminine and sensitive. Guinan, played by the innovative actor Whoopi Goldberg, is the wise woman, providing not only the listening function, but the role of interventionary adviser. She is the Yoda of 'Star Trek'. Yet throughout the first two incarnations of *Star Trek*, women disrupt men's friendships. Even in the twenty-fourth century, married women take on their husband's name. The rarity of deep female friendships remains an obvious and poignant absence from 'Star Trek'.[15]

Rand, Chapel, Uhura, Troi and Crusher hold surrogate power. They are the women behind the men behind Starfleet. It is 'Deep Space Nine' that presented the next generation of 'Star Trek' women: Kira and Dax. As Captain Sisko's second and third-in-command, they change the way power is distributed. Nana Visitor, who was Major Kira, stated that 'to play a strong woman on television, or in any medium, really, is unusual, very rare, and is a huge joy for me'.[16] Both Kira and Dax are complex, sexual, passionate women. Also, the deep bond of friendship between them marks moments of female collectivity.

'Star Trek' has always relied on a gimmick. The 'Original Series' had Spock, 'The Next Generation' had Data and 'Deep Space Nine' featured the streamlined shapeshifter, Odo. For 'Voyager', the gimmick is a woman — a woman in leadership.

CAPTAIN'S PERSONAL LOG, STARDATE 8101.2

I remember my congealed terror at the start of 2000. Some women appear to thrive on ambition fuelled by the intoxicating aura of a two-piece linen suit. They seem propelled to climb over broken bodies, scramble over the double shift and hoist themselves up the corporate ladder. I was more comfortable on the incline of a step machine. I despise those men and women who want their bosses to *see them working*, rather than simply wanting to get the job done. I find meetings a bizarre ritual of corporate management, used to justify little more than the need to have … corporate managers. It is a characteristic of our age that the person who is running a meeting invariably has no skills in running a meeting. Passing the talking stick is not the basis of human resource management.

There I was, a happy Senior Lecturer, minding my own business, when a Professor took a year's sabbatical and an Associate Professor took another job. This turn of events was frantically revealed within two weeks. I was the only senior staff member left. Therefore, I had to be Chair of the programme. It became clear in the changeover that there was no file of precedents. Actually, there was no file. All I had was a university handbook and a queue of students needing concrete information about their enrolment. Now.

This situation is every Generation Xer's nightmare. We have spent our entire lives listening to REM, thinking that we will always be outside the establishment. We are satisfied with our Macjobs, hiding in the light. Suddenly, I had the sick realisation that I could not duck, run or hole up. And I was on this stage without a script. REM only taught us how to lose and moan about it.

I had to work out very quickly what women in leadership actually means. The Margaret Thatcher mode of management would not go over well with either my colleagues or hairdresser. And Wonder Woman was nurtured by Amazons. Instead, I had been trained by male historians at an elite Australian university.

I went for a walk. I bought embarrassing books, such as *Calm at Work* and *Life Strategies*. They did not help my current situation, but I remembered why I despised American psychologists. I tried yoga and bought essential oils. Besides strengthening my ankles and making my house smell like the Queen's Hotel after a heavy night, the kinaesthetic and olfactory therapies were not helping. I talked to other women: this did help, but they were as busy as I was. Their crouched frames shadowing their keyboards spoke of too many emails received but not sent. Once more I was drawn to television.

Then I remembered Captain Kathryn Janeway. She was placed in an impossible situation, managing a starship in a foreign environment. With Starfleet a quadrant away, she had to make new rules to suit her style and truths. I also really liked her hair.

Janeway made mistakes. She affirmed that the key of leadership is to know how to handle them. Information and knowledge come from experience, but quality of work is derived from respect, creativity, humour and imagination.

Janeway taught me that.

Janeway remains as much an alien as an emotionally-torn Vulcan, poker-playing Android, or lovesick Shapeshifter. It was so unusual to have a woman as the lead actor in a non-comic series that televisual descriptions were lacking. Steven Eramo described Janeway as 'Trek's First Lady'.[17] This is an inaccurate description: after all, who is her husband/president? The notion of a woman possessing autonomous power was almost too much for Trekwriters. This one character blew apart the accepted role of women in science fiction, television drama and everyday life.

Jon Wagner and Jan Lundeen have argued that 'the fact that Voyager's captain is a woman seldom affects the story lines in any significant way'.[18] This interpretation is mistaken. Sexual difference is the basis of the humour, plot conflict and interaction with aliens. Janeway also demonstrates, perhaps more effectively than any other popular culture figure, the difficulty of women being in power *and* sexually active. While all the Starfleet Captains expect the complete allegiance of the crew, it is the relationship with the second-in-command that is the closest.[19] Voyager, like the other vessels, has a male Number One, Chakotay. With a female Captain though, romantic intrigue has peppered many of the episodes. Kate Mulgrew, the actress who plays Janeway, argued against a sexual relationship being enacted:

> I felt it would be far more interesting and far more genuine if they had a deep and intimate and wonderful relationship and they didn't go to bed. She loses her nobility.[20]

Obviously this decision has solidified her authority and integrity. A similar decision was made in Scully's case in 'The X-Files'. The sexual propriety has generated enormous plot possibilities. However, it does demonstrate that a woman could not attain respect *and* be sexually active. This issue never concerned Kirk or Riker. Janeway, like Scully, could not manage personal and public success. They both display the unique pressures powdering the feminine face of power.

'Voyager' unravelled this problem early in the show's run, during the first season's episode 'Resolutions'. Chakotay and Janeway were stranded on a planet to avoid dying of a deadly virus. Left alone without responsibilities, they had to determine the limits of their feelings in terms of sexuality, friendship and loyalty:

Janeway:	We have to talk about this.
Chakotay:	Alright.
Janeway:	I think we need to define some parameters about us.
Chakotay:	I'm not sure I can define parameters. But I can tell you a story. An ancient legend among my people. It's about an angry warrior who lived his life in conflict with the rest of his tribe. A man who couldn't find peace, even with the help of his spirit guide. For years, he struggled with his discontent. The greatest satisfaction he ever got was when he was in battle. This made him a hero among his tribe, but the warrior still struggled for peace within himself. One day, he and his war party were captured by a neighbouring tribe, lead by a woman warrior. She called on him to join her because her tribe was too small and weak to defend itself against all its enemies. The warrior was brave and beautiful and wise. The angry warrior swore to himself that he would stay by her side, making her burden lighter.

From that point on, her needs would come
first. And in that way, the warrior began to
know the true meaning of peace.

Janeway: Is that really an ancient legend?
Chakotay: No. But it made it easier to say.[21]

This scene is a remarkably honest and highly intimate discussion of women, men and power. Perhaps most significantly, while Janeway tried to create an agreed series of limits, Chakotay reminded her that she must define the terms of their relationship, to which he would agree, because 'her needs would come first'. He therefore confirmed her authority, affirmed his own and stated that he was prepared to accept her guidelines. That this discussion of women's power had to be enclosed in an indigenous legend is provocative and troubling. But the dialogue does confirm Janeway's leadership and how men move and change in response to it. The relationship between femininity, sexuality and leadership is awkward and confusing. It takes the introduction of another character, Seven of Nine, to release a blast of sexuality on 'Voyager'.

Sexual innuendo is an added item in the clutch purse of women in leadership. There is no way out of this ideological bag. Single, childless women are lacking compassion and depth; childless married women are selfish and driven; childbearing married women are unable to be fully committed to the workplace. Put simply, the standards of behaviour are higher for women and the judgments of that behaviour are more ruthless. Dianne Kaseman noticed that 'too often women see few role models and confounding situations'.[22] To change these perceptions, there is a need to align the causes of women with the goals of organisations. A few women will have to do it tough, weather the stares, the gossip and the claims of tokenism to demonstrate that women can lead and maintain competence.

'Star Trek' performs these difficulties clearly, presenting sexuality very awkwardly. Troi and Riker never managed to bypass shining space bunnies to renew a committed relationship. Kirk moved between a series of different women/different dress/same eyeliner dalliances. Picard tried (too hard) to ignore women and ended up confusing anger and intimacy. He avoided all the attractive, balanced, sensible women in his path. But if there was a dangerous alien who would damage either the ship or his crew, then he would find her irresistible. He even dated a lawyer who was a prosecutor in his only court martial.

As expected, 'DS9' offered more complex gender and sexual relationships. Being trapped on an ageing station at the edge of the quadrant meant that it was difficult to avoid conflict, so relationship troubles had to be hand-wringingly discussed. The show featured numerous nagging women pestering men to make a decision. The best example of this was the married couple Chief O'Brien and his biologist wife, Keiko. While both served on the Enterprise, the station had no use for a scientist, therefore the Chief took the promotion, but left his wife stranded with little to occupy her time. The first season featured Keiko harassing O'Brien about the mistake that he had made and the costs to her career. He would then retract to the bar. Their marital problems echoed throughout the station. 'DS9' had more gossip, rumour and intrigue than an episode of 'The Bold and the Beautiful'.

For much of the series, Odo the shapeshifter hid his unresolved longing and desire for Major Kira. Odo, our molten Mulder, pined for his best friend and colleague. Luckily, before the series ended he got his resistance fighter. Other characters wooed each other, culminating in the 1997 'DS9' episode 'You are cordially invited', which featured the first marriage of two central 'Star Trek' characters presented on screen.[23] 'Voyager' needed the soap journey of 'DS9' to activate a more intricate presentation of sex and relationships.

If there is a characteristic of proto-Janeway 'Trek' women, it is their unexplored potential. Uhura has offered enormous possibilities. Through humour, she also remained vibrant. In 'The Naked Time', she stood her ground:

Sulu: I'll protect you, fair lady.
Uhura: Sorry, neither.[24]

The humour was a significant method to deflect the threat. The physical intimidation of a security officer, rather than a communication specialist, was far more difficult to decentre. The character, Lieutenant Tasha Yar, was killed at the end of the first season of 'The Next Generation'.[25] She was physically tough and able to control men. Therefore, she was difficult to include in scripts and removed herself from the series because of a lack of use. Her role as Chief of Security was replaced by the hyper-masculine Lieutenant Worf. After her loss, Deanna Troi and Beverly Crusher took on the feminine, nurturing role.

The real difficulty faced by women with power is that they are rarely operating in a context that affirms and welcomes their differences. That is why the images of women in power are jarring. Both Thatcher and Bhutto were rarely supported or pictured with other women, but were action-oriented. They were (de)gendered by the action of fighting a war. Contextualising women in power reveals systemic flaws in human resource management and access to information and education. Janeway remained a concerned, cool observer of love and sex, but could not balance power and romance.[26] She had to focus on more important details, like choosing a hairstyle.

IT IS A HAIR BRUSH, NOT A MAGIC WAND, LOVE

Captain's Log: Star date 483.15: has anyone seen my styling wand? If so,
please return to the quarters of Captain Janeway, Starfleet commander, USS Voyager …
I don't like Janeway's hair … Nor do I like her much. Over-played by American
actress Kate Mulgrew, she is a bizarre mix of the austere and
melodramatic.[27]

Sandra McLean

For the first season of 'Voyager', Janeway was more of a hairstyle than a character in a major television series. She did everything right, delivering blistering, impassioned speeches and making an iconographic first impression. Journalists, though, wanted to lampoon the locks. Attention to her hair demonstrates the great difficulty involved in women presenting a façade of competence[28] and an attitude of leadership.[29] Critics found her tresses 'so 19th century'.[30] We have become accustomed to the blandly flicked and over-treated hair of older women who are trying to look much younger. Notions of beauty, particularly for women over forty, were skewed between Heather Locklear's 'I'm worth it' mane and Cher's wild hairpieces. The leadership literature could have predicted this problem.

The movement away from nuclear families through divorces and remarriages has increased the acceptable roles available for women. Leadership models too often revert back to earlier maternal notions of co-operation and consensus-building — a process orientation rather than a masculine, result-focussed direction. Hybrid leadership styles are only being sketched. 'Star Trek' has offered useful trajectories of future management modes and has produced best-selling books triggered by the programme.[31] Many appreciate Janeway's incredible efforts:

> Mulgrew, as Kathryn Janeway, is a splendid captain. We see her mind watch itself think in split seconds, as if hesitation were a form of sloth. She was born to command, with hair swept up like Edith Wharton's, eyes narrowed like a basilisk's, the best jaw on television this side of Karen Sillas; she's so crisp she crackles like a graviton, so svelte in her Federation woollens that she seems to chuck herself into action like a spear.[32]

The confluence between leadership and masculinity is one of the last untouched bastions of the patriarchy. Yet linking Janeway with Katharine Hepburn or discussing her hair or jawline are ways to place her in popular culture rather than public leadership.

Leadership is never based on a single man in power, but springs from both an organisational position and a culture of support. While individual women may be promoted, this does not transform the faces of power. Women executives possess competences that are not valued within organisations.[33] While new paradigms are emerging about how we work and learn, to affirm leadership development for women is a highly optimistic trajectory. They must overcome the social difficulties of the second shift in the domestic sphere and also transgress the accustomed roles of feminine assistants, administrators and secretaries. In our culture of disposable woman — sometimes labelled supermodels — there is a superfluous, competing agenda confronting every woman as she walks into every meeting.

Women operate in an environment where men, perhaps for the first time, must contemplate that the rules are changing. The primary sites of competition in this culture — sport, war, politics, academia and business — are generally closed off to women. The unilateral models of management are no longer working. With much of the employed population being overworked, underpaid and fearful of 'downsizing', loyalty, commitment and compassion are rare. The new models of leadership, invoking consultation, consensus and collaboration, are having an impact.

Janeway broadens both the image and discourse of leadership. Being neither a superwoman nor a supermodel, she works the hours of the other Captains, is tired most of the time and is 'mothered' by her second-in-command. This tendency was also shown by Spock, Riker and Kira towards their own (male) Captains. She exhibits deep remorse, but also great humour. Kirk, Picard and Sisko, as Captains, rarely express moments of doubt. They are definitive and precise in their judgments. The difference is that Janeway, during the pilot episode, made a decision that doomed her crew to a lifetime of exile from the Federation. She destroyed the only cultural force that could return them to Earth. Perhaps the most remarkable episode in the 'Star Trek' canon is the story where Janeway is lost in a deep depression, unable to leave her quarters for months. Commander Chakotay assumes the Captaincy, while Janeway wanders in a morass of the mind, blind with guilt and reliving the decision that has doomed her crew to a lifetime of travel. Without counsellors to monitor her condition, she becomes sick.[34] Janeway speaks from the corner of a blackened room:

Chakotay:	You've picked a bad time to isolate yourself from the crew. This ship needs a Captain, especially now …
Janeway:	How did we end up here, Chakotay? Answer me.
Chakotay:	We were faced with a difficult choice. We had the means to get home, but it would have put an innocent people at risk. So we decided to stay.
Janeway:	No. No. I decided to stay. I made that choice for everyone.

Chakotay:	We're alive and well. And we've gathered enough data to keep Federation scientists busy for decades. Our mission has been a success.
Janeway:	Those are the same words I've been telling myself for the last four years. But then we hit this void. And I started to realise how empty those words sound.
Chakotay:	Kathryn.
Janeway:	It was an arrogant judgment, Chakotay. It was arrogant and it was selfish. All of us are paying for my mistake … If the crew asks for me, tell them the Captain sends her regards.[35]

This is a powerful exchange. After four years of their voyage, Janeway had been established as a strong leader. She had actually accorded enough credibility and competence so that weakness, doubt and reflexivity could be revealed. Working against simplistic portrayals of a silently suffering superwoman, or 'the best man for the job', there was a desire to move beyond the oddity of female leadership. Instead, layers of complexity and texture are established around a Captain, who happens to be a woman. Importantly for the 'Star Trek' discourse, a presentation of command decisions displayed the workings of power.

The final episodes of 'Voyager' performed the process of leadership decisions with clarity and relish. Janeway is tempted by the ultimate shortcut to return her crew to Earth with speed and safety. Her older self — Admiral Janeway — returns in time to change Voyager's history and offer advice to the younger Captain. However, the crew are confronted once more with a decision that will either help themselves or serve the greater good. The older Janeway argues for self-interest. The younger Captain once more affirms the need for social justice: in this case, destroying a centre of Borg power. With the Admiral sacrificing herself for a better, different future, the Captain and crew of Voyager return home with the help of the older Janeway's strategy, but are safeguarded by the younger Janeway's principles.[36]

It is not surprising that journalists and cultural theorists rarely acknowledge this degree of complexity. Instead, Janeway has been described using the only accustomed mode of feminine power: 'the ship's matriarch … keep[ing] together her eclectic "family" against the odds'.[37] This description is following a soap opera narrative rather than creating alternative modes of authority. Kate Mulgrew made clear the difficulties in establishing and maintaining a position of authority not only as a Starfleet Captain, but in handling Twentieth Century Fox executives:

> It took me a long time to get my sea legs, because of all the pressure that I felt I was under: Can I get this command thing to the point where everybody will be satisfied and comfortable? You've no idea the scrutiny I was under. I had suits just staring at me every day — can she deliver? Does she have any natural authority? I spent the first two seasons establishing command, and I think I sacrificed what is very becoming to me as a person, and as an actress, which is my humour, my humanity, my levity, my depth.[38]

With unbelievable candour, Mulgrew believed that she had to sacrifice her humanity to claim authority. Her forty-something age is also framed as marking her distinct from 'Hollywood's predictable and tired portrayal of young, unnaturally beautiful and spineless women'.[39] Her appearance — her beauty — is undermined and she becomes only 'a woman of intellect and determination'.[40] If a woman is smart, then she must be drained of emotion, passion and body. We must stop assessing women's success in cost–benefit terms: winning a career but losing a husband, exhibiting intelligence but paying for it with the charge card of beauty. Women's realities must be re-languaged.

A characteristic of a leader is the treatment of hurdles as ongoing challenges. Women must persevere, with frequently little feedback or acknowledgment. With few role models or mentors, female networks are decentred by organisational structures. Women are riding through a difficult few years. Popular culture is a relatively positive force, but only to a degree. Jane Tennison, for example, the 'Prime Suspect' crime-solver, is a powerful female leader. But the costs of her promotion are great. She is successful, but eats alone on TV dinners accompanied by a whisky chaser. In the shift from liberation to leadership, the imperative of activism remains. To be admired as beautiful is to be dependent on the beholder. To be marked as an intelligent woman is condescending, a contradiction rather than a tautology. Only by granting women space to reconfigure and reconnect the body and mind may a new face of femininity be exposed.

Perhaps more worryingly, one of the 'Star Trek' creators, Rick Berman, was fearful of a woman in leadership losing her femininity. The conservatism of his attitude is disturbing:

> The problem with a female captain obviously is that you're always balancing … you don't want to turn this woman into a man. You don't want to make it a man's role that you happen to have a female actor playing. You don't want to take away her feminine qualities. You don't want to take away her nurturing and emotional qualities.[41]

This producer, even though rightly claiming credit for 'The Next

Generation', should not have been let near a female starship Captain. The traditional, binarised thinking may be useful in casting an earth mother, but not a scientist in Starfleet. As Stephen Poe claimed, all the creators of 'Star Trek' have thirty years of experience with male starship Captains, but none with women in the same role.[42] Therefore, women occupying public, televisual space in a position of leadership tested the truths of the audience. At times, this power may create a crisis of cultural authority. Charting the familiar terrain of mother and Amazon, it was Mulgrew's performance that granted the programme texture, particularly in the first season. She was able to monitor excessive emotions, be aggressive, but offer an affective path into the material. Her femininity, which was meant to be a weakness, has been a great strength. This is exhibited by her handling of a recurrent Trek enemy. Q's relationship with the Captain was highly gendered. He transported himself into her bedroom and addressed her as Kathy and Madame Captain:

Q:	To us.
Janeway:	There is no us, Q.
Q:	The night is young and the sheets are satin.
Janeway:	I want you out, but first — get rid of this bed.
Q:	Oh, Kathy, don't be such a prude. You have to admit, it's been a while.
Janeway:	And it's going to be a while longer.[43]

This is one of the few occasions in the Trek discourse where sex becomes a site of humour. The episode from which it is taken, 'Q and the Grey', features a seduction between an omnipotent being wishing to have a child with Janeway. Yet discussions about size, responsibility, jealousy and courtship are rendered nodes of bright and bold repartee, not seen in any of the other Trek series. Janeway was able to perform power and control through words, not by firing phasers or the threat of violence. Janeway rarely lugged around guns. She did not use her physicality like Buffy, Xena, Charlie's Angels or the Bionic Woman. This makes Janeway's aura of toughness even more significant. As Sherrie Inness has demonstrated:

> ... studying Janeway, the first woman captain featured on a *Star Trek* show, can reveal a great deal about the increased acceptance of non-traditional tough women in the media and the persistent cultural fears about such women.[44]

A woman in power is an easy target for demonising detractors. Through attacking her voice, clothes, hair, attitude or private life, she may be demeaned or discredited.

It took Captain Janeway one season to establish her leadership, ascendancy and popularity. Even more than Kirk, who always shared the light with Spock, Janeway became the character most associated with the show. This visual dominance only ended when Seven of Nine (and her lycra catsuit) entered the series. While Janeway maintained a maternal relationship with a young female traveller on the ship, Kes, Seven of Nine was never the suppliant follower of the Captain.[45] Instead, a *My Fair Lady* relationship was established between the holographic Doctor and Seven.[46] However, through the sorties, fights and confusion, Seven claimed Janeway as the most significant role model of her life.[47]

It took time, but Janeway did naturalise leadership for women and change the principles and practices of Kirk and Picard. She also granted the show distinction in a stable of great male leaders. Janeway changed television. When 'Voyager' commenced, there were no female leads in prime-time, hour-long action adventures.[48] She was successful, but as Poe confirmed, she could possess all the attributes of leadership and authority and 'we will always be able to nit-pick her hair'.[49]

I SENSE MUCH ANGER

It is in the realm of women and feminism that 'Star Trek' has been a major political disappointment. The character of Councillor Deanna Troi, from 'The Next Generation', is Pop Psychology 101. As an empath from the planet Betazoid, she is a walking panopticon. The consequences of her presence are vast. As Richards grasped, 'there is ultimately no privacy on the Enterprise … through the offices of Counsellor Troi, Starfleet is always eavesdropping on the lives of its characters'.[50] Advising the Captain on mind matters, Troi is granted less status than Data, Crusher, La Forge and Riker, who are information givers. It is as if every episode of 'The Next Generation' has been co-written by Antonio Gramsci. It remains hegemony central. Or, stated another way, it was feminine peripheral.[51]

Troi is the embodiment of the ambivalent and contradictory relationship between 'Star Trek' and feminism. 'The Next Generation' ran for seven years and 178 hours of television. The producers had plenty of opportunity to stretch and test the limits of masculinity and femininity. Yet the 'measure of a man'[52] was a continual motif, visualised through the actions of Commander Data and the maturation of Wesley Crusher. They questioned and (conservatively) revealed some of the issues active in the public domain at the time. 'The Next Generation' presented the issues dividing feminism throughout the 1980s, best embodied by 'The Child', an episode in which Troi was 'raped'[53] and carries an alien baby to term. Confronted with her crew's desire that she abort the foetus, she continues the pregnancy. The birth was a beautiful and painless experience. She did not even smear her mascara.

The crew of the enterprise aided this working mother with childcare, a supportive boss and 24-hour medical facilities. Troi remains as Roberts has framed her: 'the most obvious and consistent symbol of the feminine on the show'.[54] With all credit to Marina Sirtis, who played Troi, she grasped every opportunity presented to her and fought for more through the press:

> Ever since Denise Crosby — [who played Tasha Yar] left the show the two women that are left are both doctors in the caring professions. You don't see women in the power positions. You do see female admirals, but I have to say the fans don't really care about our guest stars. They care about the regulars and what they want to see are the regular women having more power.[55]

She knew her character was the most underdeveloped of the regular cast members and she claimed this as a feminist issue. Once more, at a point of professional disempowerment, a woman was able to use popular culture to renegotiate her social position.[56]

The atomisation of female power results in older women not being acknowledged for their wisdom and experience. Dr Crusher was replaced by another female, Dr Pulaski, who was far more in the McCoy mould[57] — argumentative, irascible and fickle, but ruthlessly honest. She commented on everything, had a fondness for the bar and played a strong poker hand. At times, her character screamed out for a large Churchillian cigar. Yet the conflicts between the male Captain and a stroppy female doctor only lasted a season. The debates between Kirk and Bones were maintained for thirty years, becoming one of the most enduring male friendships on the screen. Such a critical dialogue could not be maintained between men and women. The traditional modes of working have therefore disenfranchised the strong, difficult women. There is a need for new power tools. While men continue to possess a greater network of managing positions and are only familiar with verbal styles like their own, women will be decentred from leadership positions.

Although theorists adore 'The Next Generation' and there is no question of its quality and scripting, it is important to note that the two female characters that challenged the masculine discourse — Yar and Pulaski — were removed after one season. The series featured a reconciliation between The Federation and Klingon Empire, one-time cold war enemies. A cyborg officer provided an innovative site to fathom human subjectivity. New ways emerged for thinking about technology, science, militarism and colonialism. The woman question was unaddressed.

Leadership is attainable by all women. It is not defined by position. Still, women are rewarded for feminine behaviour: being supportive, submissive and needy. This is why it is so easy for us to be shut out of power and shunted away from leadership. Women have been encouraged to slot into male structures, having to aim lower through expectations of subservience and submission. The people are not the problem. The process is the problem.

CAPTAIN'S PERSONAL LOG, STARDATE 8012.8

I have just survived a nasty day. This week's tutorial topic — feminism through the twentieth century — has produced the most disturbing comments I have ever confronted while teaching. Women in power were described by a young white man as 'chicks wanting dicks'. University education for women was seen by another man as a waste of time as 'they will just go and get pregnant'. I thought such statements were the stuff of 1970s consciousness-raising. That such maxims could emerge now, with a female lecturer in the room and surrounded by female peers, is remarkable.

The female students remained silent. While men were delivering the most caustic of comments, the young women were quiet. None of the twenty students in the tutorial described themselves as feminists. Not one. And yet this lack of commitment resulted in an acceptance of sexism in its most ruthless and raw of forms. They simply remarked that 'we' no longer needed feminism. *Those* feminists were ugly, hairy and irrelevant. I refuse to protect the interests of quiescent female students. I am not their white knight. But I am frightened what will happen to them in the workplace.

Interspersing these Monday tutorials was a series of meetings at my university. I kept on walking into rooms of men twenty-five years older than me. I frequently attended meetings as the only woman in the room. My words sank through the floor like stale air. I wondered if my students would ever be in this position. Would they ever understand how profoundly difficult it is for women to occupy a position of authority? Express too much emotion and be labelled hysterical. Express too little emotion and become a heartless bitch. Comment on the issues and we take over the meeting. Avoid commenting on the issues and we demonstrate our lack of knowledge and attention to detail. I hope this situation becomes easier for my students.

When a man says no it is the end of a conversation. When a woman says no it is the start of a negotiation. Perhaps what makes Janeway such a strong leader is that she lives and speaks in the present, finding a way forward in the worst situations.

THIS IS FANTASY

During *Star Trek III: The Search for Spock*, Uhura confronted a man undermining her life and experience as an older woman. He asked her if she had her lost mind. She replied, 'this is not reality. This is fantasy'. She then pulled out a phaser and locked him in a closet.[58]

Women are rewarded for being quiet and are, correspondingly, placed in support positions. Working hard will not ensure success. Good politics does not lead to promotion. Only an attention to leadership allows women to set an agenda. Janeway is an example of what a successful woman can be. She is not satisfied in a feminine work ghetto of health, education or retail. With confidence and a clear sense of purpose, she has integrity, but grasps the context and consequences of her decisions.

It has taken thirty years of 'Star Trek' programmes to finally focus on the issue of women in leadership. The irony is that through the show's run, it is the female fans that have been the most dedicated and visible. They have kept the series alive commercially and televisually. They have often been disappointed with 'Star Trek' and have expressed this dissatisfaction with its gendered nature:[59]

> Please try not to carry our 20th century prejudices into the 24th century. Although there's been male crew members of all shapes and sizes, all the females seem to conform to the current ideal: tall, thin, beautiful, and under 30. I think it would be much more realistic to include women who represent a broader segment of the average human population ... Remember IDIC [Infinite Diversity in Infinite Combinations] and Live Long and Prosper.[60]

Feminists, as dedicated daughters of Frankenstein rather than the bride of the monster, continue to enjoy and use science fiction. The generic framework, which suspends disbelief, offers an imagining space that agitates gendered, raced or classed truths.

Science fiction offers alternative ways of thinking. While there are both utopic and dystopic inscriptions of technology and science, the genre shows that many of our social discourses of medicine and law still remain potent. When a seductive female robot walked from the platform in Fritz Lang's *Metropolis*, it was obvious that while the future may be female, theories of the future will need some feminism. Gerda Lerner reminded us that 'any movement that cannot be sustained for fifty or a hundred years is not likely to accomplish its goal'.[61] Science fiction, as a way of thinking about the future, shows that feminism will be both relevant and necessary far beyond Lerner's timetable. Captain Janeway captures a chance to move from revolution to revelation, from identity politics to leadership. She unpicked the frock of feminism and restitched it in a new style. 'Voyager' is so pedagogic and useful because it is messy. Characters make mistakes, they argue, they toss around the limits of power. Feminist popular culture must be fought for and contested. It is not only an issue of representation, but of the ways institutional structures either reveal or stifle women's voices. From the beginning, 'Star Trek' presented an integrated cast. This has been the basis of all the cultural productions. It offers a multicultural utopia and a critique of xenophobia. It shows the best and worse of science fiction's capacity to be a tool for thinking about the future. Offering both vision and a social impetus, it is entertainment with an agenda.

There remains a nostalgia for the 'Original Series' and 'The Next Generation'. Their simpler, clearer, patriarchal voyages have much support. 'Deep Space Nine' and 'Voyager' show that all organisations have a history. Trek has moved from small to big screen, old media to new media, print magazines to costuming and art. Theorists have become more critical with each instalment in the Trek stable. Bernardi, for example, stated that 'I enjoy most of the films and all four television series, even *Voyager*'.[62] The use of 'even' is useful here. *Even* a programme with a female Captain can be pleasant. By persisting with narrativising difference, socially-just communication is formed. Nichelle Nichols may have possessed a minor role in the 'Original Series', but she was later hired by NASA to recruit minorities and women into the space programme.[63] While we may view her as Starfleet's receptionist, she was much more. She was an aura of our future. Involved with words, languages, translations and linguistics, she showed that communication would be the crucial skill of the future. She opened the hailing frequencies. Thirty years later, Janeway could use them.

SYLVIA TEACHES

No other job in the world could possibly dispossess one so completely as this job of teaching. You could stand all day in a laundry, for instance, still in possession of your mind. But this teaching utterly obliterates you. It cuts right into your being; essentially, it takes over your spirit. It drags it out from where it would hide.[1]

Sylvia Ashton-Warner

One of the most innovative, creative television commercials I have ever seen is for a soft drink. Not for Coke or Pepsi, Sprite or even Fanta; this soft drink is derived from a little company, from a slightly larger country, and advertises a product that cannot be bought anywhere else in the world. The L & P (Lemon and Paeroa) commercial features the 'highlights' of Paeroa, the Kiwi town that forms part of the product's name. Residents, filled to the gills with irony and humour, affirm that their home is not known for its big game fishing, cuisine, rugby, yacht club or royal family. Instead, Paeroa has something better, and 'we *are* famous'. It is the home of a soft drink. This feat alone makes the residents of the town 'World Famous in New Zealand'. This slogan has always represented the best and worst of the nation. It is quirky, self-reflexive and funny. It is also self-absorbed, insular and backward.

Sylvia Ashton-Warner is world famous outside New Zealand. She was born in Stratford in 1908 and died in Tauranga in 1984. Living most of her life in the most Antipodean of nations, she became renowned for her teaching of the Maori, but hateful of the context that triggered this work. Her unprecedented fame in the United States has built a legacy, a bequest with little understanding of the specificity of colonialism or the dual histories of Aotearoa/New Zealand. While the myth of her teaching is saturating, the actual impact of her classroom strategies remains more ambiguous and blighted. Quite appropriately, there is a convoluted intertwining of her fiction and non-fiction.[2] She moulded her life imaginatively and reconstituted her life creatively. Self-absorbed, she created a teaching method that demonstrated individual care and respect for each child. Therefore, biographers and critics have a fascinating task: piecing together a life of profound internal contradictions, of shadow-boxing intellectual phantoms and an anti-establishment bias even within a supportive governmental institution. Lynley Hood best captured this disjunction:

> The potency of her ideas, and her astonishing power to polarise her audience, lives on beyond death. At the mention of her name, down-to-earth people turn misty-eyed with adoration, and mild-mannered individuals explode into rage. What is the secret of her impact? What life-force enables her to move people so?[3]

Ashton-Warner was a mediocre teacher, but a profound theorist of teaching. This chapter unravels the form of this paradox, while also discussing the role, place and importance of women in teaching. Through this practice, these tough women change the world one student at a time. These everyday victories of reading, writing and social justice are rarely valued or awarded. My study of difficult women would be incomplete without attention to this female-dominated profession.[4] Women in classrooms through the nineteenth and twentieth centuries managed complex changes to notions of literacy, numeracy, race and gender. These difficult women rarely left records of their lives, or a trace of their ethics or moral choices. If Australian and New Zealand citizens are to address their colonial legacy, or critique ageism or sexism, then the building blocks of this reconciliation will be undertaken by women with chalk dust in their nails, overhead pens staining their wrists and a gaze aimed at a better future.

One of the most important lessons of life is that teachers are everywhere and they arrive precisely when we need them. Sometimes these teachers speak with anger or hostility. Frequently, the most innovative of educators threaten the foundational truths of society. Schools are institutions different from any other in society. During the time of Ashton-Warner's teaching, they were places of children and spinsters: two groups who are rarely brought together.[5] A teacher's function can vary from mentor and model to counsellor, manager, resource or judge. Similarly, students' responses are cut with compliance and resistance.

Teaching is difficult to write about. It must not be assumed — for one moment — that a good teacher is a person who merely applies the methodologies taught in universities. Basic principles rendered acceptable by American publishers must be translated, reframed and reordered for the remainder of the world. Ironically, those same American publishers take the intellectual fodder derived from the rest of the planet and assume that it will work in their schools. Ashton-Warner exhibited this intellectual colonisation at its best. After publishing her books outside of New Zealand and inflecting abuse and ridicule at her home nation, she was asked late in life to teach in Colorado.

MEN DREAM WHILE WOMEN CLEAN

My dreams are too heavy.[6]

Sylvia-Ashton Warner

Ashton-Warner played the role of wife and mother, but never quite managed the part. Not surprisingly, her books and personal correspondence show that she was drawn to spinsters. In New Zealand, as in Australia, generations of boys and girls have been taught by committed single women who dedicate their lives to teaching:

> These saintly maiden ladies that detective story writers make up in books ... these unmarried free untrammelled people whose lives belong to no man and who dedicate themselves to their work.[7]

While viewing — and living — the treatment of married women, Ashton-Warner perceived that spinsters, although viewed as objects of misfortune, were actually granted a freedom not permissible to a 'Mrs'. Ashton-Warner's mother had been the primary breadwinner throughout her life, as she had married a 'gentleman' who could not, and would not, work. Sylvia Ashton-Warner, on the other hand, wedded a man prepared to work conscientiously. Keith Henderson was a highly respected teacher and headmaster who spent much of his life apologising for his wife. She demonstrated a highly erratic attendance in the classroom, very little curriculum development or lesson planning[8] and by 1950 was exhibiting erratic alcohol consumption. Ashton-Warner was unable to manage the ruthless discipline and attention to detail that is necessary to teach consistently and well:

> We had our grading this week. The men were well marked, Tom and K., but as usual I was very low. There's no doubt about it. I am a very low-ability teacher. My sister Daphne says on this matter that it would be a disgrace for a woman in my position to be a good teacher. As for myself, maybe it is a distinction of some kind to be unacceptable in New Zealand teaching. I walk alone, like Edmund Burke. We are 'rogues', the term critics give to people they can't classify. That's the alternative assumption. I use both.[9]

Ashton-Warner presented this statement on page 99 of her book, after detailing to her reading public a scheme of such freshness and innovation that all readers run symbolically to her rescue. Obviously, she was not a low-ability teacher. Perhaps that was her greatest problem. She had enormous ability, but little skill in applying her ideas. After all, writing about teaching is safe. Actually having to stand up in a class and persistently activate a pedagogic scheme takes courage. While she stated that 'when I teach people I marry them',[10] her cycles of poor attendance, resignations and moving meant that she was never committed long-term. Ashton-Warner continued to work and teach because of her husband's shielding professionalism. Her record with the New Zealand educational authorities was poor. She possessed grander, more encompassing plans about literacy, race and nation. However, Ashton-Warner was unable to temper her creativity with attention to the classroom. She continued to perform the role of the surrendering wife with much aplomb:

> I am his wife and to be a worthwhile wife I need successful expression. Everything is for him: the happiness of the children, the smooth running of the home, and it is for his sake that I have so severely reorganised my program.[11]

Playing the self-sacrificing artist suited her narrative of femininity. Ashton-Warner was unable to construct a more complex model of being a woman, wife, mother and teacher. She asked of her reader:

> Do you … aim to be a worthwhile person or only a worthwhile teacher? How do you see teaching — as a source of income or as a work of global status?[12]

This statement demonstrates an inability to fashion work and social justice, income and credibility, in an innovative and integrated way. To be an independent spirit, she needed to be institutionally harangued and socially chastised for an inability to manage a family home.

The school ma'am on the colonial frontier has been a stock character of literature and film in Australia and the United States. She is an ideal foil for the ill-mannered, uncivilised hero. In American literature and film, the spinster from the East — generally Boston — has some stock attributes. Polly Welts Kaufman shows that:

> … her genteel poverty, unbending morality, education, and independent ways make her character a useful foil for the two other female stock characters in Western literature: the prostitute with the heart of gold and the long-suffering farmer's wife.[13]

'Woman teacher' is a burdened phrase. It occupies a space alongside conventional feminine disempowerment in the workforce. Teaching is feminised, with gendered occupational structures excluding women from principal positions. It is difficult to reclaim these quiet, isolated lives. The role of education in the women's movement is to enact a dialogue of ideas and activism. A feminist pedagogy not only produces knowledge, but actually ponders the mechanism for producing subjectivity. As Adriana Hernandez has argued:

> ... this means to empower students not only in order to understand their positions, experiences, stories, and voices within the complexity of society, but also to be able to produce alternate responses that escape binary oppositions and contribute to the development of communities of solidarity.[14]

Ensuring social justice in education is not only a question of inclusive language. It is a teacher's responsibility to use the position of power so that a person or group is not systematically excluded. Further, there is a need to dislodge mainstream truths. There is little suggestion that Ashton-Warner critiqued or undermined gendered normalities in her classrooms. The focus on race meant that gender-based discussions were often decentred. Perhaps this is no surprise. Her life presents a highly conventional feminine pattern, through marriage, children and the teaching of infants.

The reason that the Hendersons taught in Maori schools, during a period when the interior of Aotearoa/New Zealand was being 'opened up', was not derived from a missionary zeal or a desire by Pakeha to understand their Maori Treaty Partners.[15] Instead, Maori schools were the only institutions where husbands and wives could teach together. A sense of paternalism did saturate her decision to teach in an indigenous setting. As Hood determined: 'How much brighter her talents would shine as a teacher among Maori, than a housewife among housewives'.[16] Such an attitude is not a surprise. Ashton-Warner was living and working in an era where British cultural values reigned supreme. The educational system was geared to the teaching of English. To introduce Maori elements into the curriculum was seen as obstructionary and contradictory. Within this new context, Ashton-Warner became a fluent Maori speaker and through such linguistic insight was able to instigate her most famous innovation: the Key Vocabulary.

THE TEACHING OUTLAW

In an explosion of understanding Sylvia both lost and found herself
in the inner lives of Maori children.[17]

Lynley Hood

Sylvia Ashton-Warner was focussed on communication and the mobilisation of mixed media. She took conventional British teaching strategies and moulded them for the needs of Maori children. She framed teaching and learning as a mutual process through which to activate lasting social change. Her infant reading texts are superb for their time. Not surprisingly, they remain heavily gendered: girls read about babies and houses, boys about trucks. She enacted disability inclusiveness, forty years before the disability movement gained visibility. When Koro, a disabled boy, arrived in her Waiomatatini classroom, he became the focus of the books. Similarly, she activated an open door policy: the community was involved in her teaching, with mothers allowed to hear children's reading.

Ashton-Warner's attention to Maori specificity was profoundly important. She stated that 'it is indispensable in conducting a young child from one culture to another, especially in New Zealand where the Maori is obliged to make the transition at so tender an age; but actually it is universal'.[18] She showed that 'organic reading' of a 'Key Vocabulary' was not a new system, but simply undermined because of the rigid colonial educational system. Because of her centred sense of self, the faith in her own creativity, Ashton-Warner was the focus of her system, rather than the books, cards, music and toys that were used. Singh has stated that Ashton-Warner 'believed that authority should be accorded to teachers rather than materials in recognition of the former's superior knowledge of the literacy process'.[19] Yet this confidence needs to be pondered more closely. Teachers must not be allowed to work alone, untempered by discussions of responsibility. Classrooms, while frequently reinforcing the status quo, must also prepare students to enter a racist, sexist society. Students must learn life skills necessary to challenge these inequalities. If a teacher is simply allowed to instigate her or his own system, then abuses may take place.

Ashton-Warner's sense of being an outsider — and working in outsider classrooms — obviously provided an impetus for change. There is something profound about the consequences of her recognition that Maori were not making effective transitions between indigenous and Pakeha life. To argue that the Maori vocabulary, life and experience were not being valued through the educational system was a politically courageous stance. Through the staffing problems and limited resources of these Maori schools, Ashton-Warner attempted to link indigenous families with the school system. This is still a radical notion, as 'the school assumes middle-class culture, attitudes and values in all its pupils'.[20] The aim is to reduce the gulf between home and classroom. This separation is even more pronounced if a linguistic difference accompanies the social and economic divide. Ashton-Warner became focussed on translation and transition, which she saw as 'a plank in the bridge from Maori to the European'.[21] The way to think about education is to ask not only what is happening in the school and what is occurring outside its walls, but how they connect. The effective temperament of that link is forged by both teachers and parents.

Education and training, from the earliest socialisation in the home through to doctoral level at university, cannot overcome multi-nodal societal inequalities. Physical capacity, gender and indigeneity are only a few markers of identity that are problematically poured into the baking dish of education. The classroom is not a societal panacea. Neither are these venues confessional boxes that permit uncritical platitudes or the expulsion of past guilt. While human development is frequently portrayed as a linear story, there are diverse narratives and trajectories unmarked within the normality and deviance models of psychology. Educational strategies that aim to be anti-racist also need to be radical and controversial. Particularly in former colonies like Australia and New Zealand, the calm surfaces of social binaries, like black/white, female/male, need to be inverted before they can be critiqued.

The ideological foundation of Ashton-Warner's ideas still survives in New Zealand. Iri Tawhiwhirangi, who was a student-teacher in her classroom, became an architect of Te Kohanga Reo:[22]

> My input into Kohanga Reo was designed very much on her method of teaching — it was concerned with the creation of a learning environment, and not just a teaching environment.[23]

This pupil-oriented approach was the trigger of the Key Vocabulary. Ashton-Warner's moment of luminous realisation was that different words for each child are contextually important. Therefore, to impose a single standard of literacy is short-sighted. With words organically tied to life, each student learns key personal vocabularies. Ashton-Warner did not frame these words as a replacement for the British curriculum, but as a way for indigenous children to enter it. This was a moment of creative radiance, a radical transformation of teaching from intellectual colonialism to a dialogue of learning. The melding of drama, dance, words, music and art is the ideal classroom environment, but one that was politically undermined in her era, and ours.

Sylvia Ashton-Warner clearly connected language and power. She showed how different speech communities use language in different ways, frequently working against institutional models of breaking up reality into discrete concepts. Some social groups cope more easily with the language of education than others. Education and teaching change radically through the recognition that communication is not about getting a message across, but considering how and why events and ideas gain meaning.[24] Literacy is a double-edged sword, wielded for the purpose of self and social empowerment, or for the purposes of repression and domination. Too often in the United States and Australia, the language of literacy is affiliated with a right-wing discourse, linking language with the economy. In the current political environment, the discussion of literacy represents a retreat from emancipatory politics, a retraction to reading, writing and arithmetic. Literacy theory, when inflected by cultural studies, provides those framed as different in the educational system — via race, gender, disability, age or class — with reading and writing skills to grant them a critical, empowered function. In this framework, literacy is never in deficit but is enmeshed in cultural capital. Therefore, a cultural policy of literacy and pedagogy is pivotal to those who are rendered silent or marginalised in the educational discourse. Young men and women have not only a right to read, but a responsibility to understand and transform their own experience, thereby constituting a beneficial relationship with their wider society.

For schools to address disadvantaged groups and ethnic minorities, both teaching styles and curriculum content must change. Promoting democracy in a classroom means disrupting business as usual. This is a particular challenge considering that schools are implicated in the reproduction of social inequalities. Sylvia Ashton-Warner was focussed on the development of excluded students and learnt their home language. She divided the school day into output and input sessions, with the Key Vocabulary generated in the output period of the morning. She ensured that these young students were not passive consumers of uniform knowledges. Instead, she marked the substantive differences between Maori and Pakeha children. As Singh has suggested, 'Ashton-Warner saw her pupils as active participants in the revitalisation, transformation and reproduction of their culture'.[25] Ashton-Warner suffered the wrath of School Inspectors not only because of her unreliability, but because she stressed a model of knowledge and language demeaned through the colonial process. Mass-produced reading schemes could never critique or problematise the hegemonic normalities of the social order. Yet it is not only indigenous students who must be prepared for a bicultural New Zealand; the curriculum must also change for middle-class Pakeha. Without this dialogue, the disempowered — who are educated within a discredited knowledge system — are further disempowered. Choices are not freely distributed. While there has been an increasing push to teach all New Zealand children the Maori language, a shortage of Maori language teachers makes it difficult to activate such a plan without governmental support. Pakeha learning some Maori phrases is not enough. Structural, systematic change must be activated.[26]

The Key Vocabulary was a moment of intellectual lightning that arrived as teaching and learning were being restructured in line with the post-war economy. While international education was morphing, New Zealand was not shifting quickly enough to satisfy Ashton-Warner's sense of creativity and change. Her book *Teacher* was a conflictual infusion of fact and fiction. She re-imagined her treatment by New Zealand School Inspectors and New Zealand publishers to build the narrative of her righteous fight against the establishment. For

American teachers being trained through the 1960s, her method seemed an ideal way to change the world. Her narrative of disquiet seemed to — and still seems to — activate an emotional resonance in teachers who feel cheated or un(der)appreciated by 'the system'. Her bitterness was an integral way to build her fame:

> I have been trying to get this Creative Teaching Scheme published in my country for seven eventful years. I kept it here these seven years, trying, hoping, waiting, crippled with family loyalty. I stubbornly wanted it to come out in my own country in my own lifetime ... not after ... Take what you want from life, but pay for it in blood. I took what I wanted and paid.[27]

Reading her anger still flares an anti-authority imperative. The Antipodean puritanism also sparks the polarisation of gender differences. While she affirmed humane and creative schooling — a motherhood statement in our current era — Ashton-Warner did not maintain an attendance at work that actually allowed the organic vocabulary to be facilitated. Therefore, the odd nature of New Zealand nationalism — formed through the ambivalent end to British colonialism — has been activated against the teacher. This janus-like reading of the world peppers much of New Zealand culture. As Finlay MacDonald explained:

> Fear and self-loathing: media constructs or a genuine national neurosis? Hard to say, but the willingness ... to put the slipper into ourselves whenever things went against us was deeply unattractive and probably unhealthy. It was the flipside of our similarly unlovely tendency to lose perspective and gloat when we win. Either way, it is the callow self-absorption of the culturally adolescent and not to be tolerated or encouraged.[28]

Ashton-Warner is part of this schizophrenic fixation on national identity. Although the New Zealand context forged her system, she believed that educational institutions also discredited her advances. Her use of the word 'organic' is significant, detailing the interaction of observation, critique and testing. The results of such a scheme would always be difficult to chart or measure. School Inspectors, fellow teachers and students therefore possess volatile memories of her work as an educator. The respect for her teaching came from a distance.

PROFESSIONAL BLACK EYE

I've hated New Zealand so much ... I still hate it and I suppose I always will.[29]

Sylvia Ashton-Warner

Part of the excitement and tragedy of teaching excellence is that it is of the moment. Once the hour has ended, the overhead is turned off and the staff and students have dispersed, the teaching experience dissipates. The best teachers, while enacting life changes, are decentred or forgotten. While Ashton-Warner's teaching guides, notes and experiences are lost, the novels and non-fictional works 'record' her practices. These documents have survived, thrived and forged her reputation.

Her fame in the United States was building, so when her husband died in early 1969 she left New Zealand within three months, promising never to return. She was hired as the infants' teacher for the Aspen Community School in 1970. The experience was a complete failure. Hood stated — bluntly — that 'as a working teacher Sylvia had lacked the commitment, and the administrative and interpersonal skills, to run an established school in her own country'.[30] Yet the Aspen Board was not hiring a real teacher: they were employing a myth. It is horrifying to transform the gleaming façade of myth into the sagging flesh of reality.

Once more though, Ashton-Warner, as educational theorist, rewrote and re-imagined her actual teaching in *Spearpoint*, which conveyed her interpretation of the Aspen experience. The great irony, considering her anti-authoritarian stance throughout her life, is the level of profound conservatism of this book: 'Authority, equality, freedom. Yet someone did use the word 'Responsible' one day'.[31] By this stage, Ashton-Warner was seventy-two years old and resentful of the creative freedom granted to teachers at the time, a freedom that she had craved twenty years earlier. She was anti-technological change, nostalgic and rigidly attempted to impose her New Zealand methods on a very different time and place. When actually teaching in the United States, she was a major disappointment to both her colleagues and the school board.

Ashton-Warner was a fine writer and a superb novelist of the teaching experience. Her results as a teacher were more debatable. The florid prose romanticised teaching. She built a conspiracy of the New Zealand educational establishment against her work. This narrative has been replayed and restated by others as fact:

> I've been fascinated by this book [*Teacher*], and its author, ever since a friend lent it to me during my university days. Sylvia Ashton-Warner was a New Zealander whose contradictory and tortured private life somehow didn't prevent her from being an incredible and inspiring teacher and author … She invited both adoration and loathing for her refusal to play by the established (often totally unsuitable) educational rules, instead determinedly developing her own methods.[32]

Certainly she created remarkable methods, particularly for the teaching of very young children. Ironically for a woman who never constructed detailed educational methods, she has become the basis of numerous classes on pedagogy and lesson planning. Julia Brady Ratliff has restated the myth and applied it to her Internet-based learning site:

> Sylvia Ashton-Warner, a teacher in New Zealand, wrote a book about the thing she knew best. The book is called *Teacher*. It has inspired me always. In lesson 28, I said that we all learn the unknown from the well known. In *Teacher*, Mrs. Warner said that a child's first reading vocabulary should come individually.[33]

This is the basis of the organic vocabulary. Words should come from the child, not from the teacher. This general anti-planning principle is now structured in a lesson plan and placed on the Internet for a global audience (of Americans). The creativity and play of Ashton-Warner has been structured, encoded and uploaded.

FAST-FORWARD FEMINISM

Without a doubt, Ashton-Warner moved our mind furniture. Many women affirm that she has inspired and changed their lives. Margaret Whalen made the fascinating judgment that:

> Expert teachers of young children know that teaching can get in the way of learning — one of the best writings to make this point is a book called SPINSTER — by SYLVIA ASHTON-WARNER originally published by Simon & Schuster. Ashton Warner was an expert teacher.[34]

As a young teacher, there is a desperate need to arch beyond stressful daily demands of worksheets, photocopying, rolls and parent consultations to enhance the nature of educational life. There is always a desire for resources that open out the possibilities of alternative strategies for managing an intellectual life. Ashton-Warner's work is suited to that task.

While reflexive education has become a cliché of teaching courses, it refers to a very basic process. Educators need to make sense of their experience, learn from difficulties or errors, to ensure that the problem does not resurface. In this way, information can be transformed into knowledge and finally into wisdom. While much critical thinking is based on ontological distinctions between the reality of teaching and the socially constructed value of education, there also needs to be a space to explore the technical, social and economic elements of teaching. By forming practice-centred theorising, teachers are not battered by impossibly high idealism, drained of the contextual reality by an educational system in which they are placed. That is my fear of Ashton-Warner's words. She writes of glorious ideals, deep resistances and wide-ranging systemic change. Most of the teachers reading her words do not enjoy the protection of a headmaster who was also her husband, or a condescending school system with a care/free/less attitude to Maori education. While she has reorganised and reconstructed her experiences, she has not admitted her inability to manage the routine tasks that clog up the creativity and options of other teachers. Carol Philips' easy celebration of her work should breed disquiet:

> Who are better inspirations than other teachers? We are lucky that teachers who have gone before us, as well as some who still teach now, have recorded their struggles and success. Choose a classic like Sylvia Ashton-Warner's *Teacher*.[35]

Teaching is difficult work. It is ruthlessly corrosive of innovation. Women in particular, without the benefits of seniority or leadership, are left with the routine tasks that dominate life in isolated classrooms. The great Oxford scholar of letters CS Lewis, for example, believed that his teaching task involved inculcating 'the peaceful pleasures of reading and thinking'.[36] Of course, only those who have been advantaged by the system see no reason to change it. Educational development is a historical and social formation. Through the white-heat speed of a one-year teaching diploma, there is a rigid need to teach students how to respond to 'normal' and 'deviant' development (with or without the inverted commas). When pondering these departures from the normal, we notice the narrow and constricting nature of education. While categorising development issues into four bands — physical, cognitive, linguistic and aesthetic — the cross-cultural consequences of these demarcations are rarely fully revealed. Categories and labels possess social currency, but are also flick knives into the self. Through the 1970s, there was an integration of abilities in classrooms, as embodied in the 1975 United Nations Declaration of the Rights of the Child. The languages of learning changed. The new imperatives were de-institutionalisation, mainstreaming, integration and normalisation. While the terminology has altered, many of the assumptions remain. When difference is placed into language, it is also embedded into a power structure and controlled.

To activate social justice requires action and intervention. Sylvia Ashton-Warner provided beautiful words, a revolution of the mind. But as Wieck has affirmed, 'we need more than just words — we need consistency in action'.[37] Sylvia Ashton-Warner was a creative woman. Yet to claim her as an icon of teaching undermines the daily struggles of the world's educators, most of whom are women. Like Karl Marx, she was an architect of a revolution, but we need a Lenin to visualise and produce the results. We also need an Engels to pay the bills. Teaching is frequently a conservative practice, often not by design. The pressure of marking, course design, meetings, administrative duties and disciplinary action means that attention to the bigger issues of difference, justice and change must wait until tomorrow, next semester, next year. Ashton-Warner was able to dream of a better world because she did not fulfill the teaching responsibilities of her age. The difficulty is that her books are part of a wider cultural trend that glorifies a particular type of teaching sacrifice: *Mr Holland's Opus*, *Goodbye Mr Chips*, *Stand and Deliver*, *Dead Poets Society* and *To Sir, with love*. These texts tell of struggle and the noble forfeiture of private life. Importantly, these cinematic teachers are not only inspirational, but all men. Ashton-Warner's books are one of the few feminine interventions in the representations of teachers.

Teaching is deeply familiar and taken for granted. Such informal fluency is a social blockage to more complex renderings of the practice. Because of universal education, the efforts of individual teachers become squashed under the boulder of memory. Popular culture fills the gaps in half-remembered childhoods and the empty vessels of teachers. Education is the context for a suite of films and the early seasons of 'Beverley Hills 90210', 'Buffy' and 'Dawson's Creek', while being the fodder of humour in 'Welcome back, Kotter'. The impact of *The Breakfast Club* and *Ferris Bueller's Day Off* serves to render invisible the female teacher from popular culture. Therefore, we require a critical stance to education, an intervention in the consciousness of teachers. All educators, whatever their level, must note that we 'enter a classroom that is already laden with representation, both in their own heads as well as in the heads of their students'.[38] The visions and views of Mr Keating, Mr Thackeray and Mr Escalante have shaped the images of a teacher, reinforcing the highly conservative views of education. The notion that one individual can fight a system, with little economic or social support, is placing high-level demands on the current generation of student-teachers. The masculine nature of these representations, when impressed upon the highly feminine reality of most children's experience of teachers, results in an awkward dance between theory and praxis. Teachers require the right to have an identity, rather than a public sacrifice of their private life. The difficulty with these filmic educators and the books of Ashton-Warner is that teaching becomes 'sudden enlightenment, divine intervention, or the "aha" experience'.[39] The effort, discipline and routine aspects of learning and teaching dissipate.

The aim of this chapter has not only been to connect personal biography with wider historical events. Those interested in a feminist education learn much from Ashton-Warner. She rarely focussed on the nature of being a woman, but rather on the structures of oppression derived from the system in which she was working. To rephrase Virginia Woolf, Ashton-Warner focussed on the view, not the room.

Yet the methods for cutting through the burdens of disadvantage remain debateable. How is a discrimination discerned legally and socially as a discrimination?

If Sylvia Ashton-Warner had been a male professor of education, she would now be lauded as one of the greatest and most innovative theorists of the twentieth century. Instead, she was a married woman and an infants' teacher in Maori schools in New Zealand. She was unable to manage the incredible demands of teaching in the dense, conformist environment of colonial New Zealand. What makes her case so interesting and so unlike the quiet desperations of millions of female teachers is that she re-wrote and re-created her life for publication.

Compare the Ashton-Warner case to that of Professor Bruce Biggs. He began teaching Maori Studies at Auckland University in 1951, suffering enormous condescension from the professors of English, French, Latin and Greek. He, like Ashton-Warner, was trained as a teacher. Biggs and his wife, Joy, taught together in Te Kao, then Wairongomai from 1945 to 1950. However, a friend sent him an advertisement for an Anthropology Lectureship at Auckland University College. He gained the job, as a Pakeha, with an unfinished degree and an interest in the Maori language. The other two candidates, Mat Te Hau and Maharaia Winiata, were not only native speakers, but held Bachelor degrees.

From this opportunity, he attained a Master of Arts and a PhD from the United States. He wrote Maori dictionaries and extended Maori Studies at Auckland to a PhD level. He was never seen as an inspiring lecturer, but was a prolific writer and scholar. He, like Ashton-Warner, disagreed radically with the establishment. He stated that 'My trouble … is that I am congenitally incapable of following a fashion'.[40] Through his foundational work, more Kiwi students study Maori than any European language. Similarly, Maori Studies is one of the booming departments in many of New Zealand's troubled universities. Biggs possessed many similarities with Ashton-Warner, but also differences. He was able to move from secondary schools to tertiary level and also survived mediocre teaching praxis for a brilliant publishing career. Yet Professor Biggs remains unknown outside of New Zealand intellectual and Maori circles. Ashton-Warner, through her real or imagined struggles, became so much more than significant, influential or important. She became famous — world famous *outside* New Zealand.

MAKING IT BIG: JULIE BURCHILL, BITCH POLITICS AND WRITING IN PUBLIC

I am a Thatcherite bitch, I hear, which is middle-class liberal shorthand for a working class girl who has made it … I refuse to lose, I refuse to be anyone's hard-luck story. Coming from where I did, the most rebellious thing I could have done was to make it big. And I did.[1]

Julie Burchill

That woman seems to be everywhere these days — hardening political allegiances with her infuriating contradictions. I even have daydreams of Julie Burchill replacing Greta Garbo and acting out the final scene of *Camille*. You know the bit — gaunt blonde, consumptive cough, waiting to see her lover for the last time so that she may die in his arms. A picturesque ending to a *fin de siecle* melodrama, with the femme fatale only redeemed through death. But in our *fin de siecle*, with Julie Burchill in the lead, Camille becomes a corpulent, raven-haired, level-headed courtesan. The climactic ending would involve Julie informing her lover that he was inadequate and she, in response, was now exploring her 'sapphic side'. So much for dreams.

Burchill is dangerous, particularly in a political climate of self-help and individualism. Burchill's 'pulling herself up by her shoulder pads' attitude provides a living example that the 1980s and 1990s were eras that rewarded the talented. Her political positioning is confusing: radically conservative but working-class, a woman yet misogynistic. Burchill cannot simply be dismissed as a Conservative sympathiser who has 'nothing to say' to the Left, feminism or cultural studies. She writes with clarity and boldness during a time of conviction politics and the betrayal of the welfare state. Burchill has worn many identities: the scribe of English punk, Thatcherite sympathiser, lipsticked feminist and 1990s woman journeying through (and out of) the lesbian continuum. It is her public prose and iconic status that is explored in this chapter.

Some readers may not have heard of Julie Burchill. That lack of knowledge is not surprising, considering her intense Englishness. Burchill is the most famous journalist in Britain. She was born in 1959; at sixteen, she was writing for the *New Musical Express*. She also co-authored a book with her soon-to-be ex-husband Tony Parsons (remember him?) that actually forged the meaning of punk in Britain. Like a safety pin through a garbage bag, *The Book Looked at Johnny* pierced the boundaries of acceptable commentary on cultural phenomena. Burchill enacted every woman's revenge: to become better and so much more successful than her mediocre, bitter ex-husband. Besides suffering a brilliant, articulate ex-wife with an excellent memory, Parsons had other problems:

> Lament for a middle-class wannabe. Late-night on middle-class BBC2 cultural affairs programme, he sits uncomfortably alongside Melvyn Bragg to discuss literature and … football? Mid-week, in a double-page spread in the middle-class Daily Mail/Express he patronisingly mourns the passing of the traditional 'working class.' Early evening on Channel 4's middle class Without Walls programme, he irritatingly does the same with emphasis on his pseudo-cockney, quasi-intellectual delivery. Bi-monthly in a trendy, middle-class lifestyle magazine for men, he churns out uniformly, self-indulgent polemic. Through all of this he struggles to look 'at ease' in the clothes of Giorgio Armani, fashion hero to the middle-classes. And then he has the cheek to ask, 'Who would be middle class?' (Arena 44). Well, you for one Tony Parsons … but do they really deserve you?[2]

Being a Matthew Arnold for the lads, Parsons found his niche in civilising the post-*Face* style-lifers. His ex-wife possesses few of his angst-ridden political views and a capacity to manage living and walking through the cultural landscape without an Armani crutch.

Through the 1980s and 1990s, Burchill moved from *The Face* to *The Mail on Sunday* and *The Guardian*.[3] Although she has written novels set in post-1989 Czechoslovakia and others based in South America, she has never left the United Kingdom. Burchill is an unreconstructed little Englander. More specifically, she remains a London girl.

London is a city of de Certeau's imagining, only gaining meaning by beginning the journey with footsteps. London is simultaneously pluralistic, playful, ironic, schizoid and mockingly solemn. Its spaces can be mapped via the underground stations, sporting facilities or the homeless sleeping in cardboard boxes around Piccadilly Circus. Burchill offered a distinct rendering:

The country was for cows; the country was where you ran away from, or retired to, not where you lived, when you were young and almost beautiful. She loved the city, she needed the city, she belonged to the city ...

And now the city belonged to her.[4]

Burchill has suggested that London is a place of experience, fantasy and community. The city has offered an escape from the country for a group that Burchill described as 'the lost tribe':

I was one of the lost tribe of London; the kids from the sticks who sleep with a map of the Underground over their bed. Notting Hill Gate Holland Park White City — the stations of the cross! I go through the agonising limbo (is that an oxymoron?) of my teenage years by believing that London would belong to me one day. But she doesn't.[5]

From the politicised city of the Greater London Council to Burchill's dreams of the Underground, London's multiplicity has offered an incisive venue for social exploration and political challenges. The Underground remains a powerful metaphor through which to consider the limits and boundaries of Burchill's world.

But before we buy our ticket departing from Euston Station, we need to glance at Burchill's watch. Something, indeed, is very odd with Burchilltime. A protagonist from her 1993 novel *No Exit* made the realisation that he was 'longing for a place which, unlike England, he could never go back to. It was a longing for the easy, sexy, greedy Eighties'.[6] A decade remains an elastic concept. Thatcher's Britain encompassed 11-and-a-half years. The marks and traces of the decade inscribed the bodies that circulated through that time. The 'eighties person' was viewed by Burchill as eternally trapped within the decade of excesses. As she commented in *No Exit*, 'You could take the boy out of the Eighties — but you couldn't take the Eighties out of the boy'.[7] This eighties of the mind, from the perspective of a new century, appears bloated and gaudy and Burchill knows it. By 1999, the main character in her novel *Married Alive* chastened that 'I hate people who are out of control like that — it's so Eighties'.[8] There is something in that craziness and excess that still draws attention. Even in a proto-Republic Australia, Thatcher's vision of England remains tantalising.

Thatcherism was never simply an economic doctrine; it was a mood, a set of values and a way of writing and behaving in public. Thatcher played with twentieth-century history and shamelessly poached ideas, iconography and imaginings. However, like the British Prime Ministers who had preceded her, Thatcher stressed the relationship with the United States and the Commonwealth and did

not recognise the changing world socio-political order; she continued the post-war trend of underestimating Europe's place in Britain's
future. Appropriately then, it was her view on Europe that lead to her
downfall.

Julie Burchill admired Margaret Thatcher. Her respect for the
other Iron Lady gushed through the journalist's prose. As she
remarked in the *Spectator* at the conclusion of the Thatcherite rule in
November 1990:

> But I'll think of Mrs Thatcher and the gory, glorious 1980s,
> whenever I hear the songs of Madonna (her crooning counter-
> part). In many ways, she was the first pop prime minister: her
> impatience, frustration and misfit's will to triumph spoke with the
> same tongue as a million rebel records. Under her, the 1980s
> belonged to us — all the weird, wonderful, dislocated, self-made
> Outsiders. How very bland politics will be without her, now that
> the grey men of all parties have taken back the power — now that
> the Bores are back in town.[9]

There are numerous problems with Burchill's self-help, self-made ideology. Her 'us' and 'them' divide is, however, appropriate to understanding the Thatcher years. Burchill's description of the 1980s as
'gory' and 'glorious' offers an evocative and powerful reminder of the
lavish scale of apocalyptic consumerism.

Burchill lived through the central concerns and contradictions of
the 1980s, relating to sex, sensibility and a woman's sense of self.
Burchill, like Thatcher, is dangerous — politically, socially and theoretically. As difficult women, they seduce us into trying to understand
this decade that makes less sense the further we are removed from it.
Both women are outside heterosexual, masculine, middle-class normality. Both are cultural figures who defined the nature of the 1980s.
The contradictory, fragmented, confrontational temperament of the
time was best embodied in the Burchill question: 'Is this decade at the
end of the world, or just another excuse for a party?'.[10] Of course, for
many feminists the 1980s did signal an end to the imaginary unity of a
single sisterhood. Julie Burchill and Suzanne Moore were part of the
generational challenge. The dispute, however, did not reach public
attention until Moore and Germaine Greer engaged in a feud within
the pages of the *Guardian* newspaper. Burchill became embroiled as a
fellow member of lipstick feminism.

Burchill had a closer involvement with an even more controversial
figure in feminist theory and politics. She entered into a 'fax war' with
Camille Paglia who, like Wilhelm II, approached every problem with
an open mouth. Paglia and Burchill exchanged faxes about the nature
of journalism and academia, questioning the meaning of writing in

public. Faxes are odd textual sites: private correspondences that invoke mysteries about origins and end points. Those who send faxes do not know the context of reception. Those who receive faxes do not know how many hands have touched the communication at the starting point. The resultant text is a private correspondence that has been removed from the shield of an envelope. The faxes by Burchill and Paglia were published in full by *The Modern Review* and other international papers such as *The Weekend Australian*. In the latter, the headline read: 'Fax off and Die, Bitch'. The repartee between the two women was fierce and ugly, but in the catfight the working-class little Englander came out stronger and smarter than Paglia, reducing the academic to a pompous, elitist intellectual who knew little about the rules of the street. Paglia's greatest insults included calling Burchill 'completely unknown in America' and 'anti-intellectual', and commented on her 'weaknesses and limitations as a thinker and a writer'.[11] Obviously for Paglia, being completely unknown in America is the most effective scorn to be poured on a writer. Yet for those who see Paglia as intellectually overrated, arrogant and politically naïve, Burchill's reply seemed justified. After receiving three faxes filled with venom from the American professor, Burchill replied:

> I'm surprised that you were so upset by my *Spectator* review. How you of all people can complain of my 'malice' is a complete mystery to me. Now you know how Wolf and Susan Faludi and all the others must feel every time you spew up your spiel to a waiting world. I'm here to tell you that you can't come on like a street tough and then have an attack of the Victorian vapours when faced by a taste of your own style … Don't believe what you read about the English; our working class, from where I am proud to come, is the toughest in the world. I'm not too nice. I'm not as loud as you, but if push comes to shove, I'm nastier. I'm 10 years younger, two stone heavier and I haven't had my nuts taken off by academia.[12]

Paglia's reply was … well … embarrassing:

> I could have helped you far more than you could help me. I am read and translated around the world from Japan to South America, and the basis of my fame is not journalism but a scholarly book on the history of culture. You are a very local commodity, completely unknown outside of England, and you have produced nothing of global interest.[13]

Burchill merely replied: 'I'm very glad you're big in Japan'.[14] Do we cheer at this point? Has Burchill won again, while Empress Paglia's clothing appears somewhat translucent? Sadly, and actually, Burchill's victory presents disturbing consequences.

What is remarkable about this faxical interchange is that both women assumed that there was no alternative to their confidently presented world view. Such Underground Maps can make those of us in Australia and the Pacific feel decidedly lost. After all, how do we get to Piccadilly Circus from Rockhampton? How do we get to Times Square from South Auckland? For writers and readers in the Asia-Pacific, there is a strange disquiet that emerges from being such an insignificant part of the cultural map. Both Burchill and Paglia were parochial, imagining the parameters of their public in different terms. For Paglia, success means being known from Japan to South America. For Burchill, England is all that matters — the United States is simply a joke.

The clash of maps between the New York Subway and the London Underground also invokes the perceived functional divide between journalism and academia in the United States. Paglia was offended by being treated as 'a hack'.[15] She wished for a clear demarcation between the intellectual and professional writer. However, Burchill's stature in the British cultural sphere contaminates such a divide. Academics like EP Thompson, Stuart Hall and Germaine Greer have moved from research and teaching to marching on the streets and speaking at rallies. Similarly, the texts by writers like Thompson, Raphael Samuel and AJP Taylor have aimed to speak to 'the people', not above them. Being 'big in Japan' is not the issue.

Part of my tattered identity responds negatively to catfighting between women. Perhaps in the 'noughties', hoping for political unity is naïve. The 1980s was a tough decade for feminism. The 1990s was worse. The pornography debates locked the fragmented movement into a state of stagnation. The presence of Margaret Thatcher generated confusing allegiances and ambivalent politicking on the behalf of feminists. Thatcher was a binary outlaw, conveying a hyper-femininity that 'took out' masculinity on the journey through to a gendered identity. Thatcher was always a woman, but slotted many masculinities into her textual, feminine frame.

Julie Burchill's writing in public does not offer a channel for liberation. Instead, Burchill, like Angela McRobbie,[16] has instigated a subtle linking of class, gender and generation. Burchill conveyed something of this voice from the Thatcherite gen(d)eration when she stated, 'Too many of my friends' lives are ending in pregnancy at 16 (working-class women still die in great numbers in childbirth; they just die in a different way, is all.)'.[17] Poignant and powerful, Burchill's writing in public does tap into the most personal of fears and oppressions.

Julie Burchill does not, however, dwell in the sphere of her grimy working-class origins. The nature of her desiring self was contained within the title of her first novel, *Ambition*. This hunger was moulded into the primary focus of her life:

All I ever wanted from life was love and money, and from a very early age I realized that fame would provide the most pleasurable and profitable shortcut to both ... But most of all I waited in my room, waited to be Somebody; then and only then would I be Myself. My only real definition of myself was that I was Somebody, which I wasn't yet; and that, I think, is the Modern experience — that you don't really exist until you see your name in print. That you are simply not yourself till you are famous.[18]

In this extract from *The Face* article 'Burchill on Burchill', she has articulated one of the major ideological premises of writing in public. She has argued that, within the modern experience, a person does not exist until their name is in print. The consequences of this statement are problematic, both theoretically and politically. In old-fashioned feminist terms, she is allowing the private/public divide to stand. In old-fashioned class mobility terms, she desperately believes in the importance of being somebody. For Burchill, the only way to gain that stature is through writing in public.

Julie Burchill may speak and write using the language of men, but like the ventriloquist's dummy, she makes the male voice and presence a joke through her quick wit and ironic presence. Julie Burchill is risky — politically, socially and theoretically — but through her perniciousness, feminist theory, politics and writing may be renewed. She embodies much of the potential for a blending between cultural studies and cultural journalism.

Cultural journalism has its origins in the nightclub and in the High Street rather than the university. While journalists have always engaged in cultural critique, questions of style were rarely granted currency outside of fashion pages. *The Face*, however, changed the rules of British publishing. *The Face* was published from May 1980, exactly one year after Thatcher assumed office. It was so effective in its construction of an audience that it was termed 'The Magazine of the Decade' in 1985.

The Face was based in London and remains myopically focussed on the capital. The magazine's world was restricted to the pleasurable, the stylish and the ephemeral. The reasons for *The Face*'s success are many, but particular emphasis should be granted to the innovative visual literacy commenced in the pages of the magazine. The layout, which consisted of large, glossy, hard-edged colour images, was excessive, provocative and defined the nature of eighties style. *The Face* was also able to mobilise a collective of well-known and talented journalists, such as Julie Burchill and Jon Savage. This team of writers, circulating on the streets, shops and clubs of London, watched style-lifers waiting to be invented into consciousness through an article in *The Face*. This anticipation of fame has effective resonance within Burchill's piece in the May 1985 *Face*, titled 'Apocalypse now (please)':

Unfortunately having fun is not half as respectable as being deca-
dent and in decline; but now people know that there WILL NOT
be a nuclear war they try to hear the four-minute warning all over
the place — to bring back the sense of BIGNESS that the fear of
nuclear war gave them. When you've prepared yourself for the
bunker it's hard to settle for the bistro.[19]

Style journalism, as defined by *The Face*, involved a re-evaluation of the
bistro, the club and the wine bar. The generic shift changed more than
content. It was a way of placing words and images on the page and an
attitude of disinterested nonchalance.

The bratty, insolent, but upwardly mobile child of *The Face* was *The
Modern Review*. Featuring 'low culture for high brows', *The Modern
Review* became the home of ex-*Face* readers who, through the fault of
gravity, could no longer wear spandex leggings. It was edited by Toby
Young and founded and financed by Julie Burchill. Crucially too, the
connection between cultural studies and this new form of journalism
was strengthened through the presence of a cultural studies editor on
the staff, Matt fftche. Subjects varied from fashion to the Flintstones
and encompassed numerous feature film, television and book reviews.
Regular columns had titles like 'Naff things publishers do' and 'Art for
Bart's sake' (Simpson of course). The paper was knowingly (and teas-
ingly) theoretical, poaching the storytelling style of Generation Xers.
An American commentary from the letter column effectively pinpointed its ideology. '*The Modern Review* is about style not substance. (If it
was about substance, for instance, you would not have wasted a whole,
damn page on a review of The Flintstones.) What is that style?
Sardonic, disdainful.'[20] This letter writer did not grasp that the ambivalent intellectualism of *The Modern Review* was matched by a real celebration and appreciation of the popular: 'Bewitched', 'The Simpsons',
Elizabeth Hurley, Patti Smith, *Tank Girl* and *Pulp Fiction* all took ink
from *The Modern Review*'s well.

As is common within cultural studies, *The Modern Review* rendered
popular culture an intensely special form: the soundtrack to parties, the
photographs of significant moments or a cinematic trace of powerful
social or political instants. The reading practices seem lost to time, leaving only the sweat on a dance floor, anonymous people smiling out of
a photograph and torn movie tickets. To grant meaning and significance from such texts is profoundly different from an individual historian 'responding' to a dusty document. As Suzanne Moore warned,
'you can't feign an interest in popular culture and then hold back when
something gets this popular'.[21] A belief in the crucial role that popular
culture holds in defining the historical present cannot be faked. The
dynamism of the texts renders non-enthusiasts the appearance of fools
and outsiders.

Like all good clichés, *The Modern Review* had to lose its place in the semiotic sun. It ended with issue 21, from June–July 1995. The hands that created it, Toby Young and Julie Burchill, also destroyed it. In an article titled 'The end of the affair', Young told the story of how his young assistant editor, the devilishly named Charlotte Raven, and his long-time friend Julie Burchill, became lovers and tried to gain control over the *Review*. His response was to write: 'Faced with the prospect of my kingdom falling into enemy hands, and with nothing left in my treasury, I decided to torch the place'.[22] Young argued that 'the 21 issues of *The Modern Review* will come to be seen as the gold standard'.[23] Certainly, the publication offered a potent cocktail of cultural populism, political cynicism and nonchalant, street-wise ambivalence. There is something poignant and tragic about the Burchill-led destruction of *The Modern Review*. Yet I am reminded of what one reviewer termed the publication: an 'Offspring of the union between Cultural Studies and Thatcherism'.[24] It is appropriate that Burchill, the sage and muse of the Thatcher years, snuffed out a pivotal link between academia and journalism, theory and politics.

The question posed within this chapter is whether Burchill's journey through Little England offers a tactic or method to write about difficult women. This chapter has not charted a history of Thatcher's Britain. I have suggested that the real eighties will always be somewhere else. This research has not offered a biography of Julie Burchill: the scraps of journalism, fiction, faxes, articles and books do not present an authentic voice of the real Julie. Instead, I offer a broad sweep of another, significant issue.

We live in such clean times, an era of Big Kev stain removers and Spray 'n Wipe. Nothing is pristine or predictable about Burchill. Through her words we make the uncomfortable realisation that the revolution — sister — may have passed us by while we were at step aerobics. She has been unable to balance a career, children, husband(s) and a social life. Is that a surprise? Are we any different? What are we going to do about it — go back to the gym? It was no surprise that Julie Burchill was drawn to write the biography we had to have: the scribe of the 1980s presented the history of that decade's most famous face. Burchill was ideally suited to write a study of Diana. The impact of her humour and ambivalent sexuality on subjects always results in a committed combination of wit and melancholy. The marriage of a cynic and idealist is the wedding of a nightmare and a daydream. Burchill has always worked well with fairytale metaphors, and the Diana Spencer story demanded it. Diana is the Sloaning Cinderella whose handsome prince went off with the ugly stepsister. Burchill, like a chastising older sister, uses her experience to demonstrate that there could never be a happy ending.

Diana was a bride every day, with each morning promising a new frock. Burchill appreciated that, through the years of masquerade, Diana became her own best performance. Her clothes granted a confidence not provided by either her class or husband. The tough and committed professional woman of the 1980s, with shoulder pads and filofaxes in tow, was replaced by the lavender-scented, floral pin-tucked 1990s. Burchill pinpointed the hypocrisy and the losses of this decade:

> When media men welcomed the 'softer, caring nineties,' they were merely expressing the hope for softer, caring women who would drop out of the rat race and stay at home barefoot and pregnant, leaving men free to make all the money and have all the fun.[25]

The crisp image of Diana performed what has happened to women in the last twenty years. She was Britannia in Dior, who spent too many hours in gym shorts. Even after her death, our television screens and magazine covers are scored with GDP (Gratuitous Diana Pictures).

The last century produced more beautiful women than Diana Spencer and better writers than Julie Burchill. Such quantifiable assessments demonstrate little about the mattering maps of our time. These two women have shaped our consciousness. Both were ladies who lunge, difficult women who struggled with the confines of femininity. Both were unable to manage either marriage or their class. Viewing Diana's appearance is similar to reading Burchill's words: all surface, but with a tremulous pain cutting through the skin and sentence.

Burchill has transformed writing into a glamorous, provocative, feminist enterprise. The role of the writer is always multi-tasking — moving between specialist and everyday knowledges and experiences. The power of good writing, which speaks to the present with clarity and boldness, is not questioned enough within our universities or our lives. Meanwhile Burchill is getting on with business, being innovative, funny and relevant.

If we are to gain anything from Julie Burchill, then perhaps lessons are derived from her intensely public existence. Her words capture the spark of celebrity and the sheer panic and strain involved in the maintenance of rhetorical power. Without formal qualifications, the tensions of being 'an accredited intellectual' do not weigh down her prose. Burchill is a celebrity rather than a scholar, but her feminism has more to do with Fredricks of Hollywood than McRobbie of London. The desperation to leave provincial England, to get on the Underground and *go somewhere*, provides a challenge for cultural studies and feminism to leave the drab, frumpy language of the academy and just occasionally jaunt into a stylish semiosphere. Perhaps through cultural journalism, a space may be found for a Julie Burchill to make it big, inspiring others to make a future of their choosing.

ENDING

REMEMBERING
DOROTHY WREN

All women become like their mothers. That is their tragedy. No man does. That's his.[1]
Oscar Wilde, *The Importance of Being Earnest*

Most feminists, at some stage during their writing career, sit at their desk thinking and crying about their mother. Gloria Steinem wrote her best work about her mother's mental illness.[2] Germaine Greer is at her most vitriolic and horrible when mocking her mother's accent, attitude and life.[3] My story is not as grand, nor as significant, as these doyens of the women's movement, but it is poignant and painful. It makes me cry: alone and often. To write these words, I must tightly squeeze my heart valve and focus my irises on the dancing print, rather than the tremulous pain that parks behind the prose.

While most women change one name at the point of marriage, neither of my mother's names are those given at her birth. Her father changed the first name and my father the latter. Dorothy Wren became Doris Brabazon. Her current name is solid, adult and matronly. The former is playful, light and even flighty. Images saturate the vista: of ruby slippers and a small, beautiful, cheery bird. This is the mother of my experience, with the tinkle of a laugh, the piercing blue eyes and a calmness that renders even the largest personal emergency into a minor societal hiccup.

Even when I am an old lady, I will remember two images of my mother. The first is really the foremost memory of my life. I was five years old: my mother was forty-five and returned from a hospital. A malignant melanoma had just been incised from her abdomen, with slithers of flesh stripped from her thighs to graft over the wound. At the time, I was the one distraught. My father, brother and I were sitting at the dining room table, eating our evening meal. But my mother was distanced from us, looking into space and positioned away from the family. She did not speak and appeared not to move. I was told that I could not hug or hold her. She was sick. I was too young to grasp what it all meant. Now I understand some of it. But my memory is of the smell: it was unforgettable. Later, I associated it with raw flesh.

Like the women of her generation, my mother took this major personal nightmare in her stride. I can only sketch what her thoughts could have been. But how would it feel — *how would it feel* — to be a beautiful woman and have a crater created in your abdomen. Roughened grafts replace a once smooth, creamy midriff. It is no longer possible to wear bathing suits and piteous stares erupt from the orbs of every shop assistant in the country as they enter her change room. How would *your* self-worth and self-image change? Women have mastectomies every day, but reconstructive surgery can at least restore the physical shape of a breast. Her scar remains a battle wound, a record of a fight with cancer that was won, but only just.

The second story of my mother occurred nearly twenty years later. I was watching a tape of *Shirley Valentine*. I was writing a lecture on tourism and thought that the relationship between Greece and Britain presented in this film would make a useful pedagogic point. As my mother has always done, when I watch a film, she plonks herself down on the lounge suite to watch it as well. This woman loves narrative. And she has taste — she hated *The English Patient* as much as I did. But watching *Shirley Valentine* with my then 65-year-old mother was an unforgettable experience. The scene where a teary Shirley laments the loss of her identity and name is shocking to watch, but when I turned to talk to my mother about it, her cheeks were wet and eyes red-rimmed. I touched her hand. All she could say — over and over — was that 'Shirley got it right. We have lost everything'.

With some horror, I realised that this woman did not only lose one name like Shirley, but both. The rule of the father and the husband has erased the language of a self, the marker of identity. This tragedy is well-deep, hollow and in the end, pointless. These micro tears in the fabric of language result in long-term scabs in the cloth of identity. Our role as women breathing the politics of the present is to carry the memories and ideas of these women. We have an opportunity to sustain a part of their lives.

This book offers a testament to Dorothy Wren and all the women who have lost something, but had no time to mourn its passing. These women have not loudly protested their lack of rights or their societal inequalities. They have stoically stood the taunts, humiliation and unfairness with dignity, respect and integrity. Being a woman means having to confront loss, to manage with less, but to use the strands of life's tragedy to weave magic. Through the language of the father, we fabricate the sentences of the future.

Writing, at its best, summons a fractured self, a moment of affect and trauma. This self is never on or off, never present or absent. Instead, to enunciate change is to write the self onto the page. Remembering and writing are both actions of grief, a loss of the self. While a crafted sentence can convey a life-affirming moment, the deletions, errors, death and pain are rubbed out of the story like absent, weathered skin that reveals a scab. It was Helene Cixous who commanded us to 'write your self. Your body must be heard'.[4] While writing demands courage, there is more strength necessary to invoke the tales unrecorded, the tears unshed. We hide in language, endlessly deferring a mourning for a self never actualised. For women walking with a burden, writing becomes even more important. We scribe the self into being and are changed though the process.

This book has offered a palate of popular culture and shown how it plugs social and political fractures. I have trammelled through feminist history, discrediting easily separable waves, and suggested that an issue-based approach is a transitory necessity to address the major struggles of the era. In a politically retrograde time, it is frequently difficult to establish strong community-based resistance that addresses more wide-ranging concerns. *Ladies who Lunge* has revealed resonant moments and warnings of economic retractions in women's lives. It has remained steadfastly thematic rather than programmatic. Through education, fashion, cosmetics, sport, music, television and film, life is lived in the ordinary. At times, though, the extraordinary stuns us with its revelatory power.

Ladies who Lunge makes a commitment to feminism, writing and popular culture. By remembering the cuts in the body politics and the stabs in the fabric of identity, we hold on to what makes women strong and powerful. Feminists use the crumbs of a culture to build something new and important. This is not the pointless, but popular, irony of the bad girls. It is not found underneath Ally McBeal's miniskirt. It certainly will not emerge from the ever-shrieking mobile phone. The revolution is not going to arrive by email. Instead, we have a chance for societal change if we capture the pain of the past, feel it, store it, write about it — and remember it.

NOTES

INTRODUCTION: FIND A GOOD WOMAN AND DO AS YOU'RE TOLD

1   G Steinem, *Outrageous acts and everyday rebellions*, Owl Books, New York, 1995: 1983, p 4.

PART I: WOMEN MOVING

CHAPTER ONE: MY OTHER CAR IS A BROOM: MOVING WOMEN BEYOND THE HAPPINESS PATROL

1   *Fight Club*, screenplay by Jim Uhls, from a novel by Chuck Palahniuk, directed by David Fincher, Twentieth Century Fox, 1999.
2   Fortysomething, Hokitika, *New Zealand Women's Weekly*, 8 January 2001, p 46.
3   Tyler, played by Brad Pitt, *Fight Club*.
4   This is no small issue. A recent United Nations report believed that fifty million abortions occur each year, of which twenty million are unsafe, resulting in 78 000 maternal deaths. These figures are cited in Jonathan Austin's *U.N. Report: Women's unequal treatment hurts economies*, wysiwyg://9/http://www.cnn.com/ 200...20/un.population.report/index.html, [on-line], accessed on 3 October 2000.
5   E Goldman, cited in Gloria Steinem's *Outrageous acts and everyday rebellions*, Owl Books, New York, 1995: 1983, p 4.
6   Gloria Steinem claimed that 'if we look at history, the average age of a woman's self-respecting rebellion gets younger by a decade or so with each wave of feminism', *Outrageous acts and everyday rebellions*, p xi.
7   For non-Australian readers, I should translate this evocative, sexist (but very funny) Aussie slang. 'Old biddies' are older women. 'Magging' is a mode of talking, related to the loud squawking of magpies.
8   Steinem, *Outrageous acts and everyday rebellions*, p xiii.
9   Gloria Steinem realised that 'sex isn't the only reason for valuing youth in women. With age comes authority, and beauty standards are often a way of getting rid of women just as they are attaining real power', *Revolution from Within: a book of self-esteem*, Little, Brown and Company, Boston, 1992, p 220.

10 A Summers, 'Shockwaves at the Revolution', *Good Weekend, The Australian*, Saturday 18 March 1995, p 30. To observe the impact of this article, please refer to Kathy Bail, 'Introduction', *DIY Feminism*, Allen and Unwin, Sydney, 1996, p 5.

11 K Bail, 'Introduction', *DIY Feminism*, p 5. The other well-known response to Summers was Rosamund Else-Mitchell & Naomi Flutter (eds), *Talking up: young women's take on feminism*, Spinifex Press, Melbourne, 1998. To view the response from older feminist communities, please refer to Carmen Luke's 'Feminism in New times', from L Christian-Smith & K Kellor, *Everyday knowledge and uncommon truths: women in the academy*, Westview Press, Boulder, 1999, pp 1–16.

12 S Faludi, *Backlash*, Chatto and Windus, London, 1991, p 371.

13 L Walker, 'The end of feminism', *Arena Magazine*, No. 35, June–July 1998, p 33.

14 Graham Chapman and John Cleese, *Monty Python's Life of Brian*, directed by Terry Jones, theatrical release on 1 August 1979.

15 J Burchill, *Married Alive*, Orion, London, 1999, pp 210–11.

16 B Friedan, *The Fountain of Age*, Touchstone, New York, 1993.

17 Sybil Nolan has argued that Greer really needs to be recognised for her journalism. Her professional communication, with a feminist inflection, was challenging and important. Nolan states that 'Greer changed lives not because she was the first, the most correct or even the bravest second-wave feminist: what matters is that when she discussed her own experiences, feelings and views, the effect was galvanising', 'Tabloid Women', *Meanjin*, Vol. 58, No. 2, 1999, p 168.

18 For example, Greer's piece on Jimi Hendrix, 'Hey, Jimi, where you gonna run now?', was originally published in the October 1970 *Oz*, but reprinted in *The Madwoman's Underclothes*, Atlantic Monthly, New York, 1986, pp 41–44.

19 C Paglia, *Sex, Art and American Culture*, Penguin, New York, 1992, p 274.

20 G Greer, *The Change*, Ballantine Books, New York, 1991, p 24.

21 B Friedan, *Life so far*, Simon and Schuster, New York, 2000, p 88.

22 Friedan, *Life so far*, p 164.

23 Friedan, *Life so far*, p 186.

24 D Horowitz, *Betty Friedan and the making of the feminine mystique: the American left, the cold war, and modern feminism*, University of Massachusetts Press, Amherst, 1998, p 211.

25 N Wolf, *Fire with fire: the new female power and how to use it*, Fawcett Columbine, New York, 1993, p xvi.

26 Wolf, *Fire with fire*, p 58.

27 Wolf, *Fire with fire*, p 65.

28 Lyrics from 'My Generation', written by Pete Townshend and performed by The Who, from *The Who's My generation — the very best of*, Polydor, 1996, track three.

29 L Segal, *Why Feminism? Gender, Psychology, Politics*, Polity, Cambridge, 1999, acknowledgments.

30 Segal, *Why Feminism?* p 1.

31 G Greer, *The Female Eunuch*, Paladin, London, 1971, p 11.

32 E Pankhurst, 'I incite this meeting to rebellion', *Feminism: The Essential Historical Writings*, Vintage Books, New York, 1972, p 295.

33 To survey how the study of technology can be enfolded into feminism, please refer to Anna Munster's 'Is there postlife after postfeminism?', *Australian feminist studies*, Vol. 14, No. 29, 1999, pp 119–29.

34 Susan Hawthorne & Renate Klein (eds), *Cyberfeminism: connectivity, critique, creativity*, Spinifex, Melbourne, 1999.

35 Wolf, *Fire with fire*, p 77.

36 An outstanding interview was held with PJ Harvey in *Rip it Up*, December 2000/January 2001, pp 58–59. The piece was titled 'Axe-wielding bitch no more'. The interview presents a discussion of Harvey's public image.

37 Two fine articles have been written about Hole and Courtney Love. Please refer to Georgina Safe's 'Rock women get the drum', *The Australian*, 6 February 1999,

p 8 and Susan Hopkins, 'Hole lotta attitude', *Social Alternatives*, Vol. 18, No. 2, 1999, pp 11–14.

38 C Lumby, *Gotcha: life in a tabloid world*, Allen and Unwin, Sydney, 1999, pp 4–5.

39 Polly Toynbee, 'Fay plays the fool', *The Guardian*, 1 July 1998, p 20.

40 Alanis Morissette, 'You oughta know', from *Jagged little pill*, Maverick Recording Company, 1995, track two.

41 *Dogma*, written and directed by Kevin Smith, A View Askew Production, Village Roadshow, 1999.

42 E Wurtzel, *The bitch rules*, Quartet Books, London, 2000, p 42.

43 J Burchill, interviewed by Jana Wendt, '60 Minutes', Channel 9, 16 July 1995.

44 C Sommers, *Who stole feminism?* Simon and Schuster, New York, 1994, p 15.

45 For example, Carolyn Heilbrun has written a fine biography of Gloria Steinem, *The education of a woman*, Ballantine Books, New York, 1995. She states that 'Katie Roiphe, writing as one of the younger generation of feminists in the early 1990s, found those of Steinem's generation to be anti-men and anti-sex. Steinem's life indicates that this is youth ignorant of its predecessors, whose history is just beginning to be written', p xx.

46 Sommers, *Who stole feminism?* p 18.

47 Denise Riley's corrective in *Am I that name?* University of Minnesota, Minneapolis, 1988, pp 96–101, should be recognised. She asserted that women do not live their sex twenty-four hours a day. It is not surprising, therefore, that women are not always and completely a feminist. There must be contestation and conflict involved in creating an identity.

48 Friedan, *Life so far*, pp 232–34.

49 G Capp, 'Girl Power: Boys beaten in TEE and vocational subjects', *The West Australian*, 6 January 2001, p 1.

50 It is — frankly — unbelievable that the award winner was photographed with a duster. It is a way to reclaim the winner's success into a feminine realm. If she had been photographed with a set square or sander, then the process of the construction would have been revealed. By dusting the surface of her table, she is distanced from the act of production.

51 G Capp, 'Medal scorer pips his elders', *The West Australian*, 6 January 2001, p 8.

52 Lynne Thomson, Principal of St Mary's College, in Capp, 'Girl Power', p 1.

53 Pat Byrne, State School Teachers' Union president, in 'Girl Power', p 1.

54 Peter Brown, Director-General of the Education Department, in 'Girl Power', p 1.

55 This study was reported in Betty Friedan's *Beyond gender: the new politics of work and family*, Woodrow Wilson Centre Press, Washington, 1997, p 67.

56 Graham Dellar, Education Dean — Curtin University, 'Girl Power', p 1.

57 Geraldine Capp has continued this obsession, with 'Boy Troubles probe gets issue in open', a 2-page spread in *The West Australian*, 24 September 2001. Once more, experts were summoned. Ian Lillico, a 'WA boys' education specialist', recommended that 'Boys need to reconnect with nature. They need to do activities he says men were designed for — hunting, fishing, camping — to give them confidence', p 17. While the testimony of many of these 'experts' is ridiculous, it is having a structural impact. The Federal Minister for Education at the time, David Kemp, asked a House of Representative committee to develop strategies to help boys. Not surprisingly, the submissions included one from the Lone Fathers' Association in the Northern Territory, which blamed 'separatist feminism' for disadvantaging boys. Similarly, a man from Canberra placed a submission into the committee: 'I have a son of 12 who, as a future family leader, has been disadvantaged by a sexist policy in ACT [Australian Capital Territory] primary schools which favours the promotion of girl students over boy students', p 17. Similarly, a Melbourne man used the committee as an excuse to abuse his ex-wife: 'there are no books in the house and his mother occupies her spare time sewing', p 17. This continual promotion of a 'non-story' story is having a structural consequence. The 'trouble with boys' rhetoric is

allowing anti-feminist and anti-women energies to gain attention, visibility and funding under the mask of improving the system for boys.

58 Richard Yallop, 'The trouble with boys', *The Weekend Australian*, 16–17 June 2001, p 19.

59 Yallop, 'The trouble with boys', p 19.

60 B Nelson, cited in Yallop, 'The trouble with boys'.

61 For clarification of this argument, please refer to Debbie Epstein, Jannette Elwood, Valerie Hey & Janet Maw, 'Rogue males?' *Times Educational Supplement*, 1 January 1999, p A9. This fine short article presents the crisp argument that 'In the past academic failure in girls has been blamed on their own poor ability whilst failure in boys has been seen as the fault of the educational system. Girls have been able to achieve higher standards because of the change in attitude to education for women. Interest in the subject of low levels of achievement in boys has been growing due to concern over the number of unemployed youths who are seen to threaten social order in the UK'.

62 Capp, 'Medal scorer pips his elders', p 8.

63 Susan Hewitt and Sheryn Cheah respectively, 'Best girl dispels her doubts', *The West Australian*, 6 January 2001, p 9.

64 For example, Gisela Bock and Susan James (eds) constructed a collection of papers to explore these terms in *Beyond equality and difference: citizenship, feminist politics, female subjectivity*, Routledge, London, 1992.

65 N Preston & C Symes, *Schools and classrooms: a cultural studies analysis of education*, Longman Cheshire, Melbourne, 1992, p 60.

66 This economic imperative has been particularly virulent in Australia. Government policy, from the Hawke Government's White Paper on Education in 1987, pleated education and economics. For an investigation of *Education and public policy in Australia*, please refer to S Marginson, *Education and public policy in Australia*, Cambridge University Press, Melbourne, 1993.

67 J Knight, 'Social justice and effective schooling', *Education Views*, 13 May 1994, p 1.

68 Marginson, *Education and public policy in Australia*, p 13.

69 Katha Pollitt, commenting on the situation where 54 per cent of college students in the United States are women, realised that 'for all we hear about the decline of high-paid blue-collar jobs, women with a college degree average barely more than men with a high school diploma — $35 400 versus $31 200 ... If women could earn as much as men without a college degree, lots of them would probably give it a pass too'. This discussion is derived from 'Affirmative action for men?', *The Nation*, Vol. 269, Issue 22, 27 December 1999 [Electronic], accessed: Expanded Academic [A59694101], 13 February 2001.

70 C Hoff Sommers, *The war against boys: how misguided feminism is harming our young men*, Simon and Schuster, New York, 2000, p 134.

71 Hoff Sommers, *The war against boys*, p 14.

72 Hoff Sommers, *The war against boys*, p 16.

73 W Pollack, *Real Boys*, Scribe Publications, Melbourne, 1998, p xviii.

74 Pollack, *Real Boys*, p xvi.

75 J Kenway, 'Boys' education in the context of gender reform', *Curriculum perspectives*, Vol. 17, No. 1, 1997, p 59.

76 C Mclean, 'Engaging with boys' experiences of masculinity: implications for gender reform in school', *Curriculum perspectives*, Vol. 17, No. 1, 1997, p 62.

77 RW Connell, 'Men, masculinities and feminism', *Social Alternatives*, Vol. 16, No. 3, July 1997, p 7.

78 G Capp, 'Rachael's a cut above rest', *The West Australian*, 6 January 2001, p 9.

79 bell hooks, in Andrea Juno & V. Vale (eds), *Angry Women*, RE/Search Publications, New York, 1999, p 89.

80 Fifty-four per cent of students are women compared to 36 per cent of university staff.

81 For a discussion of the application of this phrase, please refer to Amy Black &

Stanley Rothman, 'Have you really come a long way? Women's access to power in the United States', *Gender Issues*, Vol. 16, No. 1–2, Winter–Spring 1998.

82 M Sullivan, 'The status of women in Australian Universities: myths and realities', *Australian Feminist Studies*, Vol. 14, No. 30, 1999, p 427.

83 These statistics are derived from Dr Clare Burton's 1997 study, cited in Joan Kirner & Moira Rayner, *The women's power handbook*, Penguin, Melbourne, 1999, p 25.

84 For a discussion of the changing relationships between gender, teaching and research, please refer to Alison Lee & Bill Green, 'Pedagogy and disciplinarity in the "New University"', *The UTS Review*, Vol. 3, No. 1, May 1997, pp 1–25.

85 Susan Faludi reported that 'Australia has a highly segregated workforce: in 1911, 84 per cent of female labour worked in disproportionately female occupations, and by 1984 the figure, at 82 per cent, had barely changed', *Backlash*, p 398.

86 Faludi, *Backlash*, p 20.

87 For example, see Carmen Luke's 'Feminism in New Times', in L Christian-Smith & K Kellor (eds) *Everyday knowledge and uncommon truths: women in the academy*, Westview Press, Boulder, 1999.

88 In 'university speak', women are on maintenance committees, not governance committees.

89 J Gore, 'Unsettling academic/feminist identity', in *Everyday knowledge and uncommon truths*, p 17.

90 William Kerrigan, from L Botstein, J Boswell, J Blythe & W Kerrigan, 'New rules about sex on campus: should professors be denied admission to students' beds?', *Harper's Magazine*, September 1993, pp 35–36.

91 B Friedan, *Beyond gender: the new politics of work and family*, Woodrow Wilson Centre Press, Washington, 1997, p 2.

92 Friedan, *Beyond gender*, p 13.

93 bell hooks, *Reel to real: race sex and class at the movies*, Routledge, New York, 1996, p 2.

94 *Notting Hill*, written by Richard Curtis and directed by Roger Michell, Polygram Filmed Entertainment Inc, 1999.

95 b hooks, *Reel to real*, p 110.

96 Elizabeth Gross enacts a discussion of the struggles involved in instigating this critique in 'What is feminist theory?', in C Pateman & E Gross (eds), *Feminist Challenges*, Allen and Unwin, Sydney, 1986, pp 190–204.

97 P Collins, *Black feminist thought*, Routledge, New York, 2000, p vii.

98 'Don't call me baby', Madison Avenue, *Polyester Embassy*, Vicious Grooves, 2000, track three.

99 'Who the hell are you?' Madison Avenue, *Polyester Embassy*, track two.

100 E Rapping, *Media-tions: forays into the culture and gender wars*, South End Press, Boston, 1994, p 265.

101 J Ussher, *Fantasies of femininity: reframing the boundaries of sex*, Penguin, London, 1997, p 180.

102 C Lumby, *Bad Girls*, Allen and Unwin, Sydney, 1997.

103 Camilla Griggers stated that 'pornographic faciality recodes the despotic face of the White Woman as accessible to everyone regardless of class or race — that is, available for mass consumption', in *Becoming-Woman*, University of Minnesota Press, Minneapolis, 1997, p 27.

104 L Irigaray, *Speculum of the other woman*, Ithaca, New York, 1985, p 229.

105 N Penn & L LaRose, *The Code*, Fireside, New York, 1996, p 26.

106 G Steinem, *Outrageous acts and everyday rebellions*, p xviii.

107 To view this tendency in Andrea Dworkin's work at its most overt, please refer to *Pornography: men possessing women*, The Women's Press, London, 1981.

108 Lyrics from 'Hey Jude', The Beatles, *Past Masters Volume Two*, EMI Records, 1988, track seven.

109 E Probyn, *Outside Belongings*, Routledge, New York, 1996, p 5.

CHAPTER TWO: WHAT WILL YOU WEAR TO THE REVOLUTION?

1   M Pople, 'What will you wear to the revolution?', *Marxism Today*, January 1987, p 45.

2   S Hall, *The Hard Road to Renewal: Thatcherism and the crisis of the Left*, Verso, London, 1988, p 165.

3   Steve Chibnall in 'Whistle and Zoot: the changing meaning of a suit of clothes', *History Workshop*, vol. 20, 1985, recognised how odd and misplaced his analysis of fashion seemed in the socialist and feminist historians' journal. He stated, 'There must have been a number of "socialist and feminist historians" who were surprised by the inclusion in their journal of an article on such an apparently frivolous topic as the zoot suit ... the analysis of style, far from being frivolous, may serve as a focus for the wider examination of processes of social action and the construction of meaning', p 57. This piece provided a provoking and engaging analysis of the relationship between the class system, style and social mobility.

4   L Negrin, 'The meaning of dress', *Arena*, No. 7, 1996, p 144.

5   Elizabeth Wilson recognised the complex relationship between popular cultural practices and postmodernism in her chapter 'Fashion and the postmodern body', in the J Ash & E Wilson edited collection, *Chic Thrills: A Fashion Reader*, Pandora, London, 1992. She stated that 'These days, cultural critics have become accustomed to take shelter under the great umbrella of postmodernism which has conveniently opened during the past decade to shelter us from the torrents of cold water so often poured upon those who attempt to take popular culture ... seriously', p 3. Wilson has recognised that rhetorics of postmodernism provided some space to conduct academic research on popular texts.

6   Beyond studies of male youth culture, there has been an increasing interest in men's clothing, particularly when it is a signifier of power. One of the finest books on the subject is the beautifully illustrated *Dressed to Kill: James Bond the suited hero*, Flammarion, Paris, 1996. Written by Jay McInerney, Nick Foulkes, Neil Norman and Nick Sullivan, it offers an analysis of suited men in filmic history. Details are obviously important in men's fashion. Andre Malan's 'Neckties, knot just for gravy stains', *The West Australian*, 26 September 1998, p 8, demonstrates the importance of ties, particularly for men in politics. He states that 'Former president Ronald Reagan moved from red ties when he first assumed office, to green and then yellow. Observers were sure that something politically significant was happening, but they did not know quite what it was'.

7   As J Finkelstein has argued, 'being fashionable may be a kind of achievement but it simultaneously traps the individual in a cycle of financial recklessness and conspicuous spending', in *Slaves of Chic*, Minerva, Melbourne, 1994, p 116.

8   Wendy Parkins has presented an innovative answer to the question, 'what is the significance ... of women "dressing up" before going off to smash windows', in her article 'What to wear to a protest march: identity politics and fashion in the suffragette movement', *Southern Review*, Vol. 28, March 1995, p 80.

9   P Sparke, *As long as it's pink*, Pandora, London, 1995, p 223.

10 Joan Fox constructs a careful analysis of the changing meanings of fashion in a colonial culture in 'Designing Differences', from V Burgmann & J Lee (eds), *Making a life*, Penguin, Melbourne, 1988, pp 18–38. She demonstrates how, in a penal colony, clothes offer a pivotal site of transference between convict and free settler.

11 T Veblen, 'Dress as an Expression of the Pecuniary Culture', from his book *The Theory of the Leisure Class: an Economic Study of Institutions*, New American Library, New York, 1899.

12 S Faludi, *Backlash*, Chatto and Windus, London, 1991, p 208.

13 Pauline Swain, 'Fit to bust', *The Dominion*, 9 July 1998, p 13.

14 Pauline Swain, 'Wearing the pants', *The Dominion*, 9 July 1998, p 14.

15 Simone de Beauvoir, *The Second Sex*, Vintage Books, New York, 1989: 1952, p 683.

16 Women's Studies Group, 'Relations of production relations of re-production',

Working Papers in Cultural Studies, No. 9, Spring 1976, p 95.

17 Angela McRobbie, *Feminism and Youth culture*, Macmillan, Houndmills, 1991.

18 Scholars in the Birmingham Centre for Contemporary Cultural Studies, particularly during the leadership of Stuart Hall, analysed the subcultural style as the interlinking of class and age. Male subcultures were universalised. Angela McRobbie's work through the 1970s and 1980s highlighted the unwillingness of the Centre's men to contemplate the experiences and ideologies of young women.

19 J Burchill, *No Exit*, Sinclair-Stevenson, London, 1993, p 6.

20 A Krisman 'Radiator girls: the opinions and experiences of working-class girls in an East London Comprehensive', *Cultural Studies*, Vol. 1, No. 2, 1987, p 225.

21 EP Thompson, *The Making of the English Working Class*, Pelican, London, 1968.

22 Sally and Jenny quoted in L Measor '"Are you coming to see some dirty films today?": Sex education and adolescent sexuality', in L Holly (ed), *Girls and Sexuality*, Milton Keynes: Open University Press, 1989, p 48.

23 Jenny quoted in Measor, '"Are you coming to see some dirty films today?"'.

24 J Canaan, 'Is "doing nothing" just boy's play?', in S Franklin, C Lury & J Stacey (eds), *Off-centre: feminism and cultural studies*, Harper Collins, London, 1991, p 120.

25 PN69 quoted in K Bhavnani, *Talking politics: a psychological framing for views from youth in Britain*, Cambridge University Press, Cambridge, 1991, p 166.

26 Andrew quoted in Canaan, 'Is "doing nothing" just boy's play?', p 114.

27 H Cixous, 'Castration or Decapitation', *Signs*, Vol. 7, 1981, p 50.

28 J Duruz, 'Dressing up daydreams: femininity, memory and narratives of fashion', *UTS Review*, Vol. 1, No. 2, 1995, p 143.

29 Cited in D Robins, *We hate humans*, Penguin, Harmondsworth, 1984, p 15.

CHAPTER THREE: BUFF PUFFING AN EMPIRE

1 N Thomas, *Colonialism's Culture*, Princeton University Press, Princeton, 1994, p 11.

2 B Fryer, 'How to succeed in business', *PC World*, Vol. 12, No. 12, December 1994, p 271.

3 Anita Roddick, 'The Body Shop Fact Sheet', The Body Shop, Melbourne, 1996, p 1.

4 'More young millionaires, please', *The Economist*, Vol. 310, No. 7588, 4 February 1989, p 13.

5 Laura Ashley is a peculiarly 1980s phenomenon. The business was famous for utilising prints and patterns of the nineteenth century so as to provide an ordered and (conservative) aesthetic to the 1980s. For a discussion of this patterning of politics, please refer to Joanne Finkelstein, *Slaves of Chic*, Minerva, Melbourne, 1994, pp 121–22.

6 J Burchill, *Diana*, Weidenfeld and Nicholson, London 1998, p 16.

7 S Smiles, *Self-Help*, John Murray, London, 1958: 1859, p 33.

8 Smiles, *Self-Help*, pp 263–64.

9 Anita Roddick, in Paul Brown, *Anita Roddick and The Body Shop*, Exley Publications, Watford, 1996, p 10.

10 'Body and Soul', *The Economist*, Vol. 321, No. 7728, 12 October 1991, p 92.

11 Anita Roddick, *Body and Soul*, Random House, London, 1991, p 23.

12 Roddick stated that 'Benetton has done ads. Benetton has done cause-related marketing. Benetton has a different agenda. Benetton wants to get cover space in newspapers', in M Phillips, 'Anita Roddick's Body Shop', *New Directions*, August 1996, p 7.

13 Brown, *Anita Roddick and The Body Shop*, p 53.

14 Roddick, *Body and Soul*, p 166.

15 Roddick, *Body and Soul*, p 219.

16 *Club World Pack* (pamphlet), The Body Shop, London, 1999, unpaginated.

17 For a discussion of how The Body Shop's waste reduction policy has influenced other

companies, including McDonald's, please refer to S Jackie Prince & Richard A Denison, 'Launching a new business ethic: the environment as a standard operating procedure', *Industrial Management*, Vol. 34, No. 6, November–December 1992, [Electronic], accessed: Expanded Academic [A13793771], 13 February 2001.

18 *This is The Body Shop — Fact Sheet*, The Body Shop, Melbourne, 1996.

19 C Bittar, 'Green Noise', *Brandweek*, Vol. 40, Issue 8, 22 February 1999, p 28.

20 The Australian material from the Mulgrave office was the stand-out packaging and promotional material, followed by the information sent from Canada.

21 This figure is derived from *Fact sheet: the Body Shop*, The Body Shop, Wake Forest, 1997.

22 *The Body Shop Canada*, The Body Shop, Don Mills, 1997.

23 *The Body Shop Canada*.

24 'Monitoring ethical policy', http://www.bized.ac.uk/compfact/bodyshop /body11b.htm, [on-line] accessed 1 December 1997.

25 *The Body Shop New Range of Shampoos and Conditioners*, The Body Shop, Melbourne, 1996.

26 *Founder's Profile — Anita Roddick OBE*, The Body Shop, Wake Forest, 1997, p 1.

27 *Your opinion counts: Social Audit*, The Body Shop, Melbourne, 1998.

28 *On Balance*, Stakeholders' Financial Statement, The Body Shop, London, 1997.

29 Roddick, *Body and Soul*, p 256.

30 O Harari, 'Strong leadership vs. autocracy: they just don't get it', *Management Review*, Vol. 85, No. 8, August 1996, [Electronic], accessed: Expanded Academic [A18546902], 13 February 2001.

31 Roddick, *Body and Soul*, p 17.

32 For information about the activities of Australian and New Zealand staff, please refer to the fact sheet, *How we give*, The Body Shop, Melbourne, 1996, p 2.

33 *On Balance*, p 9.

34 For example, see *The Body Shop Catalogue*, The Body Shop, London, 1997, unpaginated.

35 'The Body and Self Esteem', *Full Voice*, Issue 1, 1997, p 18.

36 *The Body Shop Colourings*, The Body Shop, Melbourne, 1996, p 2.

37 This image featured as the front poster for Body Shops in 1997. It was also available as a postcard and was reprinted in the first issue of *Full Voice*, pp 13–14.

38 Anita Roddick, 'What I really think', *Full Voice*, Issue 1, 1997, p 12.

39 An example is a catalogue produced under the title *New Age Beauty*, The Body Shop, Melbourne, 1999. The text reminds readers that 'The Body Shop continually recognizes and respects the values of older persons within all societies, throughout philosophies, actions and promotions', p 3. Ironically, on page four, they sell moisturisers and under-eye cream.

40 Bergamot — one sniff and you're uplifted! Body Shop Postcard, The Body Shop, London, 1997.

41 *This is The Body Shop — Fact Sheet*.

42 Anita Roddick, 'Introduction', from V Bentley et al., *Mind body soul: The Body Shop book of wellbeing*, Ebury Press, London, 1998, p 13.

43 'The Body Shop', *The Independent*, July 1992, cited in Philip Elmer-Dewitt, 'Anita the agitator', *Time*, Vol. 141, No. 4, 25 January 1993, [Electronic], accessed: Expanded Academic [A13340105], 13 February 2001.

44 Smiles, *Self-Help*, p 58.

45 Roddick, *Body and Soul*, p 17.

46 Thomas, *Colonialism's Culture*, p 30.

47 A Cvetkovich & D Kellner, 'Introduction: thinking global and local', in A Cvetkovich & D Kellner, (eds), *Articulating the global and the local*, Westview Press, Boulder, 1997, p 13.

48 Importantly, Anita Roddick stated in 2000 that 'we reorganised the company into four regions: the UK, Europe, America and Asia. The head offices remain in

Littlehampton and London', from *Business as Unusual: the triumph of Anita Roddick*, Harper Collins, London, 2000, p 263.

49 'Planet Tea Tree', The Body Shop, London, 1999, p 2.
50 Roddick, *Body and Soul*, p 219.
51 *On Balance*, p 33.
52 *On Balance*, p 33.
53 C Healy, *From the ruins of colonialism*, Cambridge University Press, Cambridge, 1997, p 1.
54 Brown, *Anita Roddick and The Body Shop*, p 51.
55 Roddick, *Body and Soul*, p 184.
56 A Cranny-Francis, *The Body in the Text*, Melbourne University Press, Melbourne, 1995, pp 46–47.
57 Please refer to Thomas, *Colonialism's Culture*, p 190.
58 *This is The Body Shop — Fact Sheet*.
59 A Roddick, 'Introduction', *The Body Shop Book*, p 13.
60 'Community Trade Programme', http://www.the-body-shop.com/trade/main.html, [on-line], accessed on 1 December 1997.
61 Roddick, *Body and Soul*, p 203.
62 As PJ Rich realised, 'The British seldom displayed any qualms about interjecting their view about every topic under the colonial sun ... That the British could visit or live in a foreign country by *right*, while the natives came to England only as invited guests after receiving *permission*, made the relationship one-sided from the start', from *Elixir of Empire*, Regency Press, London, 1989, p 101.
63 *On Balance*, p 22.
64 Roddick, *Business as Unusual*, p 186.
65 Roddick, *Business as Unusual*, p 188.
66 M Yegenoglu, *Colonial fantasies: towards a feminist reading of orientalism*, Cambridge University Press, Cambridge, 1998, p 94.
67 'The story of cocoa butter' is presented in the Community Trade Programme, http://www.the-body-shop.com/trade/cocoa_story.html, [on-line], accessed on 1 December 1997.
68 A Roddick, 'Introduction', in T Blanks (ed), *The Body Shop Book: Skin, Hair and Body Care*, Penguin, New York, 1994.
69 S Hall, *The Hard Road to renewal: Thatcherism and the crisis of the left*, Verso, London, 1988, p 68.

CHAPTER FOUR: BIT BLOKEY, EH? LES MILLS AND THE MASCULINISATION OF AEROBICS

1 There are many awkward — and interesting — fashion interventions in the history of women's sport. For example, Reebok was built on the success of aerobics. Joe Schwartz reports that 'In the early days of the fitness movement, executives at a small British athletic-shoe company noticed that growing numbers of women were going to exercise classes. The company also found that women exercised barefoot or in men's athletic shoes because they had nothing else to wear', from 'How Reebok fits shoes', *American Demographics*, Vol. 15, No. 3, May 1993, p 54. By 1991, 72 per cent of all Americans aged between thirteen and seventy-five bought athletic footwear.
2 *Participation in Sport and Physical Activity 1996–7*, Australian Bureau of Statistics, p 3; *Participation in Sport and Physical Activity 1998–9*, Australian Bureau of Statistics, p 4.
3 *Participation in Sport and Physical Activity 1996–7*, p 13.
4 *Participation in Sport and Physical Activity 1996–7*, p 14.
5 *The Oxford Companion to Australian Sport*, Oxford University Press, Melbourne, 1992, edited by Wray Vamplew, Katharine Moore, John O'Hara, Richard Cashman and Ian Jobling.

6   D Hemphill, private correspondence, 19 July 1999.
7   The FIG (Fédération Internationale de Gymnastique) is 115 years old, with Sports
     Aerobics introduced as a discipline at the Geneva Congress in 1994. The other
     three disciplines include Men's and Women's Artistic Gymnastics, Rhythmic
     Gymnastics and General Gymnastics.
8   D Rowe, *Popular Cultures*, SAGE Publications, London, 1995, p 133.
9   Rowe, *Popular Cultures*, p 107.
10   An excellent short article on spinning is Joe Kita's 'We're gonna make you sweat!',
     Bicycling, Vol. 38, No. 2, February 1997, [full-text article]. Importantly, he shows
     how diverse social practices in these classes enact a hybrid of the nightclub and the
     health club.
11   Betsy Streisand reported that '60 percent of Americans now engage in virtually
     no leisure-time physical activity', *US News and World Report*, Vol. 120, No. 19,
     13 May 1996, p 84.
12   Interestingly, this movement to muscle has required a reprogramming of women's
     obsession with the scales. Selene Yeager, in 'From fat to firm', *Prevention*, Vol. 50,
     No. 6, June 1998, p 112, told women: 'don't get hung up if the number on the
     scale goes up. Muscle weighs more than fat'.
13   An example of such an article is Joanna McMillan's 'Home Toning', *Slimming*,
     June 2000, pp 46–47. See also Michele Meyer's 'The minimal workout', *Working
     Woman*, Vol. 29, No. 6, June 1995, p 61. This is quite a remarkable piece, as it
     explores how exercise that builds muscle can alleviate levels of stress and depression
     in working women.
14   K Dutton & R Laura, 'Toward a history of bodybuilding', *Sporting Traditions*,
     Vol. 6, No. 1, November 1989, pp 25–41.
15   Krista Scott-Dixon, 'Cyborgs in the Gym: the technopolitics of female muscle',
     paper presented at *Discipline and Deviance: Gender, technologies, machines confer-
     ence* at Duke University, Durham NC, 2–4 October 1998, http://krista.tico.com/
     dukepaper.htm, [on-line], accessed on 23 July 1999.
16   N Wolf, *The Beauty Myth*, Vintage, Toronto, 1990, p 184.
17   M Sheedy, 'Editor's Letter', *Women's Health*, June 2000, p 6.
18   Miriam Nelson, *Strong Women Stay Slim*, Griffin Press, Melbourne, 1998, p 4.
19   J Ussher, *Fantasies of femininity: reframing the boundaries of sex*, Penguin, London,
     1997, p 65.
20   Gordon Campbell, 'Garden of eating', Listener, Vol. 177, No. 3165, 6 January
     2000, p 41.
21   Kathleen Woodward states that 'the surgically youthful body is the postmodern ver-
     sion of Oscar Wilde's haunting tale of Dorian Gray', from 'Youthfulness as a mas-
     querade', *Discourse*, Vol. 11, No. 1, Fall–Winter 1988–89, p 136.
22   Amanda Daley & Joanne Buchanan, 'Aerobic dance and physical self-perceptions
     in female adolescents: some implications for physical education', *Research Quarterly
     for Exercise and Sport*, June 1999, Vol. 70, Issue 2, pp 196–201 [full-text article].
23   A Farnsworth, 'True confessions: women reveal what they really want," *She*, August
     1999, p 68.
24   JD Reed, 'Sweating and sharing: for some women, aerobics provides more than a
     workout', *Time*, Vol. 132, No. 2, 10 July 1989, [Electronic], accessed: Expanded
     Academic, [A7719537], 13 February 2001.
25   Reed, 'Sweating and sharing'.
26   M Lloyd, 'Feminism, Aerobics and the politics of the body', *Body and Society*,
     Vol. 2, No. 2, 1996, p 80.
27   Lloyd, 'Feminism, Aerobics and the politics of the body', p 95.
28   A Liu, in Bordo, *Unbearable Weight: feminism, western culture and the body*,
     University of California Press, Berkeley, 1993, p 150.
29   J Rodin, *Body Traps*, Angus and Robertson, Sydney, 1992, p 225.
30   One of the worst examples of this simplistic analysis is Ramona Koval's *Eating your*

heart out: food, shape and the body industry, Penguin, Melbourne, 1986, particularly pp 134–37.

31 Naomi Wolf, for example, believed that this attention to fitness is 'not an obsession about female beauty but an obsession about female obedience', *The Beauty Myth*, 1990, p 187.

32 D Eller, 'Is aerobics dead?', *Women's Sports and Fitness*, Vol. 18, No. 1, January–February 1996, [Electronic], accessed: Expanded Academic [A17981234], 13 February 2001.

33 T Iknoian, 'Stepping across borders', *Women's sports and fitness*, Vol. 15, No. 1, January–February 1993, p 34.

34 A Newson, 'The Les Mills Phenomenon', *Ultrafit*, Annual Edition, 1999, p 43.

35 See *Body Attack: Research and development*, http://www/lesmills.com/attack/research.asp, [on-line], accessed on 25 March 2000.

36 I asked Rod Harvey, General Manager of Les Mills Australia, in a personal email, about the consciousness of using Body Pump to bring men back to aerobics. He stated that 'It was a deliberate focus and was mainly achieved by the introduction of Body Pump, then the influence of Body Combat has further increased the number of men in the classes', 23 March 2000.

37 These statistics were derived from a personal email from Rod Harvey, 7 February 2000.

38 Rod Harvey explained these pauses in the soundtrack. He stated that 'the pausing is a deliberate move to allow the instructors time to cue their attendees and give them breaks to consume liquids, along with definite tracks that work different sections of the body i.e. ab track, warm up, cool down etc'.

39 See, for example, John Mason's *Aerobic Fitness*, Kangaroo Press, Sydney, 1999, p 22. He discusses in great detail the importance of music to the aerobics experience, focussing on the routines, choreography and speed.

40 Newson, 'The Les Mills Phenomenon', p 44.

41 Pete Manuel, *Body Attack*, http://www/lesmills.com/attack/forum/showmessage. asp?messageID=444, [on-line], accessed on 25 March 2000.

42 Rod Harvey and Tara Brabazon, personal email, 7 February 2000.

43 The difficulty is that Body Step was formed to be 'simple enough for everyone'. However, for experienced steppers, the level of challenge is too low. See *What is bodystep?* http://www.lesmills.com/step/what.asp, [on-line], accessed on 25 March 2000.

44 *Les Mills Aerobics Australia Step*, http://www.lesmills.com.au/programs/bodystep/home.htm, [on-line], accessed on 25 March 2000.

45 These statistics are derived from Newson, 'The Les Mills Phenomenon', *Ultrafit*, p 44.

46 *Bodypump testimonials*, http://www.lesmills.com/pump/testimoials.asp, [on-line], accessed on 25 March 2000.

47 See, for example, *Body Attack: Les Mills Testimonials*, http://www/lesmills.com/attack/testimonials.asp, [on-line], accessed on 25 March 2000.

48 *Les Mills Aerobics Australia Pump*, http://www.lesmills.com.au/programs/bodypump/home.htm, [on-line], accessed on 25 March 2000.

49 *What is bodycombat?* http://www.lesmills.com/combat/what.asp, [on-line], accessed on 25 March 2000.

50 CS, *Body Balance*, http://www.lesmills.com/balance/testimonials.asp, [on-line], accessed on 25 March 2000.

51 Judith, Wellington, *RPM Les Mills Testimonials*, http://www.lesmills.com/rpm/testimonials.asp, [on-line], accessed on 25 March 2000.

52 Lauren B, Auckland, *Les Mills Testimonials*, http://www.lesmills.com/testimonials.asp, [on-line], accessed on 25 March 2000.

53 Lorraine, 'Loz's Corner', *The Bullcreek Bulletin*, Vol. 1, Issue 2, p 1.

PART 2: MOVING WOMEN

CHAPTER FIVE: FASTEN YOUR SEATBELTS, BUT NOT THE HIGHCHAIR: BETTE DAVIS AND SPINSTERHOOD

1   Line by Madge, played by Bette Davis, *Cabin in the Cotton*, Warner Brothers, 1932.
2   'Vogue', sung by Madonna, written by Madonna and Shep Pettibone, produced by Madonna and Shep Pettibone, from *Vogue CD Maxi-single*, Sire Records, 1990, track one. Please note that one of the remixes of 'Vogue' was actually named the 'Bette Davis Dub'.
3   J Vermilye, *Bette Davis*, Galahad, New York, 1973, p 118.
4   Her four husbands were Harmon Nelson, Arthur Farnsworth, William Grant Sherry and Gary Merrill.
5   Bette Davis actually linked the pain she felt from the publication of her daughter's 'tell all' book and her stroke. She stated, 'I will never recover as completely from B.D.'s book as I have from the stroke. They were both shattering experiences', from B Davis & M Hershowitz, *This 'n' that*, Sidgwick and Jackson, London, 1987, p 10.
6   G Hunt, 'The 100 Greatest Stars of all time', *America*, Vol. 178, No. 1, 3 January 1998, p 2.
7   B Davis, cited in Davis & Hershowitz, p 40.
8   The fame of those eyes only increased when Kim Carnes released the successful single 'Bette Davis Eyes'. This has been included on *The Eighties Collection Volume One*, EMI New Zealand, 1990, compact disc one, track four.
9   R Wagner, *Bette Davis: Biography*, produced by Stephanie Haffner, A&E Television Network, 1994.
10 Before *Of Human Bondage*, Bette Davis made fourteen films in three years for Warner Brothers. It is important to recognise that Warner's was the 'tough guy' studio at this time, with James Cagney and Humphrey Bogart the most obvious names. It is not surprising that Bette Davis became known as the female Cagney.
11 Mildred Rogers, played by Bette Davis, *Of Human Bondage*, RKO 1932.
12 Ham Nelson and James Flannagan, cited in B Leaming, *Bette Davis*, Orion, London, 1999, p 149.
13 A *Newsweek* article stated that 'men couldn't help liking her, and for women she was the first viable example of female independence to come out of Hollywood', in 'Bette Davis of Human Bondage', *Newsweek*, Vol. 131, No. 25, Summer 1998, p 64.
14 Charlotte Vale, performed by Bette Davis, *Now, Voyager*, Warner Brothers, 1942.
15 Chilla Bulbeck wrote a remarkable critique of the second/third wave division in 'Simone de Beauvoir and Generations of Feminists', *Hecate*, Vol. XXV, Issue 2, 1999, pp 5–21.
16 For example, in Sarah Gamble (ed), *Icon Critical Dictionary of Feminism and Postfeminism*, Icon Books, Cambridge, 1999, two of the chapters were titled 'Second Wave Feminism', and 'Postfeminism'. The latter was actually the analytical shell for a discussion of third wave feminism.
17 G Greer, *The Female Eunuch*, Paladin, London, 1971, p 224.
18 Katharine Hepburn articulated this paradox with great clarity: 'It was matter of becoming the best actress I could be or becoming a mother. But not both; I don't think I could do justice to both', cited in J Sherron De Hart, 'Still missing: Amelia Earhart and the search for modern feminism', *Reviews in American History*, Vol. 23, No. 1, March 1995, [full-text].
19 W Sotile & M Sotile, *Supercouple Syndrome*, John Wiley and Sons, New York, 1998.
20 L McIntosh, *Are you tired of being tired?* Hodder, Sydney, 1995.
21 Sarah Gamble described 'the primary difference between third wave and second wave feminism is that third wave feminists feel at ease with contradiction', from 'Postfeminism', in S Gamble, *The Icon Critical Dictionary of Feminism and Postfeminism*, Icon Books, Cambridge, 1999, p 52.

22 The major film that did change the way in which older women are portrayed is *How Stella got her groove back*. Starring Angela Basset and Whoopi Goldberg, the narrative critiqued the 'problem' of the older woman.

23 J Mayne, 'Feminist film theory and criticism', in D Carson, L Dittmar, J Welsch (eds), *Multiple voices in feminist film criticism*, University of Minnesota Press, Minneapolis, 1994, p 51.

24 Line from Margo Channing, played by Bette Davis, *All About Eve,* Twentieth Century Fox, 1950.

25 To observe a recent example of this tendency, please refer to Jenny Cullen's 'Mothers and Daughters', the *Australian Women's Weekly*, May 2000, pp 2–7. Throughout the text, the mothers are validated as managing both careers and family. The difficulties of motherhood are also revealed in books like Susan Maushart, *The mask of motherhood*, Vintage, Sydney, 1997. While aware of the problems confronting women, she still presents childbearing and childrearing as a default position.

26 R Mahony, *Kidding ourselves: breadwinning, babies, and bargaining power*, Harper Collins, New York, 1995.

27 Mahony, *Kidding ourselves*, p 20.

28 Mahony, *Kidding ourselves*, pp 13–14.

29 J Scutt, 'Bold Women', in J Scutt (ed), *Singular women: reclaiming spinsterhood*, Artemis Publishing, Melbourne, 1995, p 8.

30 L Still, 'A free soul', in Scutt, *Singular women*, p 125.

31 R Corliss, 'She did it the hard way', *Time*, Vol. 134, No. 16, 16 October 1989, p 49.

32 Kenneth MacKinnon described 'the act of entering old texts with new critical perspectives is termed "re-vision", sometimes "infidelity"', from *Misogyny in the movies*, Associated University Presses, Cranbury, 1990, p 24.

33 J Staiger, *Bad Women: regulating sexuality in early American Cinema*, University of Minnesota Press, Minneapolis, 1995, p 16.

34 As C Creekmur and A Doty have stated, 'historically … gays and lesbians have … related to mass culture differently', from 'Introduction', *Out in Culture*, Duke UP, Durham, 1995, p 1.

35 D Harris, 'The diva in decline', *Harper's Magazine*, Vol. 294, No. 1, January 1997, p 25.

36 R Corliss, 'Why can't a woman be a man', *Time*, Vol. 138, No. 5, 5 August 1991, p 5.

37 R Mosely, *Bette Davis: An Intimate Memoir*, Sidgwick and Jackson, London, 1989, p 73.

38 J Plymale, 'All about "All about Eve": The complete behind-the-scenes story of the bitchiest film ever made', *Library Journal*, Vol. 125, Issue 2, 1 February 2000, p 88.

39 As Davis discovered, 'there was a theatre in Greenwich Village that kept bringing it back, and you could never hear one word I said because the people in the audience knew every one of my lines and would say them out loud along with me', from Davis & Hershowitz, p 181.

40 Margo Channing, *All about Eve*.

41 Suzanne Fields, 'Harriet's back in feminist form', *Insight on the News*, Vol. 14, No. 17, 11 May 1998, p 48.

42 Ally McBeal dialogue, cited in Fields, 'Harriet's back in feminist form', p 48.

43 J Butler, *Gender Trouble*, Routledge, New York, 1990, p 4.

44 Andrew Sarris wrote an eloquent article on *My Best Friend's Wedding*, TriStar Pictures, 1997, praising both Roberts and the script's complex construction of femininity. See 'Sighs of a summer movie maven', *Film Comment*, Vol. 33, No. 6, November–December 1997, pp 26–29.

45 Line from George, played by Rupert Everett, *My Best Friend's Wedding*.

46 R Corliss described Bette Davis as one of 'The ladies who lunge', *Time*, Vol. 148, No. 17, 7 October 1996, [full-text].

47 M Morris, *Too soon too late: history in popular culture*, Indiana University Press, Bloomington, 1998, p xix.

48 These statistics are derived from Kevin Andrews & Michelle Curtis, *Changing Australia: Social, Cultural and Economic Trends shaping the nation*, The Federation Press, Sydney, 1998, p 42.

49 Greer, p 315.

50 Greer. To ensure that I do not appear to misrepresent Greer, she described women in positions of power in 'a man's world' as 'the exceptional creature who is as good as a man and much more decorative. The men capitulate'.

51 M Patenaude, 'on not having children', in Irene Reti (ed), *Childless by choice: a feminist anthology*, HerBooks, Santa Cruz, 1992, p 36.

52 This is not unusual. Leslie Cannold reckoned that 'two out of every three pregnancies in Australia are unplanned', *The Abortion Myth*, Allen and Unwin, Sydney, 1998, p xi.

53 This threat was quite real. Jan Bowen, in her 'Introduction', to *Feminist Fatale*, stated that 'Whenever she worked, if a woman became pregnant she was expected to resign or there was a high probability that she would be sacked', *Feminist Fatale*, Harper Collins, Sydney, 1998, pp xii–xiii.

54 Irene Reti, 'Introduction', in Irene Reti (ed) *Childless by choice: a feminist anthology*, HerBooks, Santa Cruz, 1992, p 1.

55 Ann Snitow, 'Motherhood — reclaiming the demon text', in Reti, *Childless by choice*, p 10.

56 These five feminist reforms were: 1. A requirement of husbands to share a family wage; 2. Dual ownership of family savings; 3. Motherhood endowment; 4. Public provision of childcare; 5. Equal pay. These reforms were listed in Marilyn Lake's *Getting Equal: The history of Australian feminism*, Allen and Unwin, Sydney, 1999, p 5.

57 Lake, *Getting Equal*, p 256.

58 Lake, *Getting Equal*, p 257.

59 Lake, *Getting Equal*, p 279.

60 Quentin Bryce, in Bowen, p 207.

61 A Rich, *Of Woman Born: Motherhood as Experience and Institution*, Virago, London, 1986: 1977, p 15.

62 Helen Coonan, from J Bowen's *Feminist fatale*, Harper Collins, Sydney, 1998, p 184. Coonan extended her argument, believing that 'you can't aim for the top and also have the sort of family responsibilities and commitments that are going to distract you and take you away from that single-minded pursuit. It is extremely competitive and if you have four children and you want to be the prime minister, that is going to be a very difficult mix to achieve', p 191.

63 C Sullivan, 'Alright, I admit it, I want a husband', *She*, October 2001, p 159. Unbelievably, the writer affirms that 'whatever you gain by being unattached, you pay for in loss of intimacy and the feeling of not being valued by someone else … Well, you can like yourself and have a strong identity, but most of us need to be part of someone else's life. Friends may be wonderful, but they have their own lives. You need someone who'll always be there to fight in your corner'. This is an extraordinary, narrow and limited judgment from a stable of magazines that used to stress autonomy and decision-making for women. It is no surprise that this article is featured alongside other notables, such as 'Is your star sign making you fat?'.

64 Rich, *Of Woman Born*.

65 Dr Caroline West, 'Are you too old to have a baby?', *Good Medicine*, September 2000, pp 30–31.

66 Wendyl Nissen, 'Hello! From the Editor', *Family Circle*, October 2000, p 9.

67 Randi Locke, 'Choosing childlessness', in Reti, *Childless by choice*, p 31.

68 This was the description that JD used of Charlotte Vale in *Now, Voyager*.
69 S Cavell, *Contesting Tears: The Hollywood Melodrama of the Unknown Woman*, University of Chicago Press, Chicago, 1996, p 131.
70 Lake, *Getting Equal*, p 276.
71 Line from Rosa Moline, *Beyond the Forest*.
72 B Leaming, *Bette Davis*, Orion, London, 1999, p 336.
73 K White, *9 secrets of women who get everything they want*, Three Rivers Press, New York, 1998.
74 Kirsten Birkett, *The Essence of Feminism*, Matthias Media, Sydney, 2000.

CHAPTER SIX: BRITAIN'S LAST LINE OF DEFENCE: MISS MONEYPENNY AND FILMIC FEMINISM

1   Lyrics from *Bitch*, CD single, performed by Meredith Brooks, written by Brooks/Peiken, Capital Records, 1997.
2   James Bond, played by George Lazenby, *On Her Majesty's Secret Service*, United Artists, 1969.
3   The contradictory and camp elements of strong female personas in film and television were discussed by Thomas Andrae in 'Television's first feminist: The Avengers and female spectatorship', *Discourse*, Vol. 18, No. 3, Spring 1996, pp 112–36.
4   The character of Q, played by Desmond Llewellen, was featured in all films except *Dr No* and *Live and Let Die*. Llewellen's death after *The world is not enough* ends this long-term commitment to the series.
5   Lois Maxwell appeared in the fourteen films following *Dr No*. Her last screen appearance was in the last Roger Moore-Bond film, *A View to a Kill*.
6   Lois Maxwell stated that 'the Moneypenny scenes have become like a Bond trademark', from P Haining, *James Bond: A Celebration*, Planet Books, London, 1987, p 193. This book described Maxwell as 'The woman who has made a cultural figure out of a tiny part', p 193.
7   J Butler, *Gender Trouble*, Routledge, New York, 1990, p 1.
8   LL Lindsey, *Gender Roles: A sociological perspective*, Prentice-Hall, Englewood Cliffs, 1994, pp 312–13.
9   B Wearing, *Gender: the pain and pleasure of difference*, Addison Wesley Longman, Melbourne 1996, p 109.
10 T Bennett & J Woollacott, *Bond and Beyond*, Macmillan, Houndsmills, 1987, p 19.
11 *Bond and Beyond*, p 242.
12 The word 'bitch' in this context is particularly active in third wave feminism, frequently linked with the UK writers Julie Burchill and Suzanne Moore. Although affirming distinct political objectives, these women claim the power and pleasures of popular culture.
13 Sean Connery and Lois Maxwell, *Dr No*, United Artists, 1962.
14 Sean Connery and Lois Maxwell, *From Russia With Love*, United Artists, 1964.
15 Sean Connery and Lois Maxwell, *Goldfinger*, United Artists, 1964.
16 J Doyle & M Paludi, *Sex and Gender*, Brown and Benchmark, Madison, 1995, p 95.
17 Sean Connery and Lois Maxwell, *You Only Live Twice*, United Artists, 1967.
18 Lazenby and Maxwell, *On Her Majesty's Secret Service*.
19 Roger Moore, *Live and Let Die*, United Artists, 1973.
20 Roger Moore and Lois Maxwell, *The Man with the Golden Gun*, United Artists, 1974.
21 Roger Moore and Lois Maxwell, *Moonraker*, United Artists, 1979.
22 Roger Moore and Lois Maxwell, *For Your Eyes Only*, United Artists, 1981.
23 G Greer, *The Female Eunuch*, Palandin, London, 1971, p 13.
24 S Faludi, *Backlash: the undeclared war against women*, Chatto and Windus, London, 1991, particularly pp 99–103.
25 Timothy Dalton and Caroline Bliss, *The Living Daylights*, United Artists, 1987.
26 Pierce Brosnan and Samantha Bond, *Goldeneye*, United Artists, 1995.
27 Doyle & Paludi, p 172.
28 Pierce Brosnan and Judi Dench, *Goldeneye*.

29   A Tolson, *The Limits of Masculinity*, Tavistock, London, 1985, p 7.

30   C Sommers, *Who stole feminism?* Simon and Schuster, New York, 1994, p 18.

31   A series of commercials in Australia and New Zealand for Nescafe Coffee from 1994 to 1997 featured the saga of a man and woman in the rural Antipodes 'moving on' from their past lives and trying to establish a relationship. The couple have never been intimate, but persist in talking through their problems, always accompanied by a cup of black Nescafe.

32   S Willis, 'Disputed territories; masculinity and social space', *Camera Obscura*, Vol. 19, 1989, p 8.

33   Lindsey, *Gender Roles,* p 315.

CHAPTER SEVEN: I'D RATHER BE IN CHYNA: WRESTLING (WITH) FEMININITY

1   N Penn & L LaRose, *The Code*, Fireside, New York, 1996, p 118.

2   Homer, Book 23, 'Funeral Games for Patroclus', *The Iliad*, translated by Robert Fagles, Penguin, New York, 1990, pp 581–82.

3   G Rice, 'Rasslin' gets a toehold', *Collier's*, No. 87, 14 March 1931, p 16.

4   To see some sense of this history, please refer to Gideon Haigh, *The summer game: Australian Test Cricket 1949–71*, Text Publishing, Melbourne, 1999. This book works in the mythical (and misunderstood) space between the Bradman years and the Chappell era.

5   N Gabler, 'God, country and professional Wrestling', *George*, Vol. 4, No. 7, July 1999, [full-text] Academic Search Elite 1999, [1410549], accessed on 5 September 2000.

6   C Heath, 'Stone Cold Steve Austin', *Rolling Stone*, No. 802–803, 25 December – 7 January 1998–99, [full-text], Academic Search Elite, [1410549].

7   J Rickard, 'The spectacle of excess: the emergence of modern professional wrestling in the United States and Australia', *Journal of Popular Culture*, Vol. 33, No. 1, 1999, [full-text], Academic Search Elite, [2535295].

8   Hunter Hearst Helmsely, quoted in John Leland, 'Why America's hooked on wrestling', *Newsweek*, Vol. 135, No. 6, 7 February 2000, p 46.

9   L Bryson, 'My 2 cents', *World Wrestling Federation Magazine*, June 2000, p 15.

10   It is also possible to date the end of a particular era of wrestling, when The Undertaker defeated Hulk Hogan on 27 November 1991. At that point the easy rhetoric of the good American wrestler overcoming all odds started to be critiqued by a more complex cultural force.

11   John Leland discusses the WWF's position in the New media through 'Why America's hooked on wrestling', *Newsweek*, Vol. 135, Issue 6, 2 July 2000, p 46.

12   J Archer, *Theater in the squared circle*, White Boucke Publishing, Lafayette, 1999, p xiii.

13   M Ball, *Professional Wrestling as ritual drama in American popular culture*, Edwin Mellen Press, New York, 1990, p 1.

14   J Senyard, 'The barracker and the spectator', *Journal of Australian Studies*, No. 62, 1999, p 46.

15   Ball, *Professional wrestling as ritual drama in American popular culture*, p 3.

16   V McMahon, quoted in J Drucker, 'King of the Ring', *Cigar Aficionado*, December 1999, p 148.

17   J Hartley, *Tele-ology: studies in television*, Routledge, London, 1992, p 18.

18   R Barthes, *Mythologies*, Hing and Want, New York, 1972, p 15.

19   J Kobler, 'Where Grandma can yell "Bum"', *Cosmopolitan*, No. 135, 12 December 1953, p 127.

20   R Lardner, 'Pity the poor wrestler', *Look*, No. 18, 9 March 1956, p 86.

21   G Stone, 'American Sports: play and dis-play', *Chicago Review*, No. 9, Fall 1955, p 97.

22   An example of this 'homoerotic reading' is John Rickard's 'The spectacle of excess', *Journal of Popular Culture*, Vol. 33, No. 1, Summer 1999. It is also a component

of Neal Gabler's 'God, country and professional Wrestling', *George*, Vol. 4, Issue 7, July 1999, [Electronic], accessed: Academic Search Elite [19994202], 5 September 2000. Vadim also used it as the focus for his 'Grappling with homosexuality', *Village Voice*, Vol. 45, Issue 18, 5 September 2000 [Electronic], accessed: Academic Search Elite [3078671], 6 September 2000. This 'queerying' of wrestling was most cleverly deployed in Roy and HG's 're-commentary' of the Greco-Roman wrestling at the Sydney 2000 Olympics. As happened during their male gymnastics re-tapings, they renamed many of the moves and postures. Perhaps their most brilliant discussion of the oddities of the sport was shown by placing a Barry White soundtrack behind the grappling action on the mat. Please refer to *The Dream with Roy and HG — Week 2*, Warner Vision, 2000.

23 Danielle, 'Talking the talk', *World Wrestling Federation Magazine*, April 2000, p 3.

24 Ashley Kosciolek, 'Talking the talk', p 3.

25 S Mazer, *Professional wrestling: sport and spectacle*, University Press of Mississippi, Jackson, 1998, p 4.

26 One of the great sub-plots of Julie Burchill's novel *Married Alive* is that her Gran spends the entire breadth of the plot watching the WWF programming. It provides an ideal counterpoint to marriage, infidelity, shopping and dinner parties. The exploits of the Undertaker actually become more sensible than buying overpriced wine for the overwrought whining of middle-class soirees.

27 J Campbell, 'Professional wrestling: why the bad guys win', *Journal of American Culture*, Vol. 19, Issue 2, Summer 1996, [Electronic], Accessed: Academic Search Elite, [970404026162], on 5 September 2000.

28 S Mazer, *Professional wrestling: sport and spectacle*, p 119.

29 A Carden-Coyne, 'Classical heroism and modern life: the bodybuilding and masculinity in the early twentieth century', *Journal of Australian Studies*, No. 63, 1999, p 141.

30 G Steinem, *Outrageous acts and everyday rebellions*, Owl books, New York, 1995: 1983, p 212.

31 For a discussion of the male body, musculature and politics, please refer to JA Mangan's edited collection, *Superman supreme: fascist body as political icon — global fascism*, Frank Class, London, 2000.

32 G Steinem, *Revolution from within: a book of self-esteem*, Little, Brown and Company, Boston, 1992, p 208.

33 'Our bodies, ourselves', the *Australian Women's Weekly*, February 2001, p 105.

34 'Our bodies, ourselves', the *Australian Women's Weekly*, p 106.

35 Janelle, 'Our bodies, ourselves', the *Australian Women's Weekly*, p 107.

36 H Lenskyj, 'Body of knowledge', in B Lea Brown, *Bringing it home: women talk about feminism in their lives*, Arsenal Pulp Press, Vancouver, 1996, p 219.

37 These limits are obviously challenged by sport more generally. Patricia Vertinsky has researched the relationship between physical education, exercise and women's liberation. Please refer to her 'Body shapes: the role of the medical establishment in informing female exercise and physical education in nineteenth-century North America', in JA Mangan & R Park (eds), *From 'Fair sex' to feminism*, Frank Class, London, 1987, pp 256–81.

38 Michael Cole, *Come Get Some: The women of the WWF*, Universal Pictures (Australasia) and Titan Sports, 1999.

39 Road Dogg, from *Come get some*.

40 It is important to note that female wrestlers, like supermodels, rarely have more than a single name. However, most of the male wrestlers, such as Kane, Undertaker and Mankind are similar. Yet each of these non-trained wrestlers brings distinct non-wrestling talents to the programme. Sable was a model, Terri was a professional dancer and Debra was an actress. Ivory and Terri also bring long-term workout and yoga histories to the ring.

41 Jackie, from *Come get some*.

42 Jackie, from *Come get some*.
43 A discussion of this Pedigree is found in the review of the 'Survivor Series', *World Wrestling Federation Magazine*, February 2000, p 48.
44 Robert Bledsoe saw her as 'the leather-clad, dark-haired beauty in boots', R Bledsoe, 'Double Trouble', *World Wrestling Federation Magazine*, January 2000, p 55.
45 The Chyna biography is only the third released from a highly successful series from the WWF. It follows the two *New York Times* Bestsellers, Mick Foley's *Have a nice day!* and The Rock's *The Rock Says*.
46 Chyna/Joanie Laurer, *If only they knew*, Harper Collins, New York, 2001, p 10.
47 Chyna/Joanie Laurer, *If only they knew*, p 12.
48 Chyna, from *Come Get Some*.
49 Chyna, from *Come Get Some*.
50 J Laurer, 'Chyna: Wrestling's mistress of muscle', *Playboy*, November 2000, p 84.
51 Jim Ross & Chyna, *Raw is War*, 25 December 2000. Shown on Fox Sports (Australia), Channel 11, 26 December 2000.
52 Chyna/Joanie Laurer, *If They Only Knew*, p 84.
53 Chyna/Joanie Laurer, *If They Only Knew*, p 192.
54 Even in the midst of this *Playboy* shoot, she stressed that Chyna is a character, a shell that encases Joanie Laurer.
55 J Laurer, 'Chyna: Wrestling's mistress of muscle', p 84.
56 J Laurer, 'Chyna: Wrestling's mistress of muscle', p 87.
57 J Laurer, 'Chyna: Wrestling's mistress of muscle', p 87.
58 Chyna/Joanie Laurer, *If They Only Knew*, p 291.
59 G Lichtenstein, 'Competition in Women's Athletics', in V Miner & H Longino (eds), *Competition: a feminist taboo?* The Feminist Press, New York, 1987, p 48.

CHAPTER EIGHT: BREASTS ON THE BRIDGE: CAPTAIN JANEWAY AND THE FEMINIST ENTERPRISE

1   As Robin Roberts has realised, 'Both French feminism theory and *Star Trek: The Next Generation* were popular at the same time … both resonated with the cultural forces at work in America in 1987–94', *Sexual Generations*, University of Illinois Press, Urbana, 1999, p 10. Her book is a singular departure from this psychoanalytic framework in analysing 'The Next Generation'.
2   This work is well represented by Daniel Leonard Bernardi, *Star Trek and History: Race-ing toward a white future*, Rutgers University Press, New Brunswick, 1998.
3   J Hartley, *Tele-ology: studies in television*, Routledge, London, 1992, p ix.
4   T Richards, *Star Trek: In myth and legend*, Orion Books, London, 1997, p 2.
5   Thomas Richards states that it is like a 'great work of literature', *Star Trek: In myth and legend*, p 5.
6   Heather Joseph-Witham compiled a short book on *Star Trek fans and costume art*, University Press of Mississippi, Jackson, 1996. Well illustrated, it shows the attention to detail and the effort that fans put into becoming authentic Klingons, Vulcans and Starfleet officers.
7   W Goldberg, quoted in JM Dallard, *Star Trek where no one has gone before: a history in pictures*, Pocket Books, New York, 1994, p 20.
8   Mike Thomas, even after the first series of 'Voyager', proclaimed it far superior to 'DS9'. Please refer to 'Voyager: Back to Basics', *TV Zone*, No. 20, April 1996, p 41.
9   Starlog Communications, 'The Maquis', in *The official Star Trek: Deep Space Nine magazine*, Vol. 8, 1994, p 61.
10 Avery Brooks, the actor who portrayed Captain Sisko, also brought a history of affirmative achievement to the part. He was the first black student to graduate with a Master of Fine Arts at Rutgers. He became a tenured faculty member of the institution.
11 Networks of friendship are the most fascinating and under-theorised part of 'Star

Trek'. Once more, the parallels between the 'Original Series' and 'Voyager' are obvious in the Kirk/Spock, Janeway/Tuvok relationships. The fact that Tuvok is played by a black actor signifies that the Vulcan population is also multi-racial.

12 D Marinaccio, *All the other things I really need to know I learned from watching Star Trek: The Next Generation*, Pocket Books, New York, 1998, p 149.

13 *Star Trek: First Contact*, directed by Jonathan Frakes, Paramount Studies, 1996.

14 A Juno, *Angry women in rock*, Juno Books, New York, 1996, p 4.

15 Also significant is the absence of relationships between Worf, Geordi, La Forge and Guinan. To evaluate the race-based absences from the 'Star Trek' discourse, please refer to Michael Pounds, *Race in space: the representation of ethnicity in Star Trek and Star Trek: The Next Generation*, The Scarecrow Press, Lanham, 1999.

16 N Visitor, quoted in JM Dillard, *Star Trek where no one has gone before: a history in pictures*, Pocket Books, New York, 1994, p 176.

17 S Eramo, 'Trek's first lady: Kate Mulgrew', *TV Zone*, No. 82, September 1996.

18 J Wagner & J Lundeen, *Deep space and sacred time: Star Trek in the American mythos*, Praeger, London, 1998, p 95.

19 Andre Willey has stated that 'Every Starship Captain needs a good, supportive First Officer', *Star Trek: The Next Generation official Poster Magazine*, No. 2, 1991, p 2.

20 K Mulgrew in 'Kate Mulgrew facing the dark frontier', *TV Zone*, Issue 112, March 1999, p 19.

21 Kate Mulgrew & Robert Beltran, 'Resolutions', 'Star Trek Voyager 2.11', written by Jeri Taylor, Paramount, 1995.

22 D Kaseman, 'Beyond the double bind: women and leadership', *Women and language*, Vol. 21, No. 2, Fall 1998, [full-text article].

23 A hypothetical marriage (and divorce) between Jean-Luc Picard and Beverley Picard (nee Crusher) was presented on 'All things must pass', the final episode of 'Star Trek: The Next Generation'.

24 'The Naked Time', 'Star Trek: Original Series', Desilu Studies, 1966–67.

25 'The Skin of Evil', 'Star Trek: The Next Generation', Paramount Pictures, 1988.

26 The intensification of this principle is exhibited in Janeway's 'holoromance' in New Haven. The only possible sexual relationship possible on 'Voyager' was with a hologram. To view this narrative, please refer to 'Fair Haven', 'Star Trek Voyager 6.6', Paramount, 2000.

27 S McLean, 'They're here', *The Courier Mail*, 4 April 1996, p 5.

28 Stated bluntly, Adrienne Mendell declared that 'in our culture, competence is not feminine — particularly if it means demonstrating greater competence than a man', *How men think: the seven essential rules for making it in a man's world*, Fawcett Columbine, New York, 1996, p 37.

29 Quite remarkably, in 'The Next Generation', instead of attention being placed on the hair (or lack thereof) of Picard, there was concern about his accent. As Patrick Stewart stated, 'In the beginning there were a number of discussions on just how Picard would pronounce. At one point, it was thought that I should try for a more American sounding voice, something a bit more neutral in terms of accent. Finally, it was decided that, since we have already painted the picture of Picard as being a European, we should go with the normal way that I speak', *Star Trek The Next Generation Magazine*, Vol. 1, December 1987–88, p 10.

30 S McLean, 'They're here', *The Courier Mail*, p 5.

31 Wes Roberts & Bill Ross, *Leadership lessons from Star Trek The Next Generation*, Pocket Books, New York, 1995.

32 J Leonard, 'The next next generation', *New York*, 30 January 1995, p 82.

33 Material is emerging on the difficulty of women lobbying and organising in their companies. Cindy Simon Rosenthal showed how institutions can produce, reproduce and subvert gender norms in 'A view of their own', *Policy Studies Journal*, Vol. 25, No. 4, Winter 1997, [Electronic], accessed: Expanded Academic

[A20791116], 13 February 2001. Also placing attention on organisational culture is Andi Moss and Laurel Rans' article, 'Executive leadership for women', *Corrections Today*, Vol. 59, No. 7, December 1997, [full-text article].

34   Marjorie Shaevitz believed that 'most women I know need to be sick before they feel justified in taking care of themselves. We keep waiting for someone else to give us a prescription to rest, or to encourage us to slow down or stop for a while, or to reassure us that it's okay, or best of all — fantasies of all fantasies — to make all of the arrangements for us', in *The confident woman*, Harmony, New York, 1999, pp 66–67.

35   Kate Mulgrew & Robert Beltran, 'Night', 'Star Trek Voyager 5.1', written by Brannon Braga and Joe Menusky, Paramount Pictures, 1999.

36   'Endgame' Parts I and II, story by Rick Berman and Kenneth Biller and Brannon Braga, directed by Allan Kroeker, first shown on 23 May 2001.

37   Unnamed interviewer, 'Kate Mulgrew facing the dark frontier', *TV Zone*, Issue 112, March 1999, p 14.

38   K Mulgrew, 'Kate Mulgrew facing the dark frontier', p 12.

39   Unnamed interviewer, 'Kate Mulgrew facing the dark frontier', p 16.

40   Unnamed interviewer, 'Kate Mulgrew facing the dark frontier', p 16.

41   Rick Berman, quoted in Stephen Poe, *Star Trek Voyager: a vision of the future*, Pocket Books, New York, 1998, p 159.

42   Poe, *Star Trek Voyager: a vision of the future*, p 315.

43   Kate Mulgrew in 'Q and the Grey', screenplay by Kenneth Biller, 'Star Trek Voyager 3.7', Paramount, 1998.

44   S Inness, *Tough girls women warriors and wonder women in popular culture*, University of Pennsylvania Press, Philadelphia, 1999, p 113.

45   The distinct relationship between Janeway, Seven of Nine and Kes is revealed in 'The Gift'. This is the last episode for Kes and the first for Seven.

46   This relationship is revealed in 'Someone to Watch over me', 'Star Trek Voyager, 5.11', story by Brannon Braga, directed by Robert Duncan McNeill, Paramount Pictures, 1999.

47   'Equinox part II', 'Star Trek Voyager 6.1', Paramount Pictures, 2000.

48   The consequences of this absence are presented in Stephen Poe's *Star Trek Voyager: A vision of the future*, Pocket Books, New York, 1998, p 122.

49   Poe, *Star Trek Voyager: a vision of the future*, p 347.

50   T Richards, *Star Trek: In myth and legend*, p 87.

51   It is significant to note that the character of Troi appeared in one episode of 'Star Trek: Voyager'. Titled 'Life line', this episode affirmed her professional abilities. She displayed more emotional depth through this episode than through much of the run in 'Star Trek: The Next Generation'. Please refer to 'Star Trek Voyager, 6.12', Paramount, 2000.

52   'The Measure of a Man', was a provocative legal exploration on 'The Next Generation' of what makes masculinity. Data was on trial to determine whether or not he possessed consciousness. The most powerful scene in the episode was an interchange between Picard and Ginan. She reminded him of the 'value' of 'disposable people'. With the slavery narrative activated in the 'Star Trek' discourse, the very basis of masculinity and civilisation were questioned.

53   Characteristically, this 1980s rape was not a definitive act of violent penetration, but was far more ambiguously determined. Deanna was actually raped again on 'The Next Generation' — again with ambiguous definitions and consequences — in 'Violations'.

54   Robin Roberts, *Sexual Generations*, University of Illinois Press, Urbana, 1999, p 95.

55   M Sirtis, quoted by M Altman in 'Marina Sirtis Ship's Counsellor', *Cinefantastique*, Vol. 22, No. 2, October 1991, p 39.

56   Importantly, her cast members also supported her treatment and the desire for change. Jonathan Frakes, who played the second-in-command on the Enterprise and is also a successful director of the programme, stated that 'I'm not sure if they hadn't written themselves into a hole with Troi because almost all of her speeches

were interchangeable from one episode to another. "I feel pain. Great pain"', from Steven Wilson 'Jonathan Frakes', *Star Trek: The Next Generation official magazine*, Vol. 5, 1989, p 8.

57 Deforest Kelly was very conscious of his function as a role model for a generation of doctors. As he told Dan Madsen, 'I must get at least 2 or 3 letters every month notifying me that they are in the medical field because of Dr. McCoy and *Star Trek*. It is a great feeling to know you've helped someone like that', from 'Deforest Kelly', *Star Trek the official fan club*, No. 54, February/March 1987, p 5.

58 Lieutenant Uhura, played by Nichelle Nichols, *Star Trek III: The search for Spock*, written and produced by Harve Bennett, directed by Leonard Nimoy, Paramount Pictures, 1984.

59 As argued by Henry Jenkins throughout his remarkable theorising of 'Star Trek' through the late 1980s and 1990s, the series' fans are textual poachers. They love the programme with such veracity that they become dissatisfied with it and re-write it for their own context and purposes. These arguments are presented through H Jenkins, *Textual Poachers*, Routledge, London, 1992 and his publication written with John Tulloch, *Science Fiction Audiences*, Routledge, London, 1995.

60 Unsigned letter, 'Readers' comments', *Star Trek the official fan club magazine*, No. 61, March/April 1988, p 1.

61 G Lerner, 'A transformational feminism', in G Hanlon (ed), *Voicing power: conversations with visionary women*, Westview Press, Boulder, 1997, p 184.

62 Bernardi, *Star Trek and History: Race-ing toward a white future*, p 141.

63 'Star Trek' and NASA have a long history of such dialogues. Not only was the Enterprise the name of the first shuttle, but Dr May Jemison, NASA astronaut and one of the first African American women in space, appeared as a transporter technician in 'The Next Generation', in the episode 'Descent Part I'. She also expressed her respects to Nichelle Nichols and the character of Uhura in each of her shifts on the shuttle. She commenced her duty station with 'Hailing Frequencies Open'.

CHAPTER NINE: SYLVIA TEACHES

1 S Ashton-Warner, *Spinster*, cited in *quoteland.com*, http://www.quoteland.com/quotes/author/555.html, accessed on 1 January 2001.

2 Sylvia Ashton-Warner produced five novels: *Spinster* (1958), *Incense to Idols* (1960), *Bell Call* (1964), *Greenstone* (1956) and *Three* (1970). There were three autobiographically-inflected non-fiction texts: *Teacher* (1963), *Myself* (1967) and *Spearpoint: 'Teacher' in America* (1972).

3 L Hood, *Sylvia! The biography of Sylvia Ashton-Warner*, Viking, Auckland, 1988, p 249.

4 The feminisation of teaching is increasing. Greg Callaghan, in 'Forword', stated that 'it's a sad, rather odd worldwide trend. Why — in an era of greater feminine equality and less stigma attacked to the reversal of traditional sex roles — are men deserting caring professions such as nursing and teaching?', *The Weekend Australian Magazine*, 29–30 September 2001.

5 To view an engaging history of these women from the *fin de siecle* through to the depression, please refer to Sheila Jeffreys' *The spinster and her enemies*, Spinifex Press, Melbourne, 1985.

6 S Ashton Warner, *I Passed This Way*, Knopf, New York, 1979, p 276.

7 S Ashton-Warner, *I Passed This Way*, p 165.

8 Of course this lack of planning or records was justified and re-configured through her organic teaching methods. As she stated in *Teacher*, Penguin, Harmondsworth, 1963, 'Teachers say they need their workbooks … I know that the preparation of a workbook may clarify to a teacher what he is thinking about. I know that the order and method of it reflect inescapably upon the minds of the children', p 72.

9 S Ashton-Warner, *Teacher*, p 99.

10 S Ashton-Warner, *Teacher*, p 171.

11 S Ashton-Warner, *Myself*, Simon and Schuster, New York, 1967, p 71.

12 S Ashton-Warner, *Myself*, p 11.

13 P Welts Kaufman, *Women teachers on the frontier*, Yale University Press, New Haven, 1984, p xvii.

14 A Hernandez, *Pedagogy, democracy and feminism*, State University of New York Press, New York, 1997, p 82.

15 The New Zealand nation was founded through the signing of The Treaty of Waitangi in 1841. While myriad versions of the document exist — in both English and Maori — the three clauses of the document granted the Maori sovereignty over the land, with the Pakeha [European coloniser] being granted governance. The third statement of the Treaty guaranteed all Maori the rights and privileges of British citizenship. For a discussion of this document and the bicultural policy that stems from it, please refer to chapter two of my book *Tracking the Jack: A retracing of the Antipodes*, UNSW Press, Sydney, 2000.

16 L Hood, *Sylvia!* p 72.

17 L Hood, *Sylvia!* p 100.

18 S Ashton-Warner, *Teacher*, p 22.

19 M Garbutcheon Singh, 'The literacy teacher as a professional: insights from the work of Sylvia Ashton-Warner', *Australian Journal of Language and Literacy*, Vol. 15, No. 4, p 280.

20 M Henry, J Knight, R Lingard, S Taylor, *Understanding schooling: an introductory sociology of Australian education*, Routledge, London, 1988, p 142.

21 S Ashton-Warner, *Teacher*, p 26.

22 The Maori-language preschools.

23 I Tawhiwhirangi, in L Hood, *Sylvia!* p 120.

24 As JW Tollefson has argued in *Planning language, planning inequality*, Longman, New York, 1991, 'Language is particularly effective in structuring inequality in this way because it seems "natural" for everyone to speak one variety for intra-group communication', p 12.

25 M Garbutcheon Singh, 'The literacy teacher as a professional: insights from the work of Sylvia Ashton-Warner', *Australian Journal of Language and Literacy*, pp 273–86.

26 For example, Charmaine Pountney, former head of Auckland Girls' Grammar and a University of Waikato dean, has stressed the importance of 'linguistic flexibility', triggered through study of the home language. Please refer to 'Teaching Maori', *Mana*, No. 37, December 2000 – January 2001, p 23.

27 S Ashton-Warner, *Teacher*, pp 18–19.

28 F MacDonald, 'Sound of a cork popping', *The Listener*, Vol. 176, No. 3164, 30 December 2000 – 5 January 2001, p 7.

29 S Ashton-Warner, quoted in L Hood, *Sylvia!* p 158.

30 L Hood, *Sylvia!* p 198.

31 S Ashton-Warner, *Spearpoint: 'Teacher' in America*, Alfred Knopf, New York, 1972, p 52.

32 'New Zealand Further information and links …', http://www2.gol.com/users/oxbow/nz/infos.htm, accessed on 13 January 2001.

33 Julia Brady Ratliff, 'Short and Sweet', Lesson #29, 15 January 1999, http://www.firsteps.com/lessons/shortsweet29.htm, accessed on 13 January 2001.

34 M Whalen, 'Expert teachers?', http://w3.cortland.edu/psydemo/messages/297.html, accessed on 13 January 2001.

35 C Philips, 'Dozens of ways to grow!', *Scholastic Instructor*, November/December 2000, p 23.

36 J Wain, 'C.S. Lewis as a teacher', in J Epstein (ed), *Masters: portraits of great teachers*, Basic Books, New York, 1981, p 238.

37 C Wieck, 'Wake Up', *Inclusion News*, 1993–94, p 2.

38 Sandra Weber & Claudia Mitchel, *'That's funny, you don't look like a teacher,'* *Interrogating images and identity in popular culture*, The Falmer Press, London, 1995, p 13.

39 Sandra Weber & Claudia Mitchel, *'That's funny, you don't look like a teacher,'* *Interrogating images and identity in popular culture*, p 89.

40 B Biggs quoted in 'He Maimai Aroha', *Mana*, No. 37, December 2000 – January 2001, p 13. This article is a fine review of Professor Biggs' life, printed as a celebration of his life, after his death at the age of 79.

CHAPTER TEN: MAKING IT BIG: JULIE BURCHILL, BITCH POLITICS AND WRITING IN PUBLIC

1 J Burchill, 'Burchill on Burchill', *The Face*, Vol. 2, No. 9, 1989, p 76.
2 M Higgins, 'Letter', *Arena*, Vol. 1, No. 45, May/June 1994, p 16.
3 These have been collected into J Burchill, *The Guardian Columns 1998–2000*, Orion, London, 2001.
4 J Burchill, *Ambition*, The Bodley Head, London, 1989, p 4.
5 J Burchill, *No Exit*, Sinclair-Stevenson, London, 1993, pp 22–23.
6 J Burchill, *No Exit*, p 155.
7 J Burchill, *No Exit*, p 1.
8 J Burchill, *Married Alive*, Orion, London, 1999, p 10.
9 J Burchill, 'The Pop P.M.', *The Spectator*, 30 November 1990, p 16.
10 J Burchill, 'Apocalypse now (please)', *The Face*, Vol. 1, No. 61, 1985, p 14.
11 C Paglia, 'Fax off and die, Bitch', *The Weekend Australian*, 8–9 July 1995, p 23.
12 J Burchill, 'Fax off and die, Bitch'.
13 C Paglia, 'Fax off and die, Bitch'.
14 J Burchill, 'Fax off and die, Bitch'.
15 C Paglia, 'Fax off and die, Bitch'.
16 To see her analysis of class, gender and generation in operation, please refer to Angela McRobbie's collection of essays, *Feminism and Youth culture*, Macmillan, Houndmills, 1991.
17 J Burchill, 'Burchill on Burchill', p 76.
18 J Burchill, 'Burchill on Burchill', p 75.
19 J Burchill, 'Apocalypse now (please)', p 16.
20 M Heller, Letters, *The Modern Review*, October–November 1994, p 5.
21 Suzanne Moore, 'Material girl', *Marxism Today*, July 1991, p 13.
22 Toby Young, 'The end of the affair', *The Modern Review*, June–July 1995, p 4.
23 Toby Young, 'The end of the affair', *The Modern Review*.
24 Review from *Casablanca*, cited in *The Modern Review*, No. 21, June–July 1995, p 5.
25 J Burchill, *Diana*, Weidenfeld and Nicholson, London, 1998.

ENDING: REMEMBERING DOROTHY WREN

1 O Wilde, *The Importance of Being Earnest*, Peerage Books, London, 1991, p 439.
2 G Steinem, 'Ruth's Song (Because she could not sing it)', *Outrageous acts and everyday rebellions*, Owl Books, New York, 1995: 1983, pp 139–60. In the second edition of this book, Steinem stated that 'In my own life, the essay "Ruth's Song" has been the greatest marker of change. For years, I couldn't bear to re-read it. Some mysterious part of myself must have had more courage to face the sadness of my mother's life than I did', p xx.
3 Kenny Fraser, in *Ornament and Silence*, Vintage Books, New York, 1998, stated that, 'in describing her mother Germaine is merciless', p 213.
4 H Cixous, 'The laugh of the Medusa', In E Manks (ed), *New French Feminisms*, Harvester, Brighton, 1980, p 250–51.

INDEX